PAINLESS
PUBLIC
SPEAKING

Painless

PUBLIC SPEAKING

A Work/Text Approach

Abné M. Eisenberg
Pace University

Teri Kwal Gamble
College of New Rochelle

UNIVERSITY
PRESS OF
AMERICA

Lanham • New York • London

Copyright © 1991 by
University Press of America®, Inc.
4720 Boston Way
Lanham, Maryland 20706

3 Henrietta Street
London WC2E 8LU England

Library of Congress Cataloging-in-Publication Data

Eisenberg, Abne M.
Painless public speaking : a work/text approach
/ Abne M. Eisenberg, Teri Kwal Gamble.
p.   cm.
Includes bibliographical references and indexes.
1. Public speaking.   I. Gamble, Teri Kwal.   II. Title.
PN4121.E38   1991
808.5'1—dc20   90–24475 CIP

ISBN 0–8191–8147–1 (paperback)

RATIONALE

This text has been developed as a practical guide for persons untrained in speech making. It is broadly organized according to the three important areas of (a) overcoming speech anxiety, (b) preparing the speech, and (c) presenting the speech. This book is unique in that it involves the student in the learning process through numerous "speech experiences." These speech experiences allow students to learn about public speaking in a personally relevant way.

The speech experiences in this text may be viewed as a specific example of a more general pedagogical strategy commonly called simulation gaming. The goal of any game is to make a real-world activity more accessible to students, normally one which is risky to experiment with outside of the classroom. Students are involved in classroom experiences that minimize risk and allow for the learning of general principles which may be applied in the outside world.

Teachers of traditional speech courses have for a long while understood the distinction between process and content orientations to teaching speech communication. If the terminal objective of a class is to get students to communicate more effectively, then an educational strategy should be employed that allows for the actual practice of communication in the classroom. This reasoning is often offered as justification for mock interviews, group decision-making exercises and public speeches as integral parts of the communication curriculum.

An interpersonal laboratory component has been added to many courses professing to teach communication skills in higher education (Bochner, 1974, p. 279). Ruben and Budd point out that:

Becoming truly competent in communicating—in communicating and being communicated with—requires a unique combination of theoretical and practical skill. Neither alone is sufficient. (1975)

While some areas of study are best taught via lectures, speech making is not one of them. The best way for people to improve their speaking ability is by practicing. The transfer of knowledge from one situation to the next (from the classroom to beyond the classroom, for example) is greatly aided by mental or actual practice (Yelon, 1974). When the teacher begins with a concrete classroom experience and develops useful generalizations with applications beyond the classroom, the students are provided with the opportunity to practice what they are learning. Alternatively, teachers who lecture often address students as a relatively passive audience and rarely call upon them to use what they have learned. The practice approach is consistent with arguments made by many educational psychologists (Ausubel, 1968; DeCecco & Crawford, 1974). They contend that the knowledge already existing in an individual's cognitive structure is the single most important factor in determining whether new knowledge will be learned and understood. Hence, if students are expected to apply in the future what they have learned, they must have the opportunity to use what they have learned in the classroom, as a way of making it a firmer part of their cognitive framework.

Research on the effectiveness of classroom simulation games has found them to be consistently motivating of students. Numerous studies have demonstrated increased positive affect resulting from the use of exercises (Cherryholmes, 1966; Chartier, 1972), including high positive ratings toward the teacher, the topic, and the class structure (Eisenberg, 1980). This finding may be especially important in the speech teaching process where negative student affect may have a serious inhibiting effect on other kinds of learning (as in the case of stage fright, mental blocks, or other emotional reactions). Other research shows somewhat more equivocal support for the cognitive effects of simulation games, with some researchers finding increased cognitive learning from games (Lindblad, 1973; Wing, 1968; Baker, 1968; Emery & Enger, 1972). Pierfy reports (1977) that "students who participated in simulation games will retain information longer than if they learned the information through more conventional approaches."

A certain caveat must accompany any presentation on classroom exercises: they cannot stand alone, just as one would not expect any teaching technique administered haphazardly to meet with great success. As Ruben correctly notes,

In many respects, the manner in which an experiential activity is implemented and debriefing (postgame discussion) is conducted is more crucial to the outcome than the properties inherent in the activity. (1977)

Once the accompanying discussions are added, however, one can expect the best—Walling (1977) notes that "the full processing teaching method (exercise with pre- and post-discussions) was more effective in producing learning at all higher cognitive levels than either the lecture alone or the game alone methods." Relating this to the previous discussion of practice, Walling further explains:

When used in conjunction with a lecture and/or a discussion, simulation games force the students to overtly practice concepts which are implicit and/or explicit in the conventional teaching methods.

Taken together, the research shows that classroom exercises stimulate learning when used in conjunction with other instructional materials. Each of the speech experiences in this book is presented along with discussions of each area of interest.

Many people believe that they are good speakers simply because they know the elements of speech making. In reality, the knowledge involved in understanding how to make a speech is quite different from the actual presentation. As Ruben (1976) points out,

Verbal-cognitive competency—the capacity to conceptualize and articulate variables, dimensions and issues that need to be taken into account to explain or predict effective functioning in a situation—may be a necessary condition for behavioral or social competence. Behavior competency—the capacity to display behaviors that are defined as appropriate or functional by others—is a sufficient condition for effective social functioning and is probably at least a minimum condition for success in many task-oriented situations.

Most speech classrooms involve a large amount of student participation. Too often the accompanying textbooks invite students to "tune out" because of their passive approach to learning and the presentation of examples not relevant to the student's life. This text encourages students to interact with the material presented and to learn the key ideas in a way which is personally meaningful. For this reason students reading *Painless Public Speaking* should have an excellent chance of improving their speech making abilities.

Eric M. Eisenberg
Michigan State University

References

Ausubel, D. P. Cognitive structure and the facilitation of meaningful verbal learning. *Journal of Teacher Education*, 1963, 14, 217–230.

Baker, E. H. A comparative study using textbook and simulation approaches in teaching junior high school American history. Unpublished doctoral dissertation, Northwestern University, 1966.

Bochner, A., and C. W. Kelly. Interpersonal competence: rationale, philosophy, and implementation of a conceptual framework. *Speech Teacher*, 1974, 23, 1–23.

Chartier, M. R. Learning Effect. *Simulations and Games*, 1972, 3.

Cherryholmes, C. H. Some current research on the effectiveness of educational simulations: implications for alternative strategies. *American Behavioral Scientist*, 1966, 10 (2).

DeCecco, J. P. and W. R. Crawford. *The psychology of learning and instruction*. Englewood Cliffs, N.J.: Prentice Hall, 1974.

Emery, E. and T. P. Enger. Computer gaming and learning in an introductory economics course. *Journal of Economic Education*, 1972, 3, 77–85.

Lindblad, S. Simulation and guidance: teaching career decision-making skills in the Swedish compulsory school. *Simulations and Games*, 1973, 4, 429–439.

Pierfy, D. A. Comparative simulation game research. *Simulations and Games*, 1977, 254–268.

Ruben, B. D. and R. W. Budd. *Human Communication Handbook: simulation and games*. New Jersey: Hayden, 1975.

Ruben, B. D. Assessing communication competency for intercultural adaptation. *Group and Organization Studies*, 1976, 3, 334–354.

Ruben, B. D., L. R. Askling, and D. J. Kealey. Cross-cultural effectiveness: an overview. In David S. Hoopes (Ed.), *Intercultural Communication: State-of-the-art Overview*. Pittsburgh: Society for Intercultural Education, Training and Research, 1977.

Walling, J. I. An experimental study of conditions which affect learning from simulation games in speech communication instruction. Unpublished doctoral dissertation, University of Illinois, 1977.

Wing, R. Two computer based economic games for sixth graders. In S. Boocock and E. O. Schild (Eds.), *Simulation and Games in Learning*. Beverly Hills, Calif.: Sage, 1968.

Yelon, S. L., R. H. Davis, and L. T. Alexander. *Learning System Design*. New York: McGraw Hill, 1974.

CONTENTS

Taking the Pain Out of Preparation

Things You Should Know About Your Audience

How to Get Your Audience to Believe You

Choosing Your Topic

CHAPTER 6

Supporting What You Say
73

CHAPTER 7

Watch Your Language
89

CHAPTER 8

Putting Your Speech Together
105

CHAPTER 9

The Sounds of Speech   123

CHAPTER 10

The Silent Side of Public Speaking   137

PART III

Taking the Pain Out of Presentation   155

CHAPTER 11

If You're Worried About Having to Give a Speech, Read This . . .   157

CHAPTER 15

The Entertainer

PAINLESS
PUBLIC
SPEAKING

PART I

Taking the Pain Out of Public Speaking

CHAPTER 5

Public Speaking in Today's World

Behavioral Objectives

After reading this chapter, you should have a clearer understanding of:

• the part speechmaking plays in your life.
• your abilities as a speaker.
• why it is important to speak up.
• how you feel about "talkers" and "nontalkers."
• the consequences of silence.
• why you are studying public speaking.

Introduction

This chapter is designed to say "hello," to help you begin thinking about yourself as a speaker, and to start you speaking in public. As you read, you will start to know and experience what it means to be a speechmaker. You will be given the chance to develop your mental and physical skills so that you will become more and more competent as a public speaker. Perhaps this picture will explain the process. Think of yourself going through a large, dark, deserted house, holding a flashlight. In order to explore your surroundings, you will need to open doors, peek into unknown corners, and walk through unfamiliar passageways. You will, however, be able to shine your light on the various things you find. After your "explorations," you can use your discoveries to enrich yourself, relate to others, and affect the nature of your inner and outer worlds.

This book contains a number of Speech Experiences (exercises) designed to make your "travels" interesting, entertaining, and challenging. During each of the Speech Experiences, you will be asked to shine your light on certain aspects of the public-communication process. As you continue your journey, you will realize that you can apply what you have discovered about the art public communication from one exploratory experience to another. Thus, the exercises serve to make your study of public speaking active as well as informative. They provide you with an opportunity to develop an understanding of basic public speaking forms, skills, and strategies while prompting you to want to share your understandings with others.

Public Speaking: Front and Center

What role does speechmaking play in the lives of each of the following?

General

- An athlete accepting an award
- A candidate for class president
- The treasurer of a club
- The football coach
- A carnival barker
- A police officer
- A news commentator
- A minister
- A teacher
- The leader of a tenant's strike
- A student delivering a report
- A student appealing a grade before a committee
- A press secretary
- A company executive
- A tour guide
- A theatre director
- A flight attendant

Particular

- Joe Namath
- Andrew Young
- Barbara Walters
- Johnny Carson
- Ted Kennedy
- Joseph Papp
- Gloria Steinem
- Mary Tyler Moore
- Pearl Bailey
- Caesar Chavez
- Mohammed Ali
- Golda Meir
- Bob Hope
- Bella Abzug
- Billy Graham
- You

If you replied that these individuals regularly stand up, speak out, and engage in public communication, you're absolutely right! The truth is that we live in a world that depends on the delivery and receipt of public messages. Public communication is with us now more than ever. Try this.

SPEECH EXPERIENCE: LOOSENING UP

1. While still seated, you will each have a chance to complete one of the following statements: "If there's one thing I can't stand, it's _school_," or "If there's one thing I'm crazy about, it's _sex_."

2. In turn, you will each have two minutes to come to the front of the room and talk to the class about anything you wish. For example, you may share a favorite story, joke, or anecdote with fellow students, or you may talk about a belief you hold, a feeling you have recently experienced, or your concerns about a personal, local, or public issue.

Questions About "LOOSENING UP"

1. What information, opinions, likes, or dislikes did you choose to transmit?

the art of living your life

2. Describe briefly the variety of student responses.

_____

_____

3. To which student talks were you most easily able to relate?

_____

_____

4. Do you believe you filled your speaking time effectively? Explain.

_____

_____

5. What are some of the things you thought and felt while you were speaking?

_____

_____

The preceding experiences let you try on the role of speechmaker. Increasingly, a wide variety of people are called upon to express an opinion, to report, to persuade, to entertain, and to question. For this reason, public speaking is rapidly becoming an important part of our lives. We are speakers. We are listeners. We are critics. Public communication is carried on *by* us, *for* us, and *all around* us. We encounter or act as public speakers in school, on the job, at religious services, while traveling, when attending a meeting, when watching television or listening to the radio, when participating in a rally, or simply when walking down the street. As public communicators, we either influence or are influenced by the messages of other people almost every minute of every day. Public discussion is an ongoing process. We compete for the attention of other people. Other people compete for our attention. In this way, we exert some control over our social, political and economic affairs.

With this in mind, read the following poem by Stephen Crane:

> A man said to the Universe:
> "Sir, I exist!"
> "However," replied the Universe,
> "The fact has not created in me
> A sense of obligation."

What was the Universe telling the man? _____

_____

Why do you think the Universe said this? _____

_____

Simply put, the Universe was telling each of us to take some responsibility for ourselves, our society, and our world. In particular, we are responsible for what we say and for listening to what others say. Presenting your ideas clearly is your responsibility. It is also your responsibility to evaluate the public communications of others. Don't expect these vital functions to be performed for you.

Our Speech-Centered Society

We live in a speech-centered society and, as a result, are compulsive talkers. For example, if you go to a party and find yourself sitting alone in a corner, someone will usually approach you and say, "What's the matter, aren't you having a good time?" In other words, people who hardly say anything are frequently thought to have "problems." Even though such behavior could be considered perfectly normal in someone with a shy and quiet personality, it still seems to bother many of us. Talkers generally get all the attention. Your own experience has probably shown you that we are inclined to admire "good talkers," provided, of course, that these individuals do not talk "too much" or "out of turn." In contrast, we seem to scorn those who do not contribute to a conversation at all. Thus, individuals who "speak up" learn very quickly that the general public associates such behavior with a successful individual. Wherever we go, we are confronted with a simple fact: If we want to succeed in life, we must learn to speak up! When we don't speak up, we give up opportunities to influence others. Do you agree? Try this.

SPEECH EXPERIENCE: To Talk or Not to Talk

1. Divide a sheet of paper into two parts. Label one side "Talkers;" the other, "Nontalkers."

2. Under each column, list words (nicknames or adjectives) that describe people who talk a lot and those who hardly talk at all. For example, if you talk a lot, you may be called "gabby;" if you don't talk very much, you may be labeled a "Silent Sam."

3. Compare and contrast your responses with the responses of other students.

Questions About "To Talk or Not to Talk"

1. What do your lists tell you about your attitudes toward those who speak up and those who do not speak up?

2. How many of your associations for talkers were positive? List them below.

3. How many of your associations for talkers were negative? List them below.

4. How many of your associations for nontalkers were positive? List them below.

5. How many of your associations for nontalkers were negative? List them below.

To give a more objective view of human speech, a creative writer named Bryng Bryngelson invented a character named Mr. Glub. Mr. Glub was a reporter for the *Venus Star*—a newspaper published on that planet. Mr. Glub's assignment was to visit Earth and report on some of our customs. Here is what he wrote:

The Earth, Nov. 20. What struck me first on my arrival on this planet was the interminable din of human voices. It appears that periods of silence and meditation required by our laws are wholly unknown here. The people on Earth talk all the time. On several occasions, however, I have observed in the public squares men and women talking when no one seemed to be listening. On inquiring into this curious situation, I was informed that they talk to hear themselves talk. To my question as to what they talked about, the invariable reply was, *nothing*. When I asked what nothing was, I was told it is talk.

They have another strange practice here of assembling vast amounts of the talk that is uttered in various places and publishing it in their newspapers and even books. I am informed that if in that form it is not generally read, it is only because the people are too busy talking to do much reading. (Here endeth Mr. Glub's dispatch.)[1]

[1] Bryng Bryngelson, "Man and His Symbol," *The Speech Teacher*, 11:2 (March 1953), pp. 81–2.

Do you agree with Mr. Glub that we here on Earth talk too much? Or, do you think we talk too little? Which of Mr. Glub's criticisms do you believe are valid? Which do you not accept? Why?

_____

_____

_____

When you were younger, do you remember either being the giver or the receiver of the "silent treatment?" Having nobody to talk to can be very painful. How long do you think you could go without talking to another person—an hour, a day, a week, or a month? How hung up are you on talking? Let's find out.

SPEECH EXPERIENCE: "The Silent Treatment"

1. For three days before performing this exercise, each member of the class is to follow these instructions:

DAY 1

Choose any two-hour period of the school day and remain perfectly silent during it.

DAY 2.

Choose any four hour period of the school day and remain perfectly silent during it.

DAY 3

Remain perfectly silent for an entire school day.

2. On the day this exercise is scheduled for class, the instructor will ask the students to arrange themselves in groups of five.

3. After the groups are formed, each of them is to begin an independent discussion growing out of answers to the following questions:

a. How much did you miss talking?

_____

_____

b. How did your not talking affect the people around you?

_____

_____

c. Did your not talking interfere with whatever you were doing? How?

_____

_____

d. How did your not talking affect your ability to listen to others?

_____

_____

e. How did your not talking affect your willingness to listen?

_____

_____

f. Did not talking make you feel nervous or calm?

_____

_____

g. What problems arose because of your silence?

_____

_____

h. How many times during each silent period did you have an urge to say something?

_____

_____

i. By not speaking, what rights did you give up?

_____

_____

j. Do you think the average person you encounter talks too *much* or too *little?*

_____

_____

k. What is your general opinion of people who talk a lot? Of those who hardly talk at all?

_____

_____

I. What did you learn from this exercise?

_____

_____

The exercise should help you determine some of the results of not talking. By speaking up, we more fully communicate our feelings and views to others. If we do not speak up, we give others the right to assume we understand their positions and agree with their statements. We lose our power to influence others. Thus, speaking up is essential. Just as arthritis can hinder our daily activities by not permitting us to move about freely and efficiently, so "silencitis" can hinder our ability to interact with those around us and can impair our relationship to our world. When we suffer from "silencitis," we simply do not get our message out and across to those who matter. As citizens, voters, members of organizations, and in our careers, we must speak up to communicate our views to others. Only by speaking effectively can you be an influence in your world.

One of the main purposes of this text is to help you eliminate "silencitis" as a problem. We want to help you become a confident, able, and effective public communicator. We want to help equip you with the skills that will let others know you exist, think, speak, and matter.

SPEECH EXPERIENCE: MY SPEAKING SELF

This inventory of your speaking self is intended to help you take stock of your speaking strengths and weaknesses.

1. Draw something that represents the image you have of yourself as a public communicator. Explain.

2. Draw something that represents the image you would like to project to others when speaking in public. Explain.

3. Identify three objects that you believe help to illustrate your communication strengths. Explain.

_____

_____

_____

4. Identify three objects that you believe help illustrate your communication weaknesses. Explain.

_____

_____

_____

Payoff for Speechmakers

Why are you studying public speaking? Before answering this question, consider the following. Imagine that you are the person in each of the cartoons. Identify how you are feeling, what you are thinking, and why.

1. A bored, distracted listener. _____

_____

_____

2. A speaker who was just hit by a tomato. _____

_____

_____

3. A speaker whose notes are all muddled. _____

_____

4. A speaker who is so nervous that he or she shakes. _____

_____

_____

Next, explain how studying public speaking may help avoid the problems depicted in each of the preceding cartoons.

Why Study Public Speaking?

People study public speaking for different reasons. Chief among them is the fact that we want to make ourselves understood. We also like to feel that when others speak to us, we know how to listen and understand what they are saying. Practically everything we do in life depends on our ability to communicate effectively. Thus, in order to be successful in any communication situation, we need to master the skills of expression and reception. Try this.

SPEECH EXPERIENCE: COMMUNICATION DETECTIVES

1. First, describe a situation in which you attempted to communicate your thoughts/feelings to another individual but you were misunderstood.
2. Next, describe a situation in which you attempted to communicate your thoughts/feelings to another individual and you were understood.
3. Finally, conduct a communication investigation by comparing and contrasting your successful and unsuccessful communication encounters. Try to figure out what caused your failure to be understood. Try to figure out what factors were responsible for your being understood. To what extent are the factors you identified also present in the situations depicted in the preceding cartoon series?

Being able to send and receive thoughts and feelings effectively is helpful in any situation.
Studying public speaking will also give you the opportunity to increase your self-understanding as well as your understanding of others. Developing the ability to understand the way you and other people perceive the world and its problems is very important. By participating in public speaking events, you can gain insight into the convictions people hold, what motivates them, and how they react when caught up in the communication process. When you study public speaking, you are also studying how to think, evaluate information or ideas, reason, draw conclusions, and formulate effective messages. These are not just skills that will benefit society; these are skills that will benefit you. In fact, people in politics, the ministry, business education, media, and sports credit much of their success to their public speaking abilities. In part, they testify that they have attained power, influence, and respect because they have learned how to effectively manage their communication skills.

SPEECH EXPERIENCE: THE SPEECHMAKER

1. Your instructor will divide you into pairs.
2. Each pair will be asked to act out one of the following situations:
    a. asking a friend to borrow his/her car.
    b. asking a banker for a loan.

c. asking the boss for a raise.

d. asking the teacher for a better grade.

3. After each role-play, discuss how the "asker" arranged, worded, and supported his or her ideas. Identify any changes or alterations in approach that could have helped increase the asker's effectiveness.

Regardless of the situation, you will be a more effective communicator if you are able to organize your ideas, develop, support, and amplify them, and deliver them so that your listeners will understand *what* you are saying and *how* you are feeling. Each time you attempt to transmit information, to persuade someone, or to entertain or amuse your friends, your greatest ally is your ability as a speechmaker.

A course in public speaking can also help you grow personally. Every time you address a group, you learn a little bit more about who you are and what you represent. Being able to speak before an audience will provide you with a sense of competence and increase your self-confidence. You show yourself that you can successfully meet the public speaker's challenge: you are willing to stand up, speak up, and—listen. Public speakers are also public listeners. By listening to the ideas of others, by examining their values, you give yourself the opportunity to develop your mind and expand your horizons. It is very difficult to listen to ideas with which you disagree. However, it can be a worthwhile and rewarding experience. What you hear may cause you to re-examine your own ideas, your own values, your own stand on an issue. The words of another individual may cause you to develop new insights or revise old beliefs. In short, public speaking can help develop a sense of personal freedom by giving you an opportunity to experience the perceptions of others. If you realize that you can like, respect, and listen to others, even if you do not agree with them, you have surely begun to grow. You owe it to yourself to grow as a thinker, as a communicator, as a person.

Summary

Public communication is an integral part of your life and intimately related to your well-being and success. In this chapter, you have been given a number of opportunities to function as a speechmaker, and you have begun to explore the feelings you have about performing this role. Hopefully, you now realize why you are studying public speaking, and have a clearer understanding of how public speaking can benefit you.

CHAPTER 2

The Nature of Public Speaking

Behavioral Objectives

After reading this chapter, you should have a better understanding of:

- the term "communication."
- the parts of the communication process.
- the ways you function as both a source and a receiver.
- why you cannot NOT communicate.
- the different ways we send and receive messages.
- what is meant by the term "noise."
- how context affects communication.
- how communication affects your life.
- the nature of feedback and how it operates.
- a communication model.
- the similarities and differences among intrapersonal, interpersonal, and public communication.

Introduction

We are all speakers—receivers—communicators. Since birth, we have been dependent upon the exchange of information. Not only have we worked at getting what went on inside our own head across to someone else, we have also worked at getting what went on in other people's heads into our own. One could say that communication is the process of sharing what an individual thinks, feels, and knows. Put another way, communication is the pooling of experience—sharing meaning. This is a simple way of defining the process of communication. As we continue our discussion, we shall add a few details to it.

SPEECH EXPERIENCE: HOME STAPLES

1. Prepare a list of items you would purchase after renting an apartment.

a. _____

b. _____

c. _____

d. _____

e. _____

Your list probably includes some of the following: a refrigerator, kitchen set, bed, and perhaps a television set. It is reasonable to assume that the items you identified were believed to be of an essential nature. It is much the same with communication.

SPEECH EXPERIENCE: COMMUNICATION STAPLES

1. Prepare a list of the elements you believe are at work in any communication situation.

a. _____

b. _____

c. _____

d. _____

e. _____

Communication Essentials

Let us now examine what we consider to be "the essentials" of communication—the elements that are present in every communicative act. Compare the items we mention with those you listed above.

People

Communication occurs between a source (a speaker) and a receiver (listener). Sources and receivers are people who send messages to themselves and to others. Although it is easy to imagine that a message begins with a source and ends with a receiver, it is important to realize that the sending and receiving process is a dynamic one. Everyone performs both source and receiver roles. There is no such thing as being solely a source or a receiver. To help you understand this, remember your experience of being totally silent. You weren't just a receiver. You added your own thoughts to what you heard. You reacted to the speaker and influenced him or her. You were a source also. We all function both as sources and receivers. In effect, we send and receive messages simultaneously.

SPEECH EXPERIENCE: I Am a Source—I Am a Receiver

1. Divide into pairs.
2. Each pair should select one of the following situations to enact:
   a. a student appealing suspension to the Dean
   b. a son or daughter asking Mother or Dad to borrow the family car.
   c. a shopper attempting to return a damaged record to a store.
3. After enacting these scenes, be prepared to discuss this question: What did your partner do or say that influenced what you did or said?

Bear in mind, that while functioning as a sender, you also interpret and react to the verbal and nonverbal messages of your listeners.

Messages

Messages that are sent and received during any communicative act may be verbal and/or nonverbal. Although we usually think of communication messages as being either oral or written, nonverbal messages are equally important. The way we walk, talk, and look advertises something about us to others. We could say that everything about the source and the receiver of a message communicates something to somebody; thus, you cannot *not* communicate.

SPEECH EXPERIENCE: MESSAGE SEARCH

    1. Spend the next sixty seconds talking with a partner on any topic.

    2. Then, list five messages you received while you were conversing. (For instance, was your partner interested in you? Did he/she enjoy this assignment? Was he/she comfortable?)

a. _____

b. _____

c. _____

d. _____

e. _____

You probably received a number of verbal messages from your partner. In other words, you reacted to your partner's words. In addition, you probably also received a number of nonverbal messages. Such cues as posture, head-nodding, facial expressions, clothing, gestures, and vocal quality were also capable of influencing you. All of these elements, taken together, comprise the communication messages you received.

Channels

Communication may be sent and received through any one or a combination of our senses. We send and receive messages of sight, sound, touch, taste, and smell.

SPEECH EXPERIENCE: CHANNEL CHANGER

    For the next sixty seconds, list all the messages you receive.

1. _____

2. _____

3. _____

4. _____

5. _____

Who or what sent them? Through what channels were they communicated? For example, you might have noticed street noise (coming to you through your sense of hearing), the teacher walking (coming to you though your sense of sight), the dryness of your mouth (coming to you through your sense of taste), someone's perfume or aftershave (coming to you through your sense of smell), and the sharpness of your pencil (coming to you through your sense of touch): Communication is a multichanneled experience.

Noise

Noise is anything that interferes with or distorts a message. If you think of noise as any disturbance, it becomes clear that noise need not be sound. There are many types of noise. For instance, when a stomachache prevents an individual from listening effectively, we can say that noise is coming from the individual's physical discomfort. When a person is described as stubborn, headstrong, or obstinate, and refuses to accept criticism, we can say that noise is coming from that individual's psychological makeup. On the other hand, a cold, damp room can also lessen effective communication. When this happens, we can say that the physical environment itself is contributing noise. Let us investigate this further.

SPEECH EXPERIENCE: NOISE NUDGERS

1. Which of the following items could serve to create noise? In each instance, identify the noise source and the ways in which the noise source could interfere with effective communication.

a. sunglasses _____

b. blurred print _____

c. a dark room _____

d. screeching brakes _____

e. a radio _____

f. static _____

g. playing with a ballpoint pen _____

h. a howling wind _____

    i. a stuffy nose _____

    j. a black eye _____

Context

Communication always occurs in a context or setting. Sometimes, the context is so familiar that we hardly notice it. Other times, the context stands out "like a sore thumb" and exerts significant control over our behavior. Various situations offer us hints which may influence the way we interact. Consider the extent to which your language, dress, and posture change depending upon whether you are at home, at work, at a friend's house or at school. Conditions and circumstances influence your behavior without you consciously realizing it. Hence, all human communication is influenced by the context of the environment, by the time and location in which it occurs. Try this.

SPEECH EXPERIENCE: CONTEXT CAPERS

    1. Compare and contrast the types of interpersonal and public encounters that could occur in each of the following settings:

    a. a funeral home _____

    b. a rock concert _____

    c. a school lecture hall _____

    d. a political street rally _____

    e. a baseball stadium _____

Context can affect communication in other ways, as well. Just as environment can influence the type of communication that will occur, it can also determine whether effective communication will occur at all. In other words, finding out such things as room size and location are a part of a public communicator's preparation. For speakers, this means finding out what the room looks like, where it is situated, how audience members are to be arranged, if a lectern is available, and whether a public address system will be used. Any of these factors can have an impact on the delivery and reception of your message.

Effect

Communication always has some effect on you or on those with whom you are relating. Every act of communication has an outcome. Communication may influence the source, the receiver, or both. Its effect may be physical or psychological. For instance, communication can produce joy, anger or sadness; it can cause you to fight, argue, or evade an issue. Communication can lead to greater understanding, or cause you to reconsider an opinion. It is also important to realize that communication effects are not always visible or immediately observable. Thus, silence, empathy (the capacity for feeling and perceiving as another person does), apathy (the lack of feeling or emotion), and delayed reactions are perfectly valid communication effects.

Feedback

Whenever we communicate, we get back information. The information we perceive functions as feedback. It lets us know how we are doing. Like communication in general, feedback can be verbal or nonverbal. On the basis of a smile, a frown, a comment, or an internal thought, we may change or modify what we say and how we say it.

Feedback frequently works in strange ways. There was once an instructor who always kept his students five to ten minutes after the class period had ended. The students would shuffle in their seats, nervously fidget with their books, and tap their fingers impatiently. The instructor failed to respond to their cues. Finally, a group of students got together and decided that, at the scheduled moment the period ended, they would all turn and stare at the front door. What do you think happened? That's right! The instructor could not avoid the message, and the class was not detained again.

A second story concerns a class of students who decided to test their instructor's feedback perceptions. The instructor had a habit of marching back and forth across the front of the room as he spoke. The habit was so pronounced that the class nicknamed him, "The Pendulum." Needless to say, it became very tiresome and somewhat humorous to watch "The Pendulum" patrol the classroom. A couple of students got together in a last ditch effort to break the instructor of his distracting habit. One morning, before the instructor entered the room, some students informed the other class members of a plan. Whenever the instructor approached the right side of the room, they would provide him with positive feedback; that is, look alert, take notes, smile and nod their heads up and down. When he approached the left side of the room, they would shower him with negative feedback in the form of talking among themselves, yawning, taking no notes, and displaying general disinterest. After the instructor entered the room and began his lecture, the students carried out their roles to perfection. By the end of twenty minutes, where do you think the instructor was standing? Correct! "The Pendulum," had ceased to swing. The instructor had finally perceived and responded to student feedback. Try this:

SPEECH EXPERIENCE: FEED ME FEEDBACK

1. Make a list of the feedback you receive during the course of an average day. Insert each message under the appropriate heading:

Positive Messages I Sent to Myself

a. _____

b. _____

c. _____

d. _____

e. _____

Negative Messages I Sent to Myself

a. _____

b. _____

c. _____

d. _____

e. _____

Positive Messages I Received from Others

a. _____

b. _____

c. _____

d. _____

e. _____

Negative Messages I Received from Others

a. _____

b. _____

c. _____

d. _____

e. _____

Questions about "FEED ME FEEDBACK"

1. How much attention do you pay to feedback?

_____

_____

2. To what types of messages do you pay the most attention? Why?

_____

_____

Communication Models

How do the elements we have identified fit together? One way to describe communication essentials is through the use of a communication model. A model is a diagram of the communication process. Just as a model airplane provides a description of an airplane and an architect's blueprint provides a description of a building, so does a communication model provide a description of the communication process. Let us now examine a few popular models of communication. Keep in mind that each of the models may be used to explain or describe either intrapersonal (communication with yourself), interpersonal (communication with another), or public communication acts.

One of the earliest models of communication was designed by the Greek philosopher Aristotle over 2300 years ago. Aristotle's model includes a number of the essential items we mentioned. (See: Fig. 2–1) What type of communication experience do you believe Aristotle's model best depicts? Why?

Aristotle's model draws heavily upon his _Rhetorica_ in which he advises speakers on how to construct their speeches for various occasions, audiences and effects. While applicable to all communication situations, Aristotle's model is most useful for public speakers.

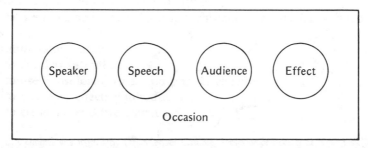

Figure 2–1. Aristotle's Model of Communication.

WHO – SAYS WHAT – TO WHOM – THROUGH WHAT
CHANNEL – WITH WHAT EFFECT?

Figure 2–2. Lasswell's Model of Communication.

Source	Message	Channel	Receiver
Communication Skills	Elements	Seeing	Communication Skills
Attitudes	Structure	Hearing	Attitudes
Knowledge	Content	Touching	Knowledge
Social System	Treatment	Smelling	Social System
Culture	Code	Tasting	Culture

Figure 2–3. Berlo's SMCR Model of Communication.

A model similar to Aristotle's comes from a contemporary scholar Harold D. Lasswell. (See: Fig. 2–2) Both models lead us to a clearer understanding of the fact that communication is designed to achieve specific purposes.

David Berlo, a speech expert, supplies us with still another communication model. (See: Fig. 2–3) Berlo's SMCR model isolates various ingredients of the communication process. Why do you think this model assigns similar elements to both source and receiver?

Next, focus on Wilbur Schramm's Model of Communication.

Schramm tells us that communication requires the active participation of

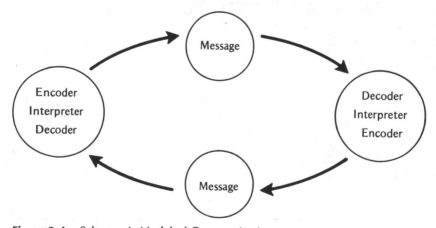

Figure 2–4. Schramm's Model of Communication.

both the source and the receiver. He also contends that both source and receiver are functions performed by each communication participant. If one views communication as a circle, it is difficult to determine who is functioning as a source and who is functioning as receiver.

SPEECH EXPERIENCE: Making a Model

1. Divide the class into small groups of equal numbers.
2. Each group should be assigned to dramatize one of the following situations or events:
   a. arguing with a storekeeper about the price of an item.
   b. delivering a lecture to a class.
   c. a committee deciding how to market a new product.
   d. daydreaming in the park.
3. After participating in the role-playing experience, each group is to create a diagram or original model that describes the type of communication situation just enacted. As you do this, seek to determine what communication elements were involved in your skit and how they related to one another.

Types of Communication

The skits and models you have created reflect each of the basic types of communication. In other words, depending on the situation, communication can be described as intrapersonal, interpersonal or public in nature. Let us examine each of these types now.

Intrapersonal communication occurs when you communicate with yourself. Basically, we communicate with ourselves on three levels: verbally, nonverbally, and vocally. To illustrate how these levels operate, picture this scene: You are backstage on the opening night of a new play. Members of the cast are nervous and this is what you see. Some are sitting or standing in a corner going over their lines without making a sound. Since they are using what is called "inner speech," it qualifies as a form of verbal intrapersonal communication. If they were observed to rehearse their lines using "outer speech," so that they could be heard, it too would be considered verbal intrapersonal communication. As long as they used organized language to communicate with themselves, it is to be classified as verbal in form.

Looking around, you might also see certain performers pacing back and forth and wringing their hands to relieve their nervousness. Actors and actresses frequently have their own characteristic ways of nonverbally communicating with themselves. Those who are superstitious confer good luck upon themselves by rubbing a rabbit's foot, knocking three times on wood, or concealing a lucky object somewhere in their costume.

A final glance at the cast before the curtain goes up should include notice of any vocal intrapersonal communication. Here the means by which performers communicate with themselves involves only the sounds they make. If you listen carefully, you might hear some of them sigh, others clear their throats, and still others hum to relieve their anxiety or stage fright.

Are there times when you prefer to be alone? It might be to think over a problem, make a decision, or figure out how to handle a new situation. Having a private sanctuary, a place where you can let your thoughts run free, can be very useful. It provides you with an opportunity to chat with yourself, about yourself, and for your own benefit. In a sense, it could be called a SELF–ish conversation. Because you don't have to explain or defend what you think or say to anyone, intrapersonal communication gives you a very special kind of personal freedom.

How do you feel about people who talk to themselves? Do you ever do it? When you have to memorize something for class, do you repeat the words over and over again to yourself out loud? For some strange reason, talking to oneself has a bad reputation. Maybe it is because people, when they think of it, picture someone walking down the street having a loud conversation with themselves. Actually, in a much less dramatic way, we all communicate with ourselves. Every time we think, we are communicating with ourselves. Many authorities today feel that people should communicate more deeply with themselves through such intrapersonal methods as meditation, contemplation, reflection, and diary-keeping. In each case, you are both the sender and receiver of information. Attempts to establish open lines of communication with yourself through these methods make several things possible. You may begin to see a problem from more than one point of view, provide a springboard for future communication with others, and sharpen your awareness of the advantages and disadvantages of a given situation. In short, how you communicate with yourself can make a big difference in how things turn out when you communicate with others. What you think about in your inner world is often a reflection of what is going on in your outer world. In order to make the two harmonize, you must take an equal interest in both.

SPEECH EXPERIENCE: Dear Diary

1. Write something personal about yourself in an imaginary diary. The entry should reveal some intrapersonal insight. For example, it might express a personal belief, attitude, feelings of love or hate. Do not sign your diary piece.

2. Pass your entry to your instructor, who will redistribute entries so that everyone in the room has someone else's.

3. Once you have someone else's message, pretend that you have discovered the diary entry fifty years in the future. Read it and register an impression of it in your mind.

Questions About "Dear Diary"

1. What does the entry reveal about the writer? _____

_____

_____

2. How could these feelings affect the individual's ability or desire to

communicate? _____

_____

_____

In contrast to intrapersonal communication, interpersonal communication occurs when you communicate with another individual or a small group verbally, nonverbally, or vocally. Thus, interpersonal communication is a circular, many leveled process in which it is often difficult to tell who is responsible for carrying on the conversation.

Too many people think that the process of communicating is simply a matter of give and take. Like a ping-pong match, they take turns speaking and listening. Although it sounds right, it isn't. The word *circular* in this definition, means that a person who is listening has not stopped communicating. While the act of listening does not include sending out verbal messages, it does include the sending out of nonverbal and vocal messages. Consequently, when any two people are engaged in interpersonal communication, the exchange is not one of stop and go, but rather, a continuous process.

Most of us spend more than half of any average day communicating with others on several levels. Talking is but one of these levels. When you are introduced to a stranger, the interpersonal communication between you and that individual probably begins before either has spoken a word. Very quickly, both parties tend to look each other over. Thus, communication has already begun on a nonverbal level. If you are close enough to each other, it may begin to function on the level of smell. This is particularly true when one or both of you is wearing a conspicuous cologne or perfume. Soon after the verbal introduction, you might also find yourself being affected by the sound of the person's voice on a vocal level. So, you see, interpersonal communication can and does operate on many levels at the same time. It also permits people to have immediate and spontaneous feedback as to how they appear to others.

Unlike intrapersonal or interpersonal communication, public communication occurs in situations where a number of listeners receive messages from a single, clearly identifiable source. It differs from what we would call an interpersonal conversation in a number of important ways. Unlike interpersonal situations, during public communication situations, the prime responsibility rests on the shoulders of the speaker. It is up to the speaker to make "continuous talk." It could be said that whenever you have the responsibility to talk to others for longer than a few minutes without interruption, you are making a speech. The size of an audience is but a secondary consideration. To illustrate, consider this scene: You meet a friend downtown. Your friend is wearing a sign which reads, "On Strike." You begin to discuss the strike with him. You inquire as to the position of the management, the working conditions, and the union's demands. Your friend responds to each of your questions. Soon, a number of other picketing workers join in the discussion. As the group grows larger, a woman striker begins to urge passersby to join the workers in their protest against the company. You, your friend, a number of other picketers, and an array of ordinary citizens begin to listen to her appeals. Somehow, what began as an interpersonal conversation suddenly has been transformed into a public communication event. The general pattern for a two-person discussion is for each individual to speak for brief periods. However, during public communication, role-taking is put aside and one individual is obliged to carry the main responsibility. That individual delivers what might be termed a speech, a monologue, or a relatively continuous address.

SPEECH EXPERIENCE: TRANSFORMATION

What could happen to convert each of the following situations into public communication events?

1. While picking up your car at the repair shop, you discover it has not been properly fixed. _____

_____

_____

2. A police officer stops you on the street and asks to see your identification. _____

_____

_____

3. A meterperson tickets your car which is legally parked at a broken meter. _____

_____

_____

4. A waiter begins to berate you because of the size of the tip you left.

_____

_____

5. You are protesting food price increases to the supermarket manager.

_____

_____

It should also be recognized that feedback received during a public communication event is usually more restricted and less immediate than the feedback received during an interpersonal communication encounter. During public communication, there is less verbal feedback offered to the communicator. The communicator is forced to rely on the positive or negative nonverbal cues received from listeners. For the most part, audience participation in the form of questions or comments are discouraged except at the end of a presentation. It is only the rude listener who interrupts a speaker during the course of a speech. In addition, the public speaker, more so than the interpersonal communicator, is apt to misinterpret the feedback messages he receives. The reason for this is that the public speaker cannot stop in the middle of a speech and ask each member of the audience if they grasp its meaning. Conversely, the interpersonal speaker can interrupt a conversation at any time to find out whether he or she is being understood.

The degree of empathy existing between speaker and listener during public communication is usually less than the amount one would find during an interpersonal communication. For this reason, the public speaking situation frequently appears to be less personal or intimate in nature. On the other hand, though the interpersonal speaker has less control over the situation on a one-to-one basis because the other party's remarks cannot be anticipated, the public speaker can prepare and rehearse a speech and be reasonably confident that his or her audience will sit quietly and not interrupt. The interpersonal communicator rarely, if ever, has the opinion of rehearsing a conversation.

Despite the differences between interpersonal and public communication, we need to realize that each form of communication springs from the desire of people to communicate. Each form involves the transmission and the receipt of messages. During each type of encounter (in a given context), some verbal and/or nonverbal messages are understood, while others may be partially or completely missed. Keep these factors in mind as we continue our study of communication.

Summary

This chapter describes and explains each of the major elements of the communication act (people, messages, channels, noise, context, effect, and feedback). Also offered were several representative models of communication which compared and contrasted intrapersonal, interpersonal, and public communication forms. We discussed the ways in which these communication elements are able to affect or alter the course, development, and outcome of any given speech experience.

PART

Taking the Pain Out of Preparation

Things You Should Know
About Your Audience

Behavioral Objectives

After reading this chapter, you should have a better understanding of:

- what is meant by the word "audience."
- why it is so important to understand your audience.
- the major obstacle to understanding an audience.
- what to analyze before delivering your speech.
- what to analyze while delivering your speech.
- what to analyze after delivering your speech.

simily like
metaphor
are

Introduction

What is an audience? It seems to be generally assumed that everyone who reads a book on public speaking or is a member of a public speaking class should be able to answer this question. After all, readers and students are members of audiences. Take a moment and write down your personal meaning for the word, "audience."

_____

_____

_____

Let us now attempt to establish some common understanding of what an audience actually is.

An audience is a group of listeners or spectators. However, unlike a mass communication event where audience members may be found in numerous and contrasting settings, the members of a public speaker's audience are usually found in one specific, definable context. Also, unlike interpersonal or small group communication where the audience is usually composed of one to five other individuals, the public speaker's audience may contain over a thousand individuals. As is common with all audiences, members of a public speaker's audience share some common purpose.

Why Should You Seek to Understand Your Audience?

In this book, we constantly stress that public speaking is neither a linear nor a one-way communication happening. Audience members are active-free-willed participants in the public speaking encounter. It is an error to assume that only the speaker communicates. In practice, speaker and audience are partners in the communication game or experience. It stands to reason that if your audience is to respond to your message in a favorable way, you need to learn many things about the individuals who make it up. Try this.

SPEECH EXPERIENCE: AUDIENCE SIMILES*

Respond to the following probe ten times, *i.e.*, without thinking, jot down whatever comes to your mind when you are confronted with the word "audience." Do not repeat answers.

Example: An audience is like a(n) fruit salad.

An audience is like a(n) _____.

An audience is like a(n) _____.

* A *simile* is an explicit comparison, generally using the words "like or as." It simply compares the qualities of one thing to the qualities of another.

An audience is like a(n) _____ .

An audience is like a(n) _____ .

An audience is like a(n) _____ .

An audience is like a(n) _____ .

An audience is like a(n) _____ .

An audience is like a(n) _____ .

An audience is like a(n) _____ .

An audience is like a(n) _____ .

Questions About "AUDIENCE SIMILES"

1. What types of words did you use to fill in the blanks? _____

_____

_____

2. What do the words you selected tell you about your understanding of

the concept "audience?"_____

_____

_____

3. How many of your associations were favorable ones? _____

_____

4. How many of your associations were unfavorable?_____

_____

The major obstacle to understanding audiences is that no two audiences are exactly alike. Audiences are as variable as the people who compose them. Audiences contain individuals who possess different personalities, beliefs, attitudes, values, hopes, dreams, and backgrounds. Therefore, one of the keys to understanding and relating to people in an audience is to recognize how they differ. Accordingly, long before you stand up to deliver a speech, you would do well to identify the differences and similarities between yourself and your listeners. After doing this, your next step is to think of ways to bridge those differences. If you perform these tasks, you will be in a better position to relate to the needs and desires of your listeners.

SPEECH EXPERIENCE: AUDIENCE AUCTION

1. Your instructor will ask you to bring a personal belonging to class. For example, you might bring in a guitar, handmade object, or a lucky charm. If desired, the actual article need not be present; pictures may be substituted. You will have two minutes to describe and sell your item to the class-audience.

2. The names of the following audience types will be written on index cards and placed in a grab bag. At the end of the preceding experience, you are to draw one of the cards at random. It is your task to adapt your original sales pitch to this new audience. A discussion of the strategies used during this exercise should follow.

Stockbrokers	Prison Inmates
Musicians	Doctors
Teenagers	Preschool Children
Teachers	Lawyers
Birdwatchers	Chefs
Scouts	Actors
Police Officers	Housewives
Airline Pilots	Bus Drivers
Farmers	Secretaries
Telephone Operators	Beauticians
Accountants	Astronauts
Athletes	Dog Lovers
Politicians	Cowboys

Questions About "AUDIENCE AUCTION"

1. How did the speakers adapt their talks to selected audiences?

_____

_____

2. Was there recognition of the fact that every audience is different?

_____

_____

3. How did the speakers display their awareness of audience differ-

ences? _____

4. To what extent did speakers attempt to identify their goals with the

interests and needs of their audience? _____

_____

_____

The ability to feel and understand what another person is feeling (empathy) is one of the most important skills a public communicator can have. If you can put yourself in someone else's shoes and see the world from behind someone else's eyes, you will be better able to communicate with that person.

Successful communicators seek to find out what their audiences need and want, and, if at all possible, they try to give it to them. Analyzing your audience will provide you with a wealth of information that will help you achieve your goal.

What to Analyze Before You Deliver Your Speech

The following model can be used to help you prepare to meet your audience.

When using this model to analyze your audience, start by examining area one. List pieces of information and bits of personal data that are known to both you and your audience. For example, are you and audience members about the same age? Are your cultural backgrounds similar? Have you had common educational experiences? Do you belong to similar socio-economic groups? Next, begin work on area two by attempting to identify information that is available to your audience, but not readily available to you. What is your audience's opinion of you? Does your audience consider you to be a trustworthy source, knowledgeable, or incompetent? If you are successful in analyzing this area, you will be able to move the information contained in it into area one. Then, proceed to

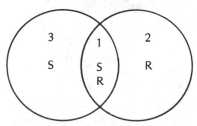

Figure 3–1. S/R Model.

area three, which contains data that only you have. Ask yourself how much of what is contained in this area you should share with your audience. In other words, what material will you have to move into area one in order to establish rapport with your audience and accomplish your purpose? It goes without saying that the larger area one becomes (the information shared by you and your audience), the greater is your chance of communicating more effectively.

When preparing to communicate in public, you should be able to answer the following questions:

1. What is the purpose of my speech?
2. Does the audience know my purpose?
3. How big is my audience?
4. What is the general age of the people in my audience?
5. Are the sexes evenly represented?
6. What is the educational background of my audience?
7. What cultural–ethnic backgrounds are represented?
8. How knowledgeable are audience members about my topic?
9. What special knowledge do I possess?
10. What special knowledge do members of my audience possess?
11. What attitudes, values, and beliefs are strongly held by the audience?
12. Do I share any of these?
13. What is my audience's probable attitude toward me?
14. What is my audience's probable attitude toward my subject?
15. What is my audience's probable attitude toward my goal?

It should be stressed that audience members carry with them a lifetime of learning and experience. So do speakers. It is your responsibility to discover how you can best make the two mesh. A "meeting of the minds" is the first important step toward removing the invisible barriers which separate speakers from their audiences.

What to Analyze During the Speech

As speechmakers, we take for granted that we will either read a speech or refer to our notes while addressing an audience. Yet, how frequently do we consider the need to also "read" our audience's reactions? All public communicators require feedback. If you are wise, you will rely on it to monitor your own talk. Let us now pay some attention to the types of messages speakers get from their audiences during the course of a public presentation.

Scene: Your instructor has assigned each student in the class either the number one or the number two. All number ones are requested to leave the room. Once outside the classroom, number ones are briefed by the instructor as follows: They are told that they will have one minute to think of a joke or story to tell to a partner (one of the remaining number twos). Unknown to the number ones, the teacher has secretly briefed the number twos. Some number twos have been told to laugh, ask questions, and look interested when their partners speak to them. Others have been told to frown, give disapproving looks, and appear bored. How do you imagine the storytellers (number ones) will feel when confronting each type of audience member? Why?

It goes without saying that we are dependent upon one another's reactions. Feedback is the process by which we adjust our messages to the responses of others. For example, what types of adjustments would the storytellers (number ones) have made when communicating with listeners who responded favorably? Unfavorably? Reading an audience's reaction helps us determine if we are communicating what we think we are communicating. Let us now consider the types of feedback an audience can provide a speaker.

Audience members can give a public speaker *positive* feedback. They can reinforce a speaker's behavior by communicating nonverbal or sometimes verbal responses of approval.

Can you think of some forms of positive reinforcement that our "storyteller" might have received? Write them on the lines below.

1. _____

2. _____

3. _____

4. _____

5. _____

If you included smiles, laughter, up and down head nods, applause, shouts of "more!," you're on the right track. Positive feedback serves to reinforce a speaker's behavior and discourage change.

Listeners also give speakers *negative* feedback. Negative feedback, if responded to properly, should have just the opposite effect. Negative feedback should serve as a corrective function, if the source is able to adjust to it. What are the means audience members can employ to alert a speaker to the need for adapting or modifying a presentation?

SPEECH EXPERIENCE: NEGATIVE PLOYS

Students should come to the front of the room and provide examples of negative feedback. Each student should demonstrate a different type.

Questions About "NEGATIVE PLOYS"

1. What forms of negative feedback occurred most often? _____

_____

_____

2. Which did you consider to be the most effective? Least effective?

Why? _____

_____

_____

Common types of negative feedback include yawns, seat-squirming, hair twirling, boos, lack of applause, and grimaces. How do you feel when someone reacts to something you are saying with such responses? How do you imagine our "storyteller" felt? What could a speaker do to reverse this type of reaction pattern? Don't expect to have much effect upon another person's thinking and behavior unless you allow that person to affect your own thinking and behavior. If you take your audience's ideas and feelings into account during the public communication event, you will increase your chance of being effective.

Since the element of feedback is essential to successful public speaking, here is a story which clearly illustrates what can happen when a speaker fails to recognize its importance.

This scene is a classroom in which a student, assigned to deliver an extemporaneous speech,* takes her place at the lectern. Without ever looking up at her audience, not even once, the speaker proceeds to mumble on and on in a monotone. The instructor, witnessing this complete disregard for any audience feedback, decides to teach the speaker a lesson in feedback she will never forget. Quietly, the instructor passes among the members of the class and, one by one, tells them to tiptoe out of the room. Soon, only the instructor remains. Imagine the speaker's surprise when, upon finishing her speech, she discovers that the audience has vanished into thin air. Needless to say, having learned a lesson in feedback the hard way, this speaker quickly developed respect for the importance of feedback from an audience.

Looking at your audience regularly, rather than at your notes, permits you to watch for and adjust to visual audience signs or reactions. Only if you observe audience feedback can you hope to adapt to it. Remember, the purpose of feedback is to help you decide what to do or say next. Should your audience's behavior suggest to you that they are puzzled or confused, you might take time to

---

* There are three basic types of speech delivery. There is the *manuscript speech* that is designed to be read verbatim from a script. An *extemporaneous speech* is thoroughly prepared, organized, and rehearsed and is then presented from memory, perhaps using notes. Finally, the *impromptu speech* is given without any advance preparation—off the top of the speaker's head.

clarify what was not clearly communicated. Or, if the feedback from your audience suggests boredom or impatience, perhaps certain segments of your talk should be shortened. Your success as a speaker will depend upon your ability to read your audience's reactions accurately.

SPEECH EXPERIENCE: FEEDBACK CHARADES

Students will be asked to go to the front of the room, one at a time, and stand facing the chalkboard. While the student's back is turned, the instructor will hold up a card on which one of the following reactions is written: anger, impatience, surprise, boredom, confusion, interest, pride, hostility, apathy, and acceptance. The class group; i.e., the audience members, are to simulate the indicated response. After turning around the "speaker" has thirty seconds to detect the audience's mood.

What to Analyze After You Give the Speech

Besides gathering information from an audience before and during a presentation, clever speakers also try to gather audience information after they have finished. You might try asking audience members how they liked what you had to say. Their reactions might surprise you. In fact, you might have completely misinterpreted the feedback messages you were sent. How do the following examples help illustrate the importance of checking your interpretations of the audience's reactions?

Example One

After he delivered the Gettysburg Address, Lincoln was extremely upset. No one had applauded. His words were met with complete silence. He interpreted this as failure. Lincoln believed that he had not moved his audience. In actuality, his audience was too deeply affected to applaud. In time, the speech earned Lincoln critical acclaim and fame.

Example Two

Ralph Nichols, co-author of *Are You Listening?*, tells this story.

One lovely spring evening, I drove to a small town in northern Minnesota. I entered the local auditorium, met the high school officials and took my seat on the platform. The audience was full of fathers, mothers, grandmothers, grandfathers, uncles, aunts, and assorted cousins. After speeches by members of the graduating class, I was introduced by the principal. I had hardly finished the introduction to my speech when a child began to cry. Soon the wails of a second child joined those of the first. Then a little boy started running up and down the aisle. The audience was distracted. A second boy started to chase the first youngster up and down the aisle. The old wooden seats in the audience creaked as people twisted around to see what was happening.

Suddenly, I was in the worst situation imaginable for a public speaker. I had no listeners. My mouth dried out and it was hard to talk. I ran through all the techniques I had learned and practiced in the past to regain my audience's attention. I tried projecting my voice more forcefully. It didn't work. I tried being humorous, but no one laughed. In a desperate effort to keep from going to pieces, I tried one last technique that I had learned long ago. I scanned my audience for a single person who was listening. Finally, I found him. He was an old gentleman seated in a row near the front. He was looking at me, nodding his head and smiling. I forgot the bedlam around the man and concentrated on him. He was a wonderful audience. My mouth stopped being dry. Slowly I pulled my speech together and proceeded to its end, feeling much better about the whole experience. After the graduation exercises, I noticed my one-man audience standing at the side of the auditorium. "That man over there," I said to the principal, "I noticed him while I was speaking. I would like to meet him." "Well, yes, I'll try to introduce you," said the principal, "but it may be a little difficult. You see, the poor fellow is stone deaf."

Positive and negative feedback can be misinterpreted. These instances illustrate that to be useful, you must analyze and evaluate carefully and accurately any and all feedback you get from your audience.

Summary

In this chapter, we have explained what an audience is, why you should seek to understand your audience, and how you can obtain needed information about your audience. We have provided you with a series of procedures you can use to gather such data before, during, and after you deliver a speech. We directed your attention to the feedback process, the need you have to be able to adapt your presentation to different audiences, and the strategies you can employ to accomplish this.

Getting Your Audience to Believe You

Behavioral Objectives

After reading this chapter, you should have a clearer understanding of:

- why it is important that an audience believes a speaker's message.
- why people believe what they see, hear, and feel.
- the kinds of evidence people accept as a basis for what they are willing to believe.
- why having an audience's undivided attention is so important to a speechmaker.
- the principles of communication a speaker must use in order to make an audience believe.
- what is meant by the term, "speech insurance."
- the relationship between boredom and believing.

Introduction

Unless your audience believes you, your purpose as a speaker is defeated. It brings to mind the saying, "The operation was successful, but the patient died." The fact that the surgeon did a beautiful job removing the patient's appendix matters little to the rest of the family if the patient died on the operating table. The same principle applies to the speechmaker; the best speech in the world falls flat on its face if the audience to whom it is directed doesn't believe what the speaker says. But, there is more to getting an audience to believe than simply speaking the truth. It is an extremely complex process. In this chapter we make every effort to simplify this process and, by so doing, help get audiences to believe what you tell them.

Values

The most direct route to communicating with your audience is to know its values before you open your mouth to speak. Your first reaction to this remark might be, "How can I know anything about an audience's values beforehand?" That's a good question and, the answer is, "You can!" Just as any serious and experienced boxer must find out as much as possible about his opponent in the next match, so must the serious and experienced speaker learn as much about the audience he or she is going to address. Whether it is in the field of sports, business, law, or international diplomacy, being thoroughly prepared to meet a new situation, or individual, is essential. In the case of an audience, it is knowing its values. For example, people who value money are always ready and willing to listen to new ways and means of making more money. Or, people who place a high value on the freedom they enjoy in this country are apt to be extremely receptive to the words of a speaker who supports such a view. What we are saying here is that, by finding out your audience's values beforehand, you are increasing the chances that they will believe you. Advertising firms and those in the field of public relations know this basic principle and, if you will look at most television commercials and highway billboards, you will notice how much they rely on values as a means of communication. Values, in plain language, apply to those things that people desire, treasure, and generally hold dear—things for which they are willing to either fight or make a sacrifice.

Audiences are not made up of people with empty heads and hearts. Every member of an audience has literally thousands of thoughts and feelings. Some they have shared with others; some have never been openly expressed to a living soul. Then, of course, there are those thoughts and feelings which are in transition—those which have come of age and stand ready to undergo a change in either course or character. So, you see, any audience you are about to address is much more than a collection of people seated before you. It is a virtual sea of values (thoughts and feelings) related to such aspects of human conditions as religion, sex, education, politics, business, health and entertainment. In whatever form these thoughts and feelings exist out there, they represent a potential sounding board for you, the speaker. If the values you advance happen to agree with those of your audience, fine! If they don't, the chances of your being believed are very slim. In short, your believability (or credibility) depends largely upon the extent to which your values and those of your audience complement one another. The question now is: "What, exactly, does a speaker do to get an audience to believe?"

Reasons Why People Believe Others

Have you ever wondered why you believe what friends tell you, what you hear on the evening news or read in the morning paper? How about the mechanic who repairs your car, the doctor who prescribes medicine for your persistent cough, and your teacher in English literature? Do you believe what they tell you? Why? People's answers will differ according to whom you ask.

SPEECH EXPERIENCE: To Tell the Truth [1]

1. On an assigned date, each student is to think up an anecdote and come to class prepared to tell it. (Time limit: 2–5 minutes) The story should either be true or false. Because it is difficult to tell a story that is completely true or false, it should be predominantly one or the other. It may be drawn from life—something that really happened—or be an outright lie.

2. With the class seated in a circle, each student should take a turn telling a story. After it is told, the teacher should take a vote by asking, "How many of you thought the story was true? Raise your hands. How many of you thought it was false? Raise your hands.

3. After each vote, students are asked to volunteer the reasons for their voting the story "true" or "false."

4. Following the voting on each story, the storyteller is to reveal whether it was, in fact, true or false.

5. Depending upon the size of the class, it may be necessary to carry this exercise over to another period. After all have had an opportunity to tell their stories, an open discussion should address itself to the following questions:

    a. Are there any nonverbal characteristics common to most liars?

    b. Do you think liars are born or made?

    c. Describe the biggest liar you have ever known.

    d. In your opinion, which is more important:

        1) why a lie was told?

[1] Adapted from: Abné M. Eisenberg, *Understanding Communication in Business and the Professions* (New York: Macmillan Publishing Co., Inc. 1978), p. 301.

2) the nature of the lie?
3) what happens because a lie was told?
Explain your answer.

Below are some of the most common reasons given for believing anything:

Because . . . I read it

There are people who believe anything they read in a book, newspaper, or magazine. Even though they are willing to admit that people make mistakes, and that whatever they read was written by people, they continue to have blind faith in anything they read. Although such an attitude seems to go against common sense, it nevertheless exists and will continue to exist as long as people have a "need to believe."

Because . . . it is logical

Logic is not a phenomenon of nature. Unlike lightning, thunder, apples, pears, and rippling brooks, logic is artificial—a manmade phenomenon. Aristotle, the Greek philosopher, was responsible for formulating the rules we still use to determine whether or not reasoning is logical. If reasoning conforms with these rules, it is said to be logical. If it does not, it is regarded as illogical.

A great many of those who worship logic are unaware of the fact that something can be logically valid but materially untrue. Take the following syllogism (a form used in logic):

• Major Premise: All dogs have two heads.
• Minor Premise: Fido is a dog.
• Conclusion: Fido has two heads.

While the conclusion that Fido has two heads was arrived at logically, it, is materially untrue because the premise—all dogs have two heads—is incorrect. Logic, like mathematics, possesses no moral code or conscience. It will serve anyone who adheres to its rules. One must, therefore, look beyond logic for reasons to believe; for the correctness of the premise and for the sincerity of the speaker.

Because . . . it is scientific

In the thinking of many people, science is a "sacred cow." It is a method that is always true and always to be trusted. But, science in a manmade methodology. It relies on human observation and is subject to human error. T.V. commercials frequently advertise their products by saying, ". . . and, it is scientific!"

They rarely go into any explanation beyond telling their viewers that their product is scientifically proven to be effective. What they do not tell you is *how* effective, under *what* circumstances, and for *whom*. But for those who worship science, the words "scientifically proven" are too often proof enough.

Because . . . everyone else believes it

Surely you know people who will believe anything everyone else believes. This is very understandable since it provides them with a great sense of security. They say to themselves, "If I am wrong, then everyone else is wrong too." If they were to believe something that went against majority belief they would run too high a psychological risk. This type of person fears feeling alone, or like an outcast or deviant. Therefore, he or she elects to follow the safe course by running with the pack—by believing whatever everyone else believes.

Because . . . statistics say so

For at least two thousand years, there have been people who believe that numbers possess mystical or magical powers. Even in the Space Age, numbers continue to exert an influence through the ancient occult system of numerology. Different numerological systems based on a person's birth date, or on the sum of the letters in one's name are subscribed to by a surprisingly large number of people.

Modern scientists continue to use numbers in research in the form of *statistics*. Statistics can be manipulated to "prove" many an untruth. Many people are woefully intimidated by numbers and are ready to believe anything "proven" by statistics. While they may think that figures don't lie, what they may not fully realize is that "liars figure."

Because . . . authorities say so

Since most of the things we know come to us secondhand, we have been conditioned to trust what authorities tell us. Doctors, lawyers, teachers, politicians, historians, geologists, and space scientists are but a few of the authorities whose opinions we have come to accept as truth. The trouble is that some of us go a little too far in believing what they say. Since we cannot personally test most of the information that comes our way, we must rely on what authorities tell us. This discourages skepticism and independent thought. Lacking knowledge with which to argue back, we often accept what we are told without questioning, without wondering whether something is good or bad, right or wrong, constructive or destructive.

Because . . . history says so

Some individuals will believe anything that has withstood the test of time. They argue that something that has been around for hundreds or even thousands of years "must" be true. They are completely unable to accept the idea that people would continue believing a myth for centuries. They strongly believe that time will tell. They look to history for truth, convinced that the longer an attitude, value, or belief exists in time, the more reliable it must be.

Because . . . people wouldn't say it if it weren't true

There are three terms which describe the people who think this way: naive, gullible, and ignorant. Because they lack information or have a certain psychological make-up, they tend to believe practically anything anyone tells them. We all know people like this.

Having examined the above reasons why people accept certain information as true, let us now look at some principles that will help you get *your* audience to believe.

Principles of Communication

Principle I: Get Your Audience's Attention

Before you can begin to relate to the members of any audience, you must first get their attention. While this is no easy task, it is a little easier than getting people to believe what you tell them. Wayne Minnick tells how a nine-year-old girl managed to attract attention. At her birthday party, all of the little boys gathered at one end of the room, ignoring the girls. "But, I got one of them to pay attention to me, alright," the little girl told her mother. "How?" asked the parent. "I knocked him down," replied the young lady.[2]

In a speech class, another young man, equally anxious to get the attention of his audience, stepped to the lectern, took out a revolver, placed it to his head—and fired! He then calmly announced, "The topic of my speech is SUICIDE." Needless to say, he had the undivided attention of everyone in the room. Whether or not he was able to hold their attention is another story.

Most audiences, as they file into auditoriums and lecture halls, are paying attention to a wide variety of things. Some are preoccupied with internal issues; e.g., the safety of their children with a new babysitter, whether they will arrive home in time to catch a late movie, if the speaker will be interesting or boring. Others are paying attention to external matters; e.g., the kinds of people around

---

[2] Wayne Minnick, *The Art of Persuasion* (Boston: Houghton Mifflin, Company, 1968), p. 52.

them, seating arrangements, wall colors, music (if any), guests of honor located on the dais. The point is that their attention, upon entering the room, is scattered. You have no way of knowing for certain what frame of mind they are in. It will be your responsibility to get them, very quickly, to be receptive to what you have to say. The nine-year-old birthday girl got her audience's attention by knocking him down. The young man whose topic was suicide put a gun to his head and fired. Both were successful because they did something that was unusual, unexpected, and attention-getting.

Practically every audience you encounter will give you an opportunity to get and hold their attention. This opportunity, however, rarely lasts more than a minute or two. If you haven't succeeded in getting attention in that short time, you probably will not get another chance. Audiences extend speakers this opportunity out of either ordinary courtesy or curiosity. If you plan to spend the first ten or fifteen minutes of your speech warming up your audience, forget it! In their eyes, your fate will probably have long since been decided. For some personal proof, think back to the first few minutes of any class at the beginning of a new semester. A teacher whom you have never met before enters the room. How long does it take you to decide whether he or she will be interesting or boring? Unless you are unusually considerate and willing to reserve your judgment, your first impression will have been formed in a matter of one or two minutes.

Another factor that determines whether or not your audiences will pay attention to you is based upon their expectations. If you come on exactly as they expect you to and say exactly what they expect, don't count on enthusiastic attention. Imagine a typical monthly Parent–Teacher Association meeting. Imagine a guest speaker whose topic is: "Getting your child to enjoy reading." Most parents who attend such monthly meetings expect that kind of subject. Now, imagine this topic: "What your eight-year-old child already knows about sex." Do you think the attention levels will be the same for both topics?

The lesson to be learned here is to plan your speech so that, while it is generally responsive to what your audience expects, it possesses some special "twist" that will cause your audience to regard it as unexpected. This can be done in a number of ways. A challenging speech title is but one way. You could, for instance, charge your audience by saying, "How many of you are neurotic?" or, "If you had to take a state examination in order to become a parent, could you pass it?" Most speechmakers speak in generalities. Rather than embarrass some member of an audience, they talk about things on an impersonal level, on a theoretical or hypothetical basis. By putting a direct question to your audience, without singling out a particular individual, you are demanding their attention.

Once you succeed in getting an audience's attention, there is no guarantee that you will be able to hold it. To do this, you must use other techniques.

Principle II: Make People Feel, Not Just Think

Most of us enjoy emotional experiences, and experienced speakers know it. Witness the average radio, television, or theatre performance. With few exceptions, the mass media has but one target—to reach people's emotions. Although thinking and feeling are difficult to separate in the human mind, people usually respond first with feelings. Perhaps this is so because feeling is a more primitive trait than thinking. If you aim your speech at the feelings of your audience, you will have a better chance of gaining and holding their attention. It is easier and quicker to engage the emotions first, and then to present your argument and support it in a logical and rational fashion.

Every speaker has a definite advantage when it comes to the "feelings" of an audience. Because all people share a common biology, they can easily identify with such basic emotions as love, hate, fear, sadness, happiness, loneliness, anxiety, and frustration. Thinking, on the other hand, involves a much more complicated mental process—and one which has greater variety. Therefore, it is harder to appeal to the thinking process.

By knowing how you feel in a variety of life situations, you have a ready reference for how others feel. While there may be some differences in terms of the quality and quantity of such feelings, you can rely on their being more alike than not. Similar feelings have a strange way of finding each other; i.e., sadness finds sadness, happiness finds happiness, loneliness finds loneliness, and so on. Keep this in mind when preparing your next speech. Rather than appealing only to your audience's ability and willingness to think, also zero in on its feelings.

Principle III: Make Mental Pictures

When you think the word *fire*, your brain does not conjure up the letters F–I–R–E. It generates a picture of a fire in your mind. Elsewhere in this book, you were told that words are symbols which merely stand for things. In any material sense, such words (or symbols) bear absolutely no relationship to the things they represent. You cannot live in the word *house*, train the word *dog*, drive the word *car*, break the word *stick*, or climb the word *mountain*. These words are simply collections of sounds which have been agreed upon by those who use them to have certain meanings. And the more definite the meaning, the more concrete they are said to be.

Words that do not generate only specifically agreed upon pictures in the mind are said to be abstract; that is, they have a range of meanings to different people. Consequently, the more abstract words you use in a speech, the less your audience will understand what you mean and the less they will be inclined to believe you. As a rule of thumb, make sure that you use words that paint pictures in the audience's mind. Instead of saying just *a house*, say *a broken-down, deserted house*; instead of saying *a patient* in a hospital bed, say an *old, shriveled woman, almost bald, and with open sores all over her body lay motionless in a hospital bed*. Making pictures in the mind feeds fuel to the emotions and lends support to belief.

Principle IV: Familiarity Breeds Belief

Have you ever had the experience of telling someone something and having him say, "Gee, I never heard of that"? Some people are convinced that if they never heard of something, it doesn't exist. Their own experience constitutes truth. Only those things which they personally have seen, heard, tasted, touched or smelled, actually exist. All else in the world does not exist until they have experienced it. For such people, only the familiar is real and can be believed. To show how erroneous the familiar can be, note these examples. At one time, some familiar beliefs were that the world was flat, blood did not circulate in the body and demons were the cause of disease. Today, we have a new assortment of familiar beliefs: the world is round, blood circulates, and bacteria and viruses cause disease. What beliefs will be familiar to the citizen of 2500 A.D.?

SPEECH EXPERIENCE: BELIEVE IT OR NOT

1. Compile a list of things you think people living in the year 2500 A.D. will believe.

a. _____

b. _____

c. _____

d. _____

e. _____

2. Choose one item from your list for further work. Prepare a two-minute speech explaining why you think people will believe as you contend.

Putting aside whether something is true or not, it is important for you to realize, as a speaker, that people are generally drawn toward the familiar and are distrustful of the unfamiliar. You can take advantage of this tendency by using material your audience will consider familiar. Also, be aware of the fact that audiences not only vary from each other, but also from one time period to another. A change in world economy could cause a substantial shift in an audience's style and values. This could seriously influence what they will and will not believe.

Principle V: Personalize Whenever You Can

[handwritten annotation: make it speaking to each individual]

Instead of talking about men, talk about "a man." Instead of talking about cars, talk about "a particular car." Audiences seem much more willing to believe what you tell them about a particular polar bear than about polar bears in general. People seem better able to identify with one member of a group rather than with large numbers. This, then, is your cue. In any speech you should make, take great care to single out one specific person or object about which you will be speaking and let your audience generalize what you say about that one to the rest.

Another technique you might try is to use yourself as an example. If your topic lends itself, see if you can change places with the hero or heroine of your story. If you are telling about what happened to a friend of yours last summer, become that friend and tell it as if it happened to you. Audiences are a curious bunch who seem to get a kick out of hearing stories firsthand from those who lived them. Secondhand stories end up in second place when it comes to being believed. So, whenever you can, personalize!

Speech Insurance

As if being afraid to give a speech were not enough, there is also the fear of having your speech fall flat on its face. There are certain things you can do to prevent your speech from failing. For our purposes, let us call it speech insurance. Essentially, it consists of things you should know and things you should do before and during your speech. Borrowing from the words of Louis Pasteur: "Chance favors the prepared mind."

Know Your Subject

Few things can destroy a speech more quickly than not knowing what you're talking about. Audiences seem able to sense when a speaker is putting them on, feeding them a lot of meaningless or empty talk, or is unfamiliar with a speech topic. Even though they may not be acquainted with the subject, they can sense from the manner in which you present yourself and your material that you don't know your subject. As insurance against this happening, be careful to choose a topic in which you are either very interested or with which you are already somewhat familiar.

Look the Part

Much of your fate will depend upon whether your audience accepts you. This involves your looking the way they expect you to look. If your subject is a serious one, dress in a serious manner. Traditionally this means a suit or sport coat and slacks for men; a dress or skirt and blouse for women. If your subject is hunting or tennis, you might consider wearing clothes appropriate to such sports. The main thing is to look like whatever you are presenting yourself to be. Naturally, dress will not apply to every subject. If your speech is on travel, building model airplanes, or collecting antiques, all you need do is look presentable.

Do Not Telegraph Your Intention *either do or don't tell*

In boxing, a fighter is said "to telegraph a punch" when he, through some subtle foot, hand or head motion, tips off his opponent as to what he is going to do. In public speaking, this same "telegraphing" occurs when a speaker tells an audience from the start of his intent to persuade them. This is not a good idea. Some people do not like to be told that they are going to have their minds changed. If it is to happen, they prefer that it happens without their being aware of it. By telling an audience, "Today, I shall try to persuade you to vote 'yes' on the new highway construction bill," you set up a competitive, rather than a cooperative, climate. While there are exceptions, of course, avoid telegraphing your intentions to persuade. Whenever feasible, seek to achieve your goal more diplomatically by avoiding the overt or extremely direct approach.

Stress the Practical Side of Things

Most audiences have a rather low tolerance for theory. They seem to prefer practical ideas and examples. If your speech should call for some theoretical explanation, do it as briefly as you can and immediately move on to its practical side. Although you may strongly feel the need for your audience to understand the *how* and *why* of something, bear in mind that they usually are preoccupied with the way its use can be of a personal benefit to them.

Let Your Audience Know Where You Stand

This is one of the exceptions referred to in telegraphing. Occasionally, an audience wants to know, up front, whether you are for them or against them. This means that you must let your audience know as soon as possible just where you stand on a particular issue. The more unclear some people are on a speaker's position, the more anxious they tend to become. This anxiety then causes them to draw hasty conclusions, which you will have to set right later on in your speech. Unfortunately, once certain audiences have arrived at an initial opinion of you, it is doubly difficult to reverse it later on.

Another suggestion you might consider as a form of speech insurance has to do with the extent to which you let your audience know where you stand on a particular issue. If you discover that your audience initially disagrees with your point of view, be sure to present both sides of the question. If, on the other hand, you discover that your audience is already on your side, present only your view. To make things even more explicit, you might also spell out what conclusion(s) you want your audience to reach. It is not uncommon to find an audience who does not know what is expected of it. Help such an audience by indicating as clearly as you can exactly what it is that you want them to think, feel or do.

Don't Overfeed Your Audience

Most untrained audiences have serious difficulty following a complicated line of reasoning. If they are confronted with too many ideas at one time, they can become confused and, as a result, become less responsive to the expectations of a speaker. Speakers who are thoroughly familiar with their subject have a distinct tendency to think in larger chunks than those who are unfamiliar with the subject. Physicians, for instance, might describe a surgical procedure without realizing that their audience lacks the ability to follow what they are saying. An automobile mechanic who is comfortable talking about motors might leave an audience behind by using too many technical terms or presenting information too quickly.

As a public speaker, you must be sensitive to what your audience can and cannot handle. You must not, under any circumstances, feed them too complex or too many ideas at one time. Small, frequent doses of information should be your watchword. If you are unsure of what your audience can handle, it is not improper to ask them during a speech, "How many of you are familiar with . . . ?" Being sensitive to whether or not your audience grasps your meaning is also a form of speech insurance. Your questions tell people that you care enough to find out if your meaning is getting through to them, or if they are having difficulty following your line of reasoning.

Repetition Is O.K., Repetition Is O.K.

With some audiences, saying something once is not enough. The reasons for this may be lazy listening habits, inattention, poor motivation, disinterest, preoccupation with other matters, or because the speaker is not clear. Repeating oneself can be a useful technique, if used discreetly. Martin Luther King used repetition effectively in his famous speech, "I Have a Dream" (see page 86). In preparing your speech, pick out those ideas which are essential to making your point and consider repeating them more than once. Although repeating yourself in everyday conversation might not be considered desirable, selective repetition in a well-constructed speech could be extremely effective.

Reward and Punishment

Every speech, to varying degrees, contains either a reward or punishment. At Weight Watcher meetings, overweight people get both. When they lose weight, they receive praise from other members. When they fail to lose weight or gain additional pounds, they experience punishment from their peers in the form of embarrassment and disappointment.

Most speeches are designed to either inform, persuade, or entertain. Depending upon the makeup of the audience, people should come away from a speech thinking or feeling something. If the audience was not moved, the speech missed the mark. In the case of the informative speech, the reward should be the receipt of additional information and insight into a particular subject. To this end, during a lecture, the speaker should point out why remembering this new information will be rewarding for the audience. With the persuasive speech, audiences again expect to be either rewarded or punished —depending upon the nature of the speech. If your audience agrees with your arguments, they will be rewarded by hearing their ideas confirmed. If they disagree, they may suffer by experiencing anxiety. Finally, the speech to entertain issues reward in the form of pleasure, but punishment in the form of boredom if the speech is not enjoyed.

Naturally, the majority of audiences prefer rewards to punishment. You must therefore give some serious thought as to how your speech will supply your audience with a reward. Above all, they must feel that they have gained something of value from listening to your speech. Force yourself to think in terms of rewarding your audience by asking this question: What is the reward my speech delivers?

Get Them to Do Something

Members of an audience should not be treated like stick figures or rag dolls neatly arranged in rows before you. Audiences wish to participate in the speechmaking process. They want to interact with you. The most successful speeches are frequently those in which the audience supplies the speaker with a great deal of feedback. Electricity fills the air when there is a dynamic interaction between speaker and audience. Not only does an enthusiastic audience response affect a speaker positively, it also excites other members of the audience.

To insure such a positive response from your audiences, try to convert them from a passive state into an active one. Do not be satisfied to have them sit quietly in their seats and listen. Encourage some kind of physical participation. You might want to hand out some literature or questionnaires to which you can later refer. You might wish to have your audience interact with one another with a hand-holding experiment, an observation, or an exchange of some general information.

Those who study audience behavior speak of something called *cohesiveness*. It is a phenomenon in which people are brought into closer contact with one another, either physically or mentally. By getting your audience to do something, you increase its cohesiveness and thereby increase your sense of oneness with it.

Boredom Burdens Believing

Few things will prevent an audience from believing more quickly than being bored.

SPEECH EXPERIENCE: THE BOREDOM BARRIER

1. Describe a situation in which you were bored. Search out those characteristics of the situation which you believe were responsible for the way you felt. *repetition + time lag*

MArketing 331

2. Describe a situation during which you bored someone else. Identify what you consider to be the factors responsible for your behavior. _____

Never

Boredom is a particularly dangerous human emotion. Not only does it afflict people of all ages, it is also a very difficult psychological condition to guard against. Think of all the defenses against boredom devised by modern society: TV, movies, books, sports, dance crazes, fashion, to name a few. Some social psychologists consider boredom a national neurosis of major proportion. Recall how often you have heard people complain that a particular theater performance or rock concert was boring.

Boredom is the enemy of every public speaker. While speakers of every description seem able to cope with the knowledge that their speech did not meet with their greatest expectations, contained some misleading information, or was of an inappropriate length, they seem to have difficulty coping with the knowledge that their speech was boring. When accused of such a thing, many are quick to blame their audience. It takes a very mature individual to accept the charge of boring an audience. Why? Because it is a speaker-centered judgment, not an audience-centered one. The moment speakers open their mouths, they must accept responsibility for boring or not boring their audiences. Audiences can rarely be held responsible for a speaker's shortcomings.

If we now agree that a bored audience is less inclined to believe a speaker than an interested one, it is appropriate that we take a closer look at some of the characteristics a bored audience displays.

Symptoms of a Bored Audience

1. Talking and whispering.
2. Feet shuffling.
3. Fidgeting.
4. Going to the restrooms or out for a smoke.
5. Looking around the room.
6. Dozing off.
7. Such disinterested postures as: hand supporting chin, arms folded across chest, arm draped over back of seat, slumping, and so on.

These actions clearly interfere with an audience's willingness to believe. They also reduce the extent to which other members of the audience are willing to believe. In short, these symptoms of boredom and the tendency they have to affect believing are contagious.

On occasion, speakers have been known to be bored with their topics. When this happens, they transmit such boredom to their audiences. When speaker and audience show recognizable signs of disbelief, they contaminate each other. In preparation for the material to be presented in Chapter 10, *The Silent Side of Public Speaking,* here are some of the more common symptoms of a bored speaker: 1) reading from a paper or script, 2) walking up to the lectern in a sluggish or lethargic manner, 3) speaking in a weak and unmodulated voice, 4) repeatedly looking at a wall clock or wristwatch, 5) beginning and ending a speech abruptly, and 6) displaying few body movements, facial expressions, or gestures. Surely if a speaker exhibits little or no interest in what he or she is saying, how can an audience be expected to behave any differently? In the public-speaking sense, believing must be a shared phenomenon in which speaker and audience focus their attention upon a particular idea or set of ideas and pool their mutual enthusiasm.

Summary

There is more to getting your audience to believe than simply speaking words at them. You must familiarize yourself with their values and the most common reasons they employ as a basis for belief *i.e.*, they read it, it is logical, it is scientific, because everyone else believes it, statistics say so, authorities say so, and people wouldn't say it if it weren't true.

You must also learn important principles of communication described in this chapter. Each is a practical method of getting your audience to believe. They include such techniques as: getting your audience's attention, making people feel as well as think, making mental pictures, stressing the familiar, and personalizing whenever possible.

Additional practical advice came in the form of speech insurance. It included: knowing your subject, looking the part, not telegraphing your intentions, stressing practicality, aligning yourself with your audience, repetition, reward and punishment, and getting your audience to participate.

In closing, we discussed boredom as a major cause of audience disbelief. Symptoms of a bored audience and a bored speaker were presented so that you will be readily able to identify the signs of a failing attempt to communicate and hopefully will be able to salvage a sinking speech.

CHAPTER 5

Choosing Your Topic

Behavioral Objectives

After reading this chapter, you should have a better understanding of:

- how to use brainstorming as a means of selecting a topic.
- how to develop a list of potential speech subjects.
- what makes a particular speech topic right for you.
- how the speaking situation affects your topic choice.
- why you should try to select a topic in which you are really interested.
- why you need to be knowledgeable about your topic.
- why it is important to inventory your abilities, background, skills, and interests.
- how your audience may affect your topic choice.
- the similarities and differences between a speech to inform, to persuade, and to entertain.

Introduction

Now that you have been introduced to speakers and audiences, it is time for you to decide what you are going to talk about. Consider this.

A grim-faced worker was standing in front of the city hall when she was approached by a stranger. "Do you know who's speaking in there now?" inquired the stranger. "Or are you just about to enter?" "No," replied the worker. "I listened for forty-five minutes. I've just left the hall. Senator Beat-about-the-Bush is delivering a talk in there." "What is he talking about?" asked the stranger. "Well," said the worker in a somewhat annoyed tone, "the Senator didn't tell us."

The first task of any public speaker is to decide on a topic. It is then up to the speaker to communicate this decision clearly and specifically to an audience. It is obvious from listening to public speeches delivered on the radio, television, or at school that the choice of topics is almost limitless. Under the proper circumstances, any conceivable subject is appropriate for some public speech. If you think that finding something to talk about to an audience is going to pose problems for you, take some time to participate in the following set of experiences.

SPEECH EXPERIENCE: THE GRAB BAG

1. Your instructor will divide you into a number of small groups.

2. A grab bag, placed at the front of the room, will contain words identical or similar to the following: lamp, record, clock, spring, skiing, paper, car, food.

3. Then, one member of each group will come to the front of the room and draw a word card from the grab bag.

4. Using the word as a stimulus, group members then have two minutes to brainstorm as many speech topic ideas as possible. NOTE: Brainstorming is a technique for generating ideas. The goal of the brainstorming process is to generate as many new ideas as possible. During idea generation, all criticism and evaluation are withheld. The initial goal is quantity; i.e., to get as many ideas out as possible. For example, while brainstorming, the word *record* might prompt topic ideas such as "radio broadcasting," "what makes a hit record," "a day in the life of a disc jockey," "the payola scandals," "how a stereo system works," and so on. The group that brainstorms the greatest number of ideas within the given time period wins.

5. At the end of this phase of the experience, group responses will be posted on the chalkboard. You will then evaluate all suggestions, and see if you can modify, add to, or otherwise enhance a posted idea.

6. Continue the game in this manner.

SPEECH EXPERIENCE: Out in the World

    1. Your instructor will divide you into groups.

    2. Each group will select a particular location to visit. For example, a group may choose to visit a neighborhood park, a zoo, a factory, a store, or a garden. While in the selected location, each group member should jot down as many particular speech topic ideas as possible. As before, quantity is your objective. Let your imagination run free. Do not compare group member responses until you return to class.

    3. Then once again attempt to pool, alter, and enrich member suggestions.

    4. Share your results with other groups.

SPEECH EXPERIENCE: Word Power

    1. This topic search strategy encourages you to play with words. Your instructor may divide you into groups or you may work individually.

    2. Each group or individual selects a class word; for example, vehicles, clothing, books, foods, games. The goal is to identify as many things that fall into the class as possible. For example, mini-bikes, scooters, trains, jets, motorcycles, cars, spaceships, and blimps all fall under the heading or class of *vehicles*.

    The preceding set of experiences should enable you to develop a list of potential subjects. Once you have compiled such a list, it is time for you to decide which ones appeal to you, that are right for the situation you will enter, and that will interest the audience you will be addressing. We will now examine more closely what makes a speech topic right for you, noting the things you should consider before finally answering the question, "What am I going to talk about?"

The Speaking Situation

Often the speaking situation will dictate your general topic. It is important that you ask yourself this question before committing yourself to a topic choice: What does the situation call for? In other words, you might be asked to speak to a particular group because they believe you know something in which they are interested. You then would be obliged to speak on that subject. Your reputation, knowledge, experience, as well as your audience's goals, all interact to influence your choice of a speech topic.

    This makes even more sense if you consider this example. Your friend's car has broken down. He knows that you know a great deal about cars. So, he asks you over to explain to him what is wrong with his car. Given this situation, and your friend's need, you would feel silly arriving at his home and talking about plant care instead of car care. The same principle applies in a public setting. A speaker must take the nature of the speaking occasion into account. He or she must understand why people are coming to listen to a particular speech. It is the unusual speaker who is permitted to ignore the demands imposed by a given situation. Try this.

SPEECH EXPERIENCE: MATCH GAME

1. Your instructor will divide the class into a number of teams.

2. Each team will be given a sheet of paper containing the following information:

    a. You are speaking before the zoological society. Members know you are an expert on African wildlife. You might speak on . . . .

    b. You are speaking before the American Library Association. Members know you are an expert on Twentieth Century Literature. You might speak on . . . .

    c. You are speaking before the American Automobile Association. Members know you are an expert on automobile safety. You might speak on . . . .

    d. You are speaking before the Executive Committee of the Diners Club. Members know you are an expert on food preparation. You might speak on . . . .

    e. You are speaking before the state Polar Bear Club. Members know you are an expert on body conditioning. You might speak on . . . .

3. The goal of each group is to generate as many specific speech topic ideas as possible. The group that has accumulated the most points at the end of play is the winner.

Most speaking situations lead a speaker in a specific direction by calling for a particular kind of subject. A college anniversary lecture series, a political convention, a literary discussion group, and a dinner club all call for different speech topics. Consequently, it should be kept in mind that a speaker's responsibility does not end with just the selection of the subject. It is also up to you to determine what aspect of a general subject you will focus on. It is necessary for all speakers to design their topics for a particular audience and to limit the topic coverage to the alotted time period. Keeping these principles in mind, try the following.

SPEECH EXPERIENCE: WHAT'S MY TOPIC?

1. Write down the name of a prominent speaker or personality.

2. Select a speech topic that you believe fits your chosen speaker. Then, identify an audience before which such a speech might be delivered. Write your selected topic on a sheet of paper.

3. One at a time, each student will come to the front of the classroom, announce the selected speaker and identify the audience. The class will have five minutes to guess the speaker's topic.

Situational rules also apply to classroom speeches. Each time you are asked to make a speech, you must remind yourself that you have to offer your listeners something. What you offer may be new information, a different way of looking at something, or a controversial idea. Above all, your speech should be on a topic that is important to your receivers, or will make them want to know more.

Consider Your Interests

Sometimes the choice of subject is left entirely to the speaker. When you have a free choice, how will you pick a topic? You must consider your interests. Select only a subject that you care about. Any other choice invites failure. Listeners can spot a phony speaker in an instant. To affect your listeners in a positive manner, you must believe in what you say. If you do, you can convince them to care about the subject too. If not, you may bore them. Even if your speech contains new insights or a novel twist, it is unlikely that you will move your audience unless they detect your own involvement in the subject.

SPEECH EXPERIENCE: TIME TO TALK

1. Your instructor will divide you into pairs.
2. Each pair has three minutes to converse on any subject.

Questions About "TIME TO TALK"

1. What did you and your partner talk about?
2. Why do you think you chose your particular topic?

Have you ever considered what you talk about during the course of a day? When speaking with friends, it is the unusual person who deliberately selects a topic of conversation. It seems that people just start talking. In actuality, the topic selection process does have structure. Even when conversing informally, we talk about subjects that interest us. What is true of our conversations is also true of our public communications. For example, Fran Tarkenton delivers speeches on football, Walter Cronkhite speaks of newsreporting, Barbara Walters conducts interviews, Betty Friedan talks about the Equal Rights Amendment, and Billy Graham speaks to audiences of religious life. Just as we speak on subjects of personal interest in private, we should exercise this same selectivity when speaking in public.

Wasting an audience's time is just as bad as wasting a friend's time. While five minutes spent talking to a friend consumes ten minutes of the time of both, five minutes spent talking before an audience of fifteen individuals consumes seventy-five minutes of their total time. How many minutes of everyone's time will you use when you deliver a speech to your class? Figure it out. With that much time at stake, we have to be certain that we are using it wisely. We have a responsibility to learn as much as we can about the subject on which we will speak. It is a waste of everyone's time to speak on a topic about which we know little, and to fail to communicate anything new or useful.

For these reasons, ask yourself what topics you are capable of handling. The answer to this question is partially one of speaker credibility. Are you able to speak with authority on your selected subject? For example, if you were an architect, you would appear foolish delivering a speech on how to use a buzz saw to a convention of carpenters, unless your goal was to familiarize them with the functions of a completely new type of buzz saw. You would be perfectly within your right, however, to speak to an audience of carpenters about the types of homes they will be called upon to build in the future. Thus, you need to select a subject about which you are knowledgeable and about which you can find additional information. Your choice can be based on the jobs you have held, your hobbies, places you have visited, courses you have taken, unusual experiences you have had, or particular skills you possess.

Let us conduct some self-research. Fill out this Self-Survey Chart.

Self-survey Chart

Instructions: This inventory of yourself deals with your abilities, your background, your skills, and your interests.

Background

Places I Have Lived

1. _____

2. _____

3. _____

Types of People I Have Known

1. _____

2. _____

3. _____

Special Experiences I Have Had

1. _____

2. _____

3. _____

Skills

What I Can Do Well

1. _____

2. _____

3. _____

Special Information I Have

1. _____

2. _____

3. _____

Interests

Hobbies I Have

1. _____

2. _____

3. _____

What I Really Care About

1. _____

2. _____

3. _____

What I Would Like to Learn More About

1. _____

2. _____

3. _____

This inventory should aid you in selecting your topic.

The Audience

The third factor to be taken into account when deciding upon a speech subject is the audience. In a previous chapter, we stressed the importance of analyzing the audience in terms of its attitudes, values, and beliefs. Whatever subject you select, it should be important to your listeners. It should relate to their needs, concerns and interests. You should also consider what your listeners are capable of understanding. When one of the authors of this text was a college student, she was fortunate (or unfortunate, perhaps) to have a scholarly theatre professor who insisted upon giving his lectures on the German playwright Brecht in German. It was the professor's belief that a lecture on Brecht sounded better in the language of the playwright rather than the language of the audience—English. Needless to say, the audience did not understand a word of what he said and learned nothing from the professor's lectures. The ultimate choice of *how* you will speak is really determined by the audience. If an audience feels your language, style, manner, or topic imposes a hardship on them, they will simply tune you out. To avoid being tuned out by your audience, take care to adapt your subject to your listeners. Make a concerted effort to determine *who* your listeners are, *why* they are coming to hear your speech, and *what* they expect to gain from it. What is more, be certain to narrow down your subject so that it conforms to your time limit. By failing to do this, you risk making your audience frustrated, restless, and angry.

Why Are You Making a Speech?

Beyond just determining *what* you are going to speak about, you must also determine *why* you are delivering a speech. Your reason for delivering your message is your *speech purpose*. Your reason for speaking is your *goal*. Once you have identified your reason for speaking, you have clarified in your own mind what you plan to do with your speech topic.

Realize that both the selection of the topic and its purpose are influenced by similar factors. Both are affected by the nature of the speaking situation, your reputation, and your audience's expectations. Imagine how annoyed a group of medical researchers would be if they paid fifty dollars each to hear a cancer-research specialist speak on "The Future of Chemotherapy" and instead were given a speech on "Comedians I Have Known and Loved." Your audience was seeking information, not amusement. Audiences do not like to be deceived or disappointed.

Generally, the speaker may choose from among three speech purposes: to inform, to persuade, and to entertain.

To Inform

Different types of speeches may be used to inform an audience. Informative talks may be lectures in a college classroom, a company's report to its stockholders, a plant foreman explaining how to use a piece of equipment, or a re-formed smoker telling others about the dangers of smoking. In each case, the goal of the speaker delivering the talk is to provide a learning experience for listeners; that is, to provide the members of the audience with information they did not have before. The informative speaker should take special care to see that the audience understands and remembers what was said. The statement of specific purpose for an informative speech should contain such words as *explain*, *report*, *instruct*, *demonstrate* or even *inform*.

Let us try this brief informative speech experience.

SPEECH EXPERIENCE: INSTRUCTIONS ON THE LOOSE

A common method of informing people involves giving instructions. Could you, for example, explain to someone who had never seen a sweater, how to put it on? Would you be able to find suitable language to establish a workable sequence? As an instructional exercise, explain to another person or group one of the following: (NOTE: You are responsible for any necessary props.)

a. How to tie a tie
b. How to put on a shoe
c. How to braid hair
d. How to construct a cube
e. How to walk
f. How to put on false eyelashes
g. How to make a peanut butter and jelly sandwich
h. How to sit in a chair

It will be helpful if you bear in mind that your subjects will do *only* what you instruct them to do.

After each attempt, analyze the instructions given by the speaker. Determine if the speaker's instructional sequence was easy to follow and if the language used was simple and direct. Speculate on how an alternative set of instructions could have been used to increase effectiveness.

To Persuade

Speeches to persuade are designed to reinforce or change an audience's beliefs. When delivering a persuasive speech, the speaker is interested in making his audience think or do something. This is accomplished by motivating people to think and act differently. Politicians, social activists, salespeople, advertisers, fundraisers, attorneys, ministers, and doctors all seek to persuade others. Here is an opportunity to try your hand at persuasion.

SPEECH EXPERIENCE: THE INFLUENCE GAME

Listed below are a number of familiar persuasive situations. Each requires that you apply the art of persuasion.

a. You want to persuade your friend not to drop out of school.
b. You want to persuade the city council that sex discrimination is still widespread.
c. You want to persuade your professor to curve the last examination.
d. You want to motivate the members of your club to contribute to your favorite charity.
e. You want to persuade a police officer that you were not speeding.
f. You want to get your classmates to vote for you in an upcoming election.

Questions About "THE INFLUENCE GAME"

1. Can you identify some persuasive strategies that work?
2. Can you identify some of the ways people resist being influenced?

To Entertain

If your goal is to entertain, you will want the members of your audience to relax and enjoy your talk. Given this as an objective, the main purpose of your speech should be to amuse, captivate, please, produce laughter, or divert. Information is only of secondary importance. In fact, if you do use information, it may be old or new, true or false, and deal with either real or ficitional material. Speeches to entertain are usually given at parties, dinners, testimonials, or roasts. The comic monologue of a performer is an example of a speech whose prime purpose is to entertain.

To deliver a successful speech to entertain, you must make an accurate prediction as to what will amuse and interest your audience. Also, be mindful of the fact that a speaker need not be funny to be considered entertaining. For example, a speaker who is able to captivate an audience with tales of adventure on the high seas is also functioning in the realm of entertainment. Try this next speech experience.

SPEECH EXPERIENCE: TICKLE MY FANCY

1. In groups, brainstorm entertainment speech topic ideas for each of the following occasions:
   a. a high school reunion
   b. a teacher's retirement party
   c. a twenty-fifth wedding anniversary party
   d. an engagement party
   e. a graduation party
   f. a sports award dinner

2. Identify the guidelines you used when making your topic choices.

3. Identify the assumptions you made about the nature of each audience.

Most speeches are not exclusively informative, persuasive, or entertaining. They often contain a mixture of elements—a little bit of each. But only one of the preceding elements should receive the bulk of your attention. The others should be used to reinforce its impact on your audience.

SPEECH EXPERIENCE: PUTTING IT TOGETHER

Generate statements of purpose which you believe effectively illustrate each of the three main speech purposes we discussed:

a. To Inform: _____

_____

_____

_____

b. To Persuade: _____

_____

_____

_____

c. To Entertain: _____

_____

_____

_____

Summary

This chapter has demonstrated how choosing a topic can be an exciting, challenging, and thought-provoking experience. You were shown how selecting a topic is interrelated with your interests, your audience's interests, and the speaking situation. You were provided with guidelines to follow when deciding whether to deliver a speech to inform, to persuade, or to entertain. You were then given the opportunity to familiarize yourself with each of these three major speech types.

CHAPTER 6

Supporting What You Say

Behavioral Objectives

After reading this chapter, you should have a better understanding of:

- why we use supporting materials.
- how to select your supporting materials.
- where to find supporting materials.
- how to use personal experience as a form of support.
- the role other people play in providing you with support.
- how to use published materials as support.
- how to use the library.
- such supporting materials as definitions, descriptions, explanations, examples, illustrations, testimonials, statistics, comparisons, contrasts, repetition and re-statement.

Figure 6–1.

Figure 6–2.

Introduction

Have you ever seen a rag doll or a scarecrow? What did you notice about them? Chances are they were soft and flexible—unable to stand unless supported by something or someone. Examine the scarecrows in Figures 6–1 and 6–2.

The scarecrow in Fig. 6–1 is unsupported. But in Fig. 6–2, it has been put on a stick (serving as a backbone) to hold it upright. People who lack support (like rag dolls and scarecrows), have been referred to as "pushovers." They have nothing with which to anchor themselves. They cannot support their ideas or influence other people. Figuratively speaking, they lack backbones.

Public communicators should not be pushovers. They should take great care to back up their statements.

Why We Use Supporting Materials

Think about your own daily experiences. Supporting your beliefs and feelings is something you do all the time.

SPEECH EXPERIENCE: Support Me, Please.

1. Consider each of the following statements:
    a. You would enjoy seeing the movie I saw last night.
    b. I'm sure you would enjoy reading this book.
    c. This record will never make the top twenty list.
    d. Getting to my house is easy.
    e. That bank gives you more for your money.
2. Next, divide into pairs and take turns explaining how you would support each of the preceding statements. When you have finished, answer the following questions:

Questions about "SUPPORT ME, PLEASE"

1. How did you persuade your partner to accept what you said in support of each statement?
2. What question(s) had to be answered?

In each case, you had to answer the question "why" to your partner's satisfaction. And, to answer such a question, you had to supply information that helped make your statement more believable. The type of information you offer in support of any statement will depend upon the person to whom you are speaking and the event in question. You would support the statement, "You would enjoy seeing the movie I saw last night" with such comments as, "Your favorite movie star is in it," or "A leading film critic called it, 'The best film of the decade.'" The data you would use to support the statement, "That bank gives you more for your money," would differ. For the latter, you might compare interest rates offered by banks, promotional gifts, and free services. In other words, the kind of specific information you offer to support a particular statement should be matched to that statement. Only by offering sound reasons can you convince your audience.

Supporting materials are needed to inform, persuade, or entertain. They serve to clarify, prove, or enliven the main points of your speech. If used to inform, supporting materials will help you explain and amplify your ideas to your listeners. If used to persuade, supporting materials will help you convince your audience that your arguments are sound, and that what you are suggesting is in their best interest. If used to entertain, supporting materials will add vitality and warmth to your comments. Thus, the wise public communicator uses supporting materials to make a speech more interesting, understandable, or believable.

Your speaking purpose or topic matters less than you think. If you are to attain your goal, your listeners have to judge you as a dynamic, competent and credible source. In order to convince your audience that you are not wasting their time, you must use evidence, data, and examples that will prompt them to pay attention and allow you to achieve your goal. For your support to be effective, it should allow your audience to understand your ideas and visualize them clearly. Abstract, general, and obscure data must be replaced by concrete, specific, and clear information. You need hardnosed support!

How to Select Your Supporting Material

A major task confronting all speechmakers is to decide what materials they will use to support their ideas. Since the amount of material generally available on any given topic far exceeds that which can or should be used, it is up to the speaker to select materials which are both relevant and appropriate. This is the type of decision we are called upon to make every day. Recall the support you used in the exercise, "Support Me, Please." In all probability, the supporting statements you used differed from the supporting statements your classmates used to buttress the same ideas. In short, we can say that each person's use of supporting material was, at least in part, based on personal judgments regarding an audience's interests. To reinforce this concept, try the following:

SPEECH EXPERIENCE: It's News to Me

1. Read the Inaugural Address of John F. Kennedy.[1]

Mr. Chief Justice, President Eisenhower, Vice President Nixon, President Truman, reverend clergy, fellow citizens, we observe today not a victory of party, but a celebration of freedom—symbolizing an end, as well as a beginning—signifying renewal, as well as change. For I have sworn before you and Almighty God the same solemn oath our forebears prescribed nearly a century and three-quarters ago.

The world is very different now. For man holds in his mortal hands the power to abolish all forms of human poverty and all forms of human life. And yet the same revolutionary beliefs for which our forebears fought are still at issue around the globe—the belief that the rights of man come not from the generosity of the state, but from the hand of God.

We dare not forget today that we are the heirs of that first revolution. Let the word go forth from this time and place, to friend and foe alike, that the torch has been passed to a new generation of Americans—born in this century, tempered by war, disciplined by a hard and bitter peace, proud of our ancient heritage—and unwilling to witness or permit the slow undoing of those human rights to which this nation has always been committed, and to which we are committed today at home and around the world.

Let every nation know, whether it wishes us well or ill, that we shall pay any price, bear any burden, meet any hardship, support any friend, oppose any foe, in order to assure the survival and the success of liberty.

This much we pledge—and more.

To those old allies whose cultural and spiritual origins we share, we pledge the loyalty of faithful friends. United, there is little we cannot do in a host of cooperative ventures. Divided, there is little we can do—for we dare not meet a powerful challenge at odds and split asunder.

To those new states whom we welcome to the ranks of the free, we pledge our words that one form of colonial control shall not have passed away merely to be replaced by a far greater iron tyranny. We shall not always expect to find them supporting our view. But we shall always hope to find them strongly supporting their own freedom—and to remember that, in the past, those who foolishly sought power by riding the back of the tiger ended up inside.

To those peoples in the huts and villages across the globe struggling to break the bonds of mass misery, we pledge our best efforts to help them help themselves, for whatever period is required—not because the Communists may be doing it, not because we seek their votes, but because it is right. If a free society cannot help the many who are poor, it cannot save the few who are rich.

To our sister republics south of our border, we offer a special pledge—to convert our good words into good deeds, in a new alliance for progress, to assist free men and

---

[1] Inaugural Address, *Presidents of the United States*, 87th Congress, 1st session, *House Document No. 218.* (Washington, D.C.: United States Government Printing Office, 1961), pp. 267–70.

free governments in casting off the chains of poverty. But this peaceful revolution of hope cannot become the prey of hostile powers. Let all our neighbors know that we shall join with them to oppose aggression or subversion anywhere in the Americas. And let every other power know that this hemisphere intends to remain the master of its own house.

To that world assembly of sovereign states, the United Nations, our last best hope in an age where the instruments of war have far outpaced the instruments of peace, we renew our pledge of support—to prevent it from becoming merely a forum for invective—to strengthen its shield of the new and the weak—and to enlarge the area in which its writ may run.

Finally, to those nations who would make themselves our adversary, we offer not a pledge but a request: that both sides begin anew the quest for peace, before the dark powers of destruction unleashed by science engulf all humanity in planned or accidental self-destruction.

We dare not tempt them with weakness. For only when our arms are sufficient beyond doubt can we be certain beyond doubt that they will never be employed.

But neither can two great and powerful groups of nations take comfort from our present course—both sides overburdened by the cost of modern weapons, both rightly alarmed by the steady spread of the deadly atom, yet both racing to alter that uncertain balance of terror that stays the hand of mankind's final war.

So let us begin anew—remembering on both sides that civility is not a sign of weakness, and sincerity is always subject to proof. Let us never negotiate out of fear. But let us never fear to negotiate.

Let both sides explore what problems unite us instead of laboring those problems which divide us.

Let both sides, for the first time, formulate serious and precise proposals for the inspection and control of arms—and bring the absolute power to destroy other nations under the absolute control of all nations.

Let both sides seek to invoke the wonders of science instead of its terrors. Together let us explore the stars, conquer the deserts, eradicate disease, tap the ocean depths, and encourage the arts and commerce.

Let both sides unite to heed in all corners of the earth the command of Isaiah—to "undo the heavy burdens and to let the oppressed go free."

And if a beachhead of cooperation may push back the jungle of suspicion, let both sides join in creating a new endeavor, not a new balance of power, but a new world of law, where the strong are just and the weak secure and the peace preserved.

All this will not be finished in the first hundred days. Nor will it be finished in the first thousand days, nor in the life of this Administration, not even perhaps in our lifetime on this planet. But let us begin.

In your hands, my fellow citizens, more than in mine, will rest the final success or failure of our course. Since this country was founded, each generation of Americans has been summoned to give testimony to its national loyalty. The graves of young Americans who answered the call to service are found around the globe.

Now the trumpet summons us again—not as a call to bear arms, though arms we need; not as a call to battle, though embattled we are; but a call to bear the burden of a long twilight struggle, year in, and year out, "rejoicing in hope, patient in tribulation"—a struggle against the common enemies of man: tyranny, poverty, disease, and war itself.

Can we forge against these enemies a grand and global alliance, north and south, east and west, that can assure a more fruitful life for all mankind? Will you join in that historic effort?

In the long history of the world, only a few generations have been granted the role of defending freedom in its hour of maximum danger. I do not shrink from this responsibility—I welcome it. I do not believe that any of us would exchange places with any other people or any other generation. The energy, the faith, the devotion which we bring to this endeavor will light our country and all who serve it—and the glow from that fire can truly light the world.

And so, my fellow Americans, ask not what your country can do for you: Ask what you can do for your country.

My fellow citizens of the world: Ask not what America will do for you, but what together we can do for the freedom of man.

Finally, whether you are citizens of America or citizens of the world, ask of us the same high standards of strength and sacrifice which we ask of you. With a good conscience our only sure reward, with history the final judge of our deeds, let us go forth to lead the land we love, asking His blessing and His help, but knowing that here on earth God's work must truly be our own.

2. **Pretend you are a reporter who covered the Inaugural. Your editor has asked you to write a 750 word news article, highlighting those elements of the speech you believe to be newsworthy.**

3. **Compare and contrast your article with the articles prepared by other students in your class. In what ways are the articles similar? How are they different? What types of support were used?**

4. **How would you change your article if, instead of writing for the general public, you were summarizing the President's speech for Congress—the military—a Republican fundraising dinner? (You will remember that Kennedy was a Democrat.)**

In each case, limitations influenced what you decided to include. Some of these limitations were imposed by us; others you imposed on yourself. Since you were not permitted to give a word by word detailing of the speech, you had to select data that you believed would be most interesting to each particular audience you addressed. These same principles are at work in public communication. Once you choose a topic, you have to consider carefully what you want to say about it and what others want to hear about it. You need to decide what aspects of the topic are important and how you can discuss them in the time allotted. Like reporters, public communicators are gatherers, evaluators, and selectors of materials that they believe will hold the interest of their audiences as well as help support the ideas contained in their speeches.

Where to Find Supporting Materials

As a speechmaker, you must determine what types of supporting materials are available to you and where they can be located. If you give your topic careful thought, you will realize that you can find relevant information to enhance your presentation within yourself, other persons, as well as in published sources.

First, you will want to search your own background and experience for materials that you might want to incorporate into your presentation. However, while the knowledge you have gained through life experience is worthwhile and important to you, be very careful not to rely on it exclusively. Too often, we assume that we know all there is to know about a topic and conclude that no additional information is needed to accomplish our task. This is seldom true. Avoid closing your mind to new sources of information. Your goal should be to keep learning. People who rely on their own knowledge and exclude all other sources of information may resemble the man in the following story who

gets to pawing around a secondhand store and picks up an old cello with one string to it. He takes it home, sits in a corner of the front room, finds a place for one finger to hold down that one string. Then, he saws back and forth with a bow. Hours on hours, every day his patient wife has to listen to him sawing back and forth on that one string and his finger always on that one place.

Weeks pass and she notices he never once changes his finger from that one place as he saws and saws back and forth on that one string. Sometimes, she went so far as to wish he would drop dead and his one finger be loosed from the place where he always held it on the string. Other times she hoped and prayed he would suddenly realize what he was doing and stand up and smash the cello and throw away the bow. But this didn't happen. He went on playing.

He had taught her to speak softly or else. So one day she said softly to him that she had watched other players playing the cello. And, more than that, they kept changing their fingers from one place to another all the time they were playing. This, she went on, she had particularly seen, they never kept one finger in the same place on one string while playing the cello.

He looked at her a slow moment. He laid down the bow and cello. He told her, "I might have expected this from you." . . . Of course the other cello players are always moving their fingers from one place to another. They're looking for the right place. I have found it![2]

This is an extreme example of closing one's mind to new possibilities. The public speaker who relies on one type or source of information, to the exclusion of all others, faces much the same problem.

While personal experience is a good ingredient to add to any presentation, the wise public communicator does not rely on it exclusively. Cautious public speakers are careful not to include unsupported personal opinions in their talks. One way to give extra weight to your personal feelings is to back them up with a detailing of observations that you have made. For instance, one speaker asked an audience to believe that middle-class adults were more apt to strip a car than were teenagers. He stated, "I believe auto strippers are composed mainly of middle-class adults." At first, this appeared to be just a personal opinion. Would you expect listeners to believe him? Probably not. There was a way, however, to back up this statement. The man had been a member of a group of researchers in New York City who studied this problem. He had opened the hood and removed the license plates from a parked car abandoned on a city street. He had watched from a hiding place to see what would occur. From his vantage point, he was able to determine that most of the auto strippers were middle-class

[2] A William Saroyan fable retold by Carl Sandburg. Copyright 1941 by Harcourt, Brace and Company, Inc. Copyright 1941 by Carl Sandburg.

adults.[3] Watching and observing and then reporting your findings can aid you in accomplishing your supportive task.

Other people can help you support the ideas contained in your speech. You can gather your information by writing to or interviewing relevant individuals. To obtain useful information from knowledgeable sources you have to analyze carefully what it is you want to know. You have to formulate specific questions that, once answered, will provide you with the information you need to accomplish the objective of your speech.

What is wrong with the following oral request that a student made to an administrator? "I have to give a speech on new courses. Please, tell me what you think about them?"

The student's question is much too broad. He has not identified what the new courses are. He has not identified what type of information is desired. For example, does the student want to know what the administrator thinks about the procedures for instituting new courses, the content of the new courses, the impact of the new courses on the present curriculum, or about the students who will be permitted to take the new courses? The question does not let us know. Neither would it let the administrator know. Thus, while other people can serve as valid and helpful sources, you need to know exactly what information you want them to give you—and be certain you are speaking to the right person. If, for example, the student had been addressing the administrator in charge of space management rather than the Dean of Instruction, it is doubtful that he would have been able to obtain the desired information.

Finally, published materials usually offer the preparing speaker a wealth of . information from which to select supporting material. A principal source of such published materials is the library. Once in the library, begin at the card catalogue. The card catalogue lists books on your topic under three headings: the name of the book, the author, and the subject. All three categories should be checked. Although you may have some books or authors in mind, don't neglect the subject cards as sources of new ideas.

Other useful resource materials include the various research indexes also located in the library. While you may never need to use *all* of these indexes, you should become familiar with the *Readers' Guide to Periodical Literature*, *The Education Index*, *The Social Science and Humanities Index*, *The New York Times Index*, *Sociological Abstracts*, and *Psychological Abstracts*. When using any of these indexes, you can employ the following guidelines:

1. Identify your topic area(s).
2. Rank the areas from the most to the least specific.
3. Begin by looking up the most specific items on your list.

[3] From a study done by: Floyd L. Ruch and Philip G. Zimbardo, *Psychology and Life*, 8th ed. (Glenview, Ill.: Scott, Foresman and Company, 1971) p. 547.

Try the following:

1. You will divide into small groups.
2. Each group will work with the following topics:
    a. The Three Mile Island Nuclear Power Plant Accident
    b. The Loch Ness Monster
    c. King Tut
    d. Women in Advertising
    e. The Assassination of Robert Kennedy
3. It is each group's task to locate as many relevant sources of supporting material for each topic as possible. The group that compiles the most extensive lists within the assigned time period is the winner.

Types of Supporting Material

Supporting material, like clothes, comes in all shapes and sizes. Just as you would not buy an item of clothing without trying it on and considering how it fits and looks, neither should you select material to support your speech without thinking about how you will use it and what purpose it will serve. Listed below are some of the types of supporting material.

Definitions

A definition tells what a thing is or what a term means. Definitions are useful whenever you use terms or concepts with which your listeners are unfamiliar or for which they have meanings that differ from your own. Unusual, abstract, obscure, or unfamiliar words should be defined. Only in this way will listeners know how you would like them to interpret your words.

A student in a public speaking course used the following definition to clarify his ideas about love for his audience: "By love, I mean the knot that ties two pieces of loose twine into one smooth, silky ribbon."

Susan B. Anthony, in a speech, "On Woman's Right to Suffrage," defined the phrase, "we, the people," as follows: "It was we, the people; not we, the white male citizens; nor yet we, the male citizens; but we, the whole people who formed the union."

Richard Nixon, in his famous "Checkers" speech, used a particular definition of the term "morally wrong" to help him achieve his purpose:

I am sure you have read the charge, and you have heard it that I, Senator Nixon, took $18,000 from a group of my supporters.

Now, was that wrong? And let me say that it was wrong. I am saying, incidentally, that it was wrong, not just illegal, because it isn't a question of whether it was legal or illegal. That isn't enough.

The question is, was it morally wrong? I say that it was morally wrong—if any of the $18,000 went to Senator Nixon, for my personal use. I say that it was morally wrong, if it was secretly given and secretly handled.

And I say that it was morally wrong if any of the contributors got special favors for the contribution they made.[4]

To demonstrate your understanding of the way in which definitions are used, try the next exercise.

SPEECH EXPERIENCE: It's Time to Define

1. Choose an abstract word like *jealousy, liberty, good, evil,* and so on.

2. In a one to two minute presentation, explain your definition of that term to the class.

Descriptions and Explanations

Descriptions and explanations help to clarify the topic: how something is done, what the present state of affairs is, or how something came to be. When used carefully, descriptions create word pictures that will enable listeners to see, taste, touch, smell, hear, and feel what you, the speaker, wish to share with them. When used wisely, explanations add clarity and precision to your message.

If you want your listeners to know how to apply for a credit card, you can use an explanation. If you want your listeners to experience your feelings regarding animal experimentation and research, you can use description. Germaine Greer, author of *The Female Eunuch,* used vivid descriptions to convey her feelings about female stereotypes to her audience:

Maybe I don't have a pretty smile, good teeth, long legs, a cheeky arse, a sexy voice. Maybe I don't know how to handle men and increase my market value, so that the rewards due to the feminine will accrue to me. Then, again, maybe I'm sick of the masquerade. I'm sick of pretending eternal youth. I'm sick of belying my own intelligence, my own will, my own sex. I'm sick of peering at the world through false eyelashes, so everything I see is mixed with a shadow of bought hairs; I'm sick of weighting my head with a dead mane, unable to move my neck freely, terrified of rain, of wind, of dancing too vigorously in case I sweat into my lacquered curls. I'm sick of the Powder Room. I'm sick of pretending that some male's self-important pronouncements are the objects of my undivided attention. I'm sick of going to films and plays when someone else wants to, and sick of having no opinions of my own about either. I'm sick of being a transvestite. I refuse to be a female impersonator. I am a woman.

---

[4] Richard M. Nixon, "My Side of the Story," *Vital Speeches of the Day,* **19**:11–12 (October 15, 1952).

Examples and Illustrations

While examples specify or identify particular instances, illustrations help to create more detailed narrative pictures. Whereas examples cite given references, illustrations recount happenings or tell stories. Both forms of support can help clarify the points you want to make and insure your being understood by your audience. One would probably not attempt discussing TV situation comedies without noting specific examples and/or telling about one situation comedy episode in greater detail. Examples and illustrations come in three basic types: factual or real—those that indicate actual circumstances; unreal or fictitious—those that refer to something that has been made up to explain a point; and hypothetical or imagined—those that provide an indication of what would or could happen if certain circumstances or conditions were met.

In a speech on child abuse, a student used a series of brief, factual examples to clarify her point:

When found in the 23″ x 52″ closet, where she had been locked for half her life, nine-year-old Patty weighed only twenty pounds, and stood less than three feet tall. When brought to the San Francisco General Hospital, eleven-year-old Gary was suffering from severe malnutrition, weighed forty-four pounds, had a temperature of just eighty-four degrees, and was in a deep coma. Gary also had suspicious marks on his wrists and ankles. The police quickly located the cause of these marks; the apartment where Gary lived with his mother and her boyfriend was littered with handcuffs, chains, and locks that had been used to immobilize him for hours at a time. When an autopsy was performed on six-week-old Alice, it disclosed that she had a ruptured spleen and liver, fourteen broken ribs, human bite marks on her cheek, bruises on her stomach, and alcohol in her bloodstream. Patty, Gary, and Alice were victims of child abuse.

In contrast, another speaker, instead of using brief examples, used a lengthier, personal illustration to make her point about rising health-care costs.

My father had lung cancer and cancer of the spinal column. He was ill for only five weeks. The last weeks of his life were spent in a hospital. He was operated on, given radiation treatments, and placed in a medical contraption that was supposed to increase his limited mobility. It didn't. The bill for his five-week stay in the hospital amounted to $20,000. My father was, by no means, a wealthy man. However, neither was he eligible for medicare. Thus, his illness consumed my parents' entire savings. There is something terribly wrong with a health care system that is permitted to inflict such a terrible blow on patients and their families. National health care has become a necessity.

Testimonials

Testimonials are statements made by a person attesting to his or her beliefs, feelings, or experiences. When you use testimonials, you are attempting to buttress your speech with favorable, interesting, and supportive opinions. Adding testimony helps you add credibility and sparkle to your ideas. It permits you to connect your ideas with the thoughts and attitudes of individuals with whom your listeners are familiar and whom they admire and respect. Testimony need not come from a present-day source. The words and beliefs of an esteemed person who lived long ago can be used to tie together today and yesterday. In any case, the worth of your testimony will vary with the reputation and credibility of the individuals you choose. Ask yourself if the individual you chose as an authority is competent and trustworthy. Also, ask if his or her words are understandable and relevant.

Another student delivered a speech on the peoples' right to know in a democracy and quoted Senator George McGovern:

Let us say to Americans, as Woodrow Wilson said in his first campaign: 'Let me inside (the government) and I will tell you everything that is going on in there."[5]

In a speech made before the House Judiciary Committee, Representative Barbara Jordan clarified her stand on the impeachment of Richard Nixon by using a quotation from President James Madison, who had written:

If the President be connected in any suspicious manner with any person and there be grounds to believe that he will shelter him, he may be impeached.[6]

Statistics

Statistics may be defined as facts expressed in numbers. They are used as quantified examples to demonstrate how things are related to other things or to indicate trends. If used properly and sparingly, statistics can clarify ideas and increase the believability of information. When using statistics, be sure to check the date when they were compiled, who compiled them, the reliability of the source, and what they actually are said to measure.

In one speech, former General Motors executive, James M. Roche, used statistical information to make his point:

Today, you can predict fairly accurately just how many alcoholics there are in a company. If there are 100 employes, there are five to ten alcoholics. If there are 100,000 employes, you will find 5,000 to 10,000 . . . alcoholics. At General Motors, we have more than 500,000 employees, so you will find 25,000 to 50,000 who are involved in an alcoholic problem.[7]

A dean of an eastern university once introduced an entering class of freshmen to university life by telling them: "Look to the right of you. Look to the left of you. One of these individuals won't make it to the sophomore class."

A member of a public speaking class included this passage in her speech in an effort to show how we must treat statistical proof with some reservations:

[5] Senator George McGovern, in his acceptance speech, Democratic National Convention, Miami Beach, Florida, July 14, 1972.
[6] Speech by Barbara Jordan before House Judiciary Committee, n.d.
[7] *Vital Speeches of the Day*, 39:120 (December 1, 1972).

Experts who counselled the builders of the baboon cage at the Los Angeles Zoo assured them that baboons were unable to jump further than ten feet. With this figure in mind, the builders gave themselves what they deemed to be ample breathing space— they made the moat surrounding the cage twelve feet across.

Much to everyone's surprise, after the cage was built, a number of baboons escaped; they simply jumped over the "secure" twelve-foot moat and ran out of the zoo. It was several days before they were recaptured. When asked how the baboons could have escaped, officials of the zoo were quoted by the Associated Press as follows: "We were informed, when we placed the animals there, that they could not jump more than ten feet. Regrettably, it appears the baboons were unfamiliar with the data."

Comparison and Contrast

When using a comparison, the speaker selects something familiar to the audience and likens it to an unknown item or concept he or she is attempting to explain. In this way, the similarities possessed by the two entities are shown. Contrast is used when a speaker wishes to stress the differences, rather than the similarities, between the two ideas or items.

William L. Laurence used comparison and contrast to describe the atomic bombing of Nagasaki:

As the first mushroom floated off into the blue, it changed its shape into a flower-like form, its grand petals curving downward, creamy white outside, rose-colored inside . . . Much living substance had gone into those rainbows. The quivering top of the pillar was protruding to a great height through the white clouds, giving the appearance of a monstrous prehistoric creature with a ruff around its neck, a fleecy ruff extending in all directions, as far as the eye could see.

Comparisons and contrasts (analogies) can be literal or figurative. In a literal comparison, two things basically alike are compared. (For example: one tree to another) In a figurative comparison, two things basically different are compared. (For example: a baby to a Volkswagon; an overbearing person to a jackhammer)

Repetition and Restatement

Public communicators employ the support devices of repetition and restatement when they repeat some of the words of their speeches verbatim, or when they repeat ideas contained in their speeches in different words.

A speaker used these devices when delivering an address on the death of the famed conductor, Arturo Toscanini:

The January 17th issue of the New York Times carried the headline, "Arturo Toscanini is dead." Newspaper boys shouted from the street corners of Milan, "The Maestro is dead." The NBC Radio Symphony in Radio City gave a concert in his honor . . .

The Maestro is dead. La Scala in Milan was closed down and a special mass was said in St. Peter's . . . the Maestro is dead.[8]

Martin Luther King, Jr. also used repetition to highlight his ideas and help his listeners remember his thoughts.

I Have a Dream[9]

I am not unmindful that some of you have come here out of great trials and tribulations. Some of you have come fresh from jail cells. Some of you have come from areas where your quest for freedom left you battered by the storms of persecution and staggered by the winds of police brutality . . .

Go back to Mississippi; go back to Alabama; go back to South Carolina; go back to Georgia; go back to Louisiana; go back to the slums and ghettoes of our Northern cities, knowing that somehow this situation can, and will be changed. Let us not wallow in the valley of despair.

I say to you today, my friends, so even though we face the difficulties of today and tomorrow, I still have a dream. It is a dream deeply rooted in the American dream. I have a dream that one day this nation will rise up . . . live out the true meaning of its creed—we hold these truths to be self-evident, that all men are created equal . . .

I have a dream that my four little children will one day live in a nation where they will not be judged by the color of their skin but by the content of their character. I have a dream today! . . .

I have a dream that one day every valley shall be exalted, and every hill and mountain shall be made low, the rough places shall be made plain, and the crooked places shall be made straight and the glory of the Lord will be revealed and all flesh shall see it together.

This is our hope. This is the faith that I go back to the South with.

With this faith we will be able to hew out of the mountain of despair a stone of hope. With this faith we will be able to transform the jangle and discords of our nation into a beautiful symphony of brotherhood.

With this faith we will be able to work together, to pray together, to struggle together, to go to jail together, to stand up for freedom together, knowing that we will be free one day. This will be the day when all of God's children will be able to sing with new meaning—"my country 'tis of thee; sweet land of liberty; of thee I sing; land where my fathers died, land of the pilgrim's pride; from every mountain side, let freedom ring"—and if America is to be a great nation, this must come true.

So let freedom ring from the prodigious hilltops of New Hampshire.

Let freedom ring from the mighty mountains of New York.

Let freedom ring from the heightening Alleghenies of Pennsylvania.

Let freedom ring from the snow-capped Rockies of Colorado.

Let freedom ring from the curvaceous slopes of California.

But not only there.

Let freedom ring from Stone Mountain of Georgia.

Let freedom ring from Lookout Mountain of Tennessee.

Let freedom ring from every hill and molehill of Mississippi, from every mountainside, let freedom ring.

And when this happens, when we allow freedom to ring, when we let it ring from every village and every hamlet, from every state and every city, we will be able to speed

---

[8] Elizabeth Langer, "An Instrument of Revelation," in Linkugel *Contemporary American Speeches*, 3d ed. (Belmont, California: Wadsworth Publishing Co., 1972), pp. 302–3.

[9] Martin Luther King, Jr. Speech given in 1963 at the Lincoln Memorial.

up that day when all of God's children—black men and white men, Jews and Gentiles, Protestants and Catholics—will be able to join hands and sing in the words of the old Negro spiritual. "Free at last, free at last, thank God Almighty, we are free at last."

Wit and Humor

Wit and humor add interest, vitality, and warmth to a speech. They can be used to increase listener appreciation.

In a speech given on the hazards of transporting dangerous materials, a speaker relaxed her audience by telling them that the following notice had recently appeared in the help wanted section of her local newspaper: "Wanted— Person to drive dynamite truck. Must be prepared to travel unexpectedly."

A Democratic president, participating in a roast, also employed humor when he delivered his remarks to the gathered newswriters:

Last year, when I spoke to this distinguished group, I started my speech by smil- ing. For the life of me, I can't remember what I was smiling about . . . I have gotten a great deal of advice from you, some of which, unfortunately, I've taken . . . Some Republicans have said that our foreign policy is a disaster. I just thought that as the ad- ministration changed, there ought to be some continuity.

Wit and humor certainly play an most important role in public discourse.

Summary

By now, you realize that giving a speech is not a simple action. One cannot simply transfer information to one's audience the way one might hand over an object. Since ideas are not so easily transferred, speeches demand support of these ideas.

In this chapter, we have examined how to find support for your topic, the major types of supporting materials available to you, and how such materials can be used to help you achieve your speaking goal.

Watch Your Language

Behavioral Objectives

After reading this chapter, you should have a better understanding of:

- how difficult it is to express yourself clearly without words.
- the nature of language.
- the origin of language.
- the relationship between words, things, and thoughts.
- how language functions as a tool.
- how language can act as a barrier to effective communication.
- the ways language can stir an audience's imagination.

Introduction

Have you ever wondered what it would be like if you were not free to use words to express your ideas? What if you were permitted to show but not to tell others what you felt or thought? To give you an idea of how it might feel, perform this exercise.

SPEECH EXPERIENCE: SHOW AND TELL

1. Divide into groups of four to five students each.
2. Each student should select one of the following topics:

Physical Fitness	Jealousy
War	Cooking
Love	History
Show Business	Beauty

3. One at a time, each participant should come to the front of the room and attempt to communicate personal thoughts and feelings on the selected subject to the class, *using only body language or visual aids* (pictures, drawings, or props).

4. Add to the presentation the element of *sound* (i.e., grunts, groans, laughter, or sighing) to clarify the message.

5. Finally, add *words*. At this point, nonverbal, vocal, and verbal communication may be used together.

Questions to Answer About "SHOW AND TELL"

1. How did you feel during each stage of the "Show and Tell" process?

_____

_____

2. How did the initial series of restrictions affect your ability to communicate?

_____

_____

3. To what extent were you able to share meaning and understanding with each other during each stage of the experience?

_____

_____

You have probably discovered how difficult it is to express yourself clearly to an audience without using words. Even audio aids (the sounds you were permitted to make), visual aids (the pictures you were permitted to draw), or physical cues (the body language and props you used) were no guarantee that you would be able to share your thoughts and feelings with your audience. In fact, we are willing to wager that intelligent, understandable, and clear communication began only when you were permitted to use words. Hopefully, this exercise has enabled you to experience the desire and need to communicate, as well as the frustration that results when one is hampered by various restrictions. You should now know, firsthand, what it feels like to have something important to say and not have a suitable way of saying it. The public speaker's nightmare is to have ideas that cannot be made understandable to others. For the first time, perhaps, you may realize how much you take your speaking abilities for granted. Too often, we fail to realize the value of something until we no longer have it or are threatened with its loss. Speech is one of the things we frequently take for granted. We depend on our speech abilities to help us communicate with others. Once we understand how speech operates, we will be in a better position to use words to help us share meaning with audiences. Let us now examine what language is and how its proper use can benefit the public communicator.

What Is Language?

If you were assigned a speech on the subject of language, you would probably discover something very interesting. While there are hundreds of books written on language, it continues to defy our understanding. Ask yourself: What is language? Are you satisfied with your answer? If you said that language is what people use when they communicate, you are off to a good start. Actually, language is a kind of "civilizing tool." Language is the means by which knowledge is presented and passed on from person to person. Or, to put it another way, human beings have gathered together a body of knowledge consisting of vocal and written symbols (words). Our symbols have meaning because we have agreed on what they will mean. This is LANGUAGE—that which sets humans apart from all other forms of life. Language is humankind's most important invention.

SPEECH EXPERIENCE: THE WORD-GO-ROUND

1. Divide into groups of four or five students.

2. Each group has ten minutes in which to create and define a new word. Then, three sentences containing the word are to be composed.

3. In turn, a representative of each group will come to the chalkboard and write the group's newly created word. He or she will then ask a member of another group to define the word.

4. The selected member may confer with teammates for fifteen seconds before giving a response. If the meaning of the word is guessed correctly, ten points are earned. If the guess is incorrect, the challenging team member will read one of his group's sentences aloud. The opposing team member then has thirty seconds more to respond with another definition. If correct, five points are earned.

5. Play continues from team to team in this manner. The team accumulating the most points at the end of play is the winner.

When we were children, we did not know that language was something people just made up. We thought there was some connection between an act or an object and the *word* that stood for it. If an adult asked us why we called a particular object "a rock," we probably would have answered, "Because it is a rock." Although most of us have left such childish views behind, we still may make this faulty connection occasionally. You may have heard a remark like, "The real name for this is 'frankfurter'[1], but I call them 'hot dogs' because everyone else around here calls them that." People who talk like this give the impression that they actually believe there is a "real" name for everything. They don't seem to realize that words are only spoken or written symbols that a group of people have agreed on as having a particular meaning.

The Origin of Language

We have all wondered where language came from. Almost every language spoken in the civilized world has been suggested as the original. Because Hebrew was the language of the people of the Old Testament, it was a favorite choice. A Swedish writer of the seventeenth century believed that in the Garden of Eden, Adam and Eve spoke Danish, the serpent spoke French, and God spoke Swedish. The list of theories goes on and on. One of the most amusing is the Royal Experiment. Three times in history, specific kings have tried an inhuman experiment to discover the nature of our original language. It was thought that if a number of small children were isolated from birth from all sound of human speech—brought up in complete silence—that they would naturally begin to speak the original language of mankind. The first king to try this experiment was the Egyptian, Psammitichos. His victims were supposed to have said first, *bekos*, which happened to be the Phrygian word for "bread." Next, Emperor Frederick II (died in 1250 A.D.) tried the same experiment but failed. The children he used died inconveniently before saying anything. Still later, King James IV of Scotland (died in 1513 A.D.) also tried this experiment and declared that the children came to speak "very good Hebrew."

The nineteenth century brought forth theories which made a bit more sense. There were four types of theories, to which scholars gave the following nicknames: *Bow-wow Theory*, *Ding-dong Theory*, *Pooh-pooh Theory*, and the *Yo-he-ho Theory*.

The Bow-wow Theory

This theory suggests that human speech began as an imitation of the noises that animals make. For example, if early humans heard a cat and imitated the

---

[1] The origin of the frankfurter: a German butcher decided to try a new version of a sandwich, placing a sausage between two pieces of bread. The city in which this sausage sandwich originated was Frankfurt, Germany: hence the name *frankfurter*.

sound, they soon connected that sound with the category *cat*. The main problem with this theory is that humans had more pressing reasons to communicate than to name animals.

The Ding-dong Theory

The idea of this theory is that the first sounds which had any meaning for humans were imitations of the sounds of nature. Sounds of the wind, falling rocks, babbling brooks, thunder, and lightning all are said to be models for the earliest form of speech. Like the Bow-wow Theory, this theory fails to account for the wide variety of reasons early people had for developing language.

The Pooh-pooh Theory

Here, the belief is that language grew out of the emotional noises early people made when they expressed their feelings. "Ow!" "mmmmm!" and "ah!" are a few examples. Unfortunately, a language consisting of sounds associated only with the emotions is, at best, very limited. Where does grammar fit in? It is difficult to imagine these noises ever giving rise to ordinary words.

The Yo-he-ho Theory

This theory focuses on the noises people make while doing physical work. People working in groups use certain sounds to coordinate their movements. For example, sailors pulling rope together on board ship and workers laying railroad track chant certain sounds to coordinate their efforts. This theory proposes that primitive chants were the origin of language. Again, like all the other theories, this one attempts to oversimplify the origin of language.

Words: The Building Blocks of Language

According to Abraham Kaplan, "Give a small boy a hammer and he will find that everything he encounters needs pounding." This same principle can be applied to words. "Give anyone the power of words and, before you know it, everything that is encountered needs naming."

Which of us, at some time, has not come into contact with a person, place, or thing and has been unable to give it a name? It can be very frustrating. How many things are there around your house you cannot name? Think how much of your education is concerned with learning the proper names for things. We seem to be constantly judging one another on the basis of how well we are able to name things correctly. Finally examinations or television quiz shows are perfect examples of this "naming" compulsion. Our whole world seems to consist of little more than *things* and *words which stand for things*. Our job is to manage these tools successfully—the words and the things they represent, and their relationships to one another.

Symbols *stand for some thing else*

We live in two different worlds and commute back and forth. One of these worlds consists of the things we experience directly. The other world consists of words and other symbols—our indirect experiences. Pavlov, the famous Russian scientist, described these two worlds in terms of communication. He spoke of two signaling systems. To illustrate what he meant by each, picture yourself sitting in a theatre. Suddenly, you smell smoke—and, in your experience, smoke means fire. On the basis of what you smell, you get up and leave the theatre. You have just responded to your surroundings through your First Signaling System. On the other hand, if you hear someone yell the word *fire* and, on the basis of it, you leave the theatre, you have responded through your Secondary Signaling System. In the first situation, you were in direct communication with the real world. In the second, you were communicating with the world indirectly; that is, through the *symbol* which members of our society have agreed stands for fire.

Although we can experience most of the world in which we live through our senses, there are a number of things we cannot experience that way. We have invented a whole stockpile of symbols to stand for abstract concepts. Examples of some of these concepts are love, grateful, satisfactory, freedom, intelligence, politics, opinion. Even the word *real* does not stand for anything we can see, hear, taste, touch, or smell. It too is an abstract concept.

SPEECH EXPERIENCE: SYMBOL SEE-SAW

1. Select an abstract concept such as friendship, hate, ugly, power.
2. Ask three to five people of different ages to tell you:
   a. What they think of when you say the word.
   b. How they explain the word's meaning.
   c. Report your findings to the class.
   d. Compare student findings.

Words do more than define abstract concepts. They are also used to describe. Words are used to communicate physical characteristics of concrete things: their size, shape, color, thickness, weight, and so on. Other words serve to communicate abstract characteristics, which cannot be physically experienced. Is the object valuable, rare, or unusual? Here you have two working sets of tools: one to describe the concrete and the other to describe the abstract.

Perhaps you will be persuaded by the following paragraph to look at words more closely. James McCrimmons argues that words are not things: they simply make people think of things.

The letters b–o–o–k make you think of this thing you are reading or of a similar thing. But, any other combination of letters could perform the same function, provided people had agreed on that combination. Because of this general agreement, the same object is known by different names in different languages. Thus, what we call a *book* in English is also referred to as *buch* (German), *bock* (Dutch), *bok* (Swedish), *bog* (Danish), *livre* (French), *libro* (Spanish), and so on. Not one of these names is the 'real' name for book. Not one of them is better than the others. In so far as they point to the thing which we choose to call a book, they are all satisfactory names.

To repeat a principle: Words are not things; they are symbols.

Thoughts

If you are searching for the most fantastic communication tool of them all, search no further. That tool is your brain. Your brain has an endless appetite. It takes the information it is fed, digests it, and comes up with such things as the theory of relativity, techniques of space travel, organ transplants, astrophysics, cloning, and electron microscopes. Its accomplishments are staggering. As if these were not enough, it also has the ability to reach backward as well as forward in time. History books, packed with information, enable us to communicate across centuries. We can enjoy and benefit from the thoughts sparked by the brains of Jesus of Nazareth, Socrates, Confucius, and Mohammed. Their thoughts are as alive today as they were in the past. This process is called, "time-binding." Keeping a diary is a form of personal time-binding. Human brains, in addition to having information from the past at their disposal, also can make predictions about the future. The brains responsible for our science-fiction literature are examples of people being able to reach out into the future with words.

Animals cannot time-bind because of the limited size and nature of their brains. They can react only to symbols as signals; whereas, we can give signals additional meaning. Lacking the highly developed brain we possess, every lower animal is "locked into the present." A walrus cannot tell its baby walrus about a particularly wise walrus who lived two thousand years ago, or what life was like for the walrus during the third century. For this reason in particular, we humans enjoy the privilege of living in a much larger universe than any other creature. With our unique brain, we have already invented machines to carry on where our senses have left off, such as microscopes, telescopes, earphones, radar, etc.

There are three ways of looking at a tool like language. You can describe its appearance, indicate its use, or tell how it works. For our purposes here, the first and second ways are less important than the third.

You have already been told that language is made up of symbols. When you manipulate these symbols inside your head, you are *thinking*. The power to think is so much a natural part of our lives that we often fail to realize it is the core of our humanity. The story of Helen Keller illustrates this dramatically. She was made blind and deaf by disease at the age of nineteen months. For the next five years, she grew up without normal word contact. Her mind was, indeed, a palace of shadows—a place where no words existed. She lived in a world of things without names. One day, while walking in the garden with her teacher, Miss Sullivan, a miraculous thing happened. Miss Sullivan's description of it was as follows:

I made Helen hold her mug under the spout while I pumped. As the cold water gushed forth, filling the mug, I spelled the word W–A–T–E–R into Helen's free hand. The word coming so close upon the sensation of cold water rushing over her hand seemed to startle her. She dropped the mug and stood as one transfixed. A new light came into her face. She spelled "water" several times. Then she dropped on the ground and asked for its name and pointed to the pump and the trellis, and suddenly turning around she asked my name . . . In a few hours, she had added thirty new words to her vocabulary.[2]

This experience caused Helen to think, to wonder at the fact that suddenly the mystery of language was revealed to her. She knew that w–a–t–e–r meant the wonderful cool something that flowed over her hand. The living word awakened her soul; gave it light, hope, joy; set it free.

Over two thousand years ago, the Greek philosopher, Socrates, had a deep insight into the nature and function of speech. He recognized that we find ourselves defined by the words we speak to other people and with which they answer. He also sensed that by revealing ourselves to others and having them reveal themselves to us, we shall know ourselves. Because she was robbed of her speech, all of this was impossible for Helen Keller. In spite of her fine brain, the ability to use it, and the vocal machinery necessary for speech—without words, Helen was a prisoner confined within her own body. Only through the magic of WORDS was she able to gain her freedom.

Language Problems

It is important to realize that words don't always set us free. In fact, unless we use them wisely, they can imprison us. Just as language can provide the key that permits us to share thought and meaning with others, so language can serve as a barrier which prevents us from communicating clearly with our listeners. Here are three common ways in which language can pose problems for us.

---

[2] Helen Keller, *The Story of My Life* (New York: Doubleday & Company, Inc. 1954), p. 257.

Forgetting That Meanings Are in People

We are apt to experience a communication breakdown if we consider only our own meanings for a word. Although the interpretations we have for particular words are usually clear to us, we fail to ask how our listeners will interpret our words. As speechmakers, it is essential that we recognize that the meaning of words may change as a result of time, place, or experience. This exercise is designed to enable you to recognize that the meaning of a word depends upon when it is used, where it is used, and who is using it.

SPEECH EXPERIENCE: THE KALEIDESCOPE OF WORDS

1. Write down your definitions for each of the following words:

   a. Pop _____

   b. Gay _____

   c. High _____

   d. Pad _____

   e. Grass _____

   f. Stoned _____

   g. Rock _____

   h. Hip _____

2. How do you think the following individuals would define the words with which they are paired?

   a. A gardener and the word "grass" _____

   _____

   b. A pilot and the word "high" _____

   _____

   c. A teacher and the word "pad" _____

   _____

  d. A resident of New York City and the word "pop" _____

_____

  e. A minister and the word "stoned" _____

_____

  f. A construction engineer and the word "rock" _____

_____

  g. A doctor and the word "hip" _____

_____

Words seldom have only a single meaning. This excerpt from an essay by William Safire will help to illustrate this point.

"Gentlemen," beams the chief executive, "I am pleased to announce that we have a gorilla."

The speaker is not a zoo keeper; nor is he the head of an underworld organization, using "gorilla" to mean "strong arm man," or "hoodlum imported for intimidation." The speaker is the boss of a music publishing business using the newest noun to denote "smash hit".

The meaning of the word *gorilla* will depend upon who uses it and how it is used. For this reason, when you use words, you need to be aware that others may not respond to a word exactly as you do. Meanings are in people, not in words or objects.

Watch Out for Jargon = *shorthand, sub-language (field specific)*

Too frequently, public communicators forget that listeners may not understand the words that are used because they are too technical. This problem is illustrated in the following example:

A plumber was aware that hydrochloric acid opened clogged drain pipes quickly and efficiently. However, he thought he had better check with the National Bureau of Standards in Washington, D.C. to determine if hydrochloric acid was safe to use in pipes. So, he wrote the Bureau a letter. A scientist at the Bureau wrote a letter back to the plumber. The scientist's letter read as follows: "The efficacy of hydrochloric acid is indisputable, but the corrosive residue is incompatible with metallic permanence."

The plumber wrote a second letter thanking the scientist for the quick reply and for giving him the okay to use hydrochloric acid.

The plumber's second letter bothered the scientist and he brought it to the attention of his supervisor. The supervisor decided to write a letter to the plumber himself. His letter read: "We cannot assume responsibility for the production of toxic and noxious residue which hydrochloric acid may produce and suggest that you use an alternative procedure."

This left the plumber somewhat confused. He dashed off a letter to the Bureau telling them that he was glad they agreed with him. "The acid was working just fine."

Upon receiving this letter, the supervisor sent it to the top boss at the Bureau. He solved the problem by writing a short note to the plumber: "Don't use hydrochloric acid. It eats the hell out of the pipes."

A good rule to follow, if you hope to achieve clarity, is to keep the jargon usage to a minimum—unless your listener is schooled in the same jargon. You want to be certain that you speak the same language as your audience. It doesn't matter how precisely we choose words to express our ideas if our listeners are unable to comprehend what the words mean. It is only when we use language to which our listeners can easily relate that we take a giant step toward shared meaning. Bear in mind that people who recieve messages are just as important as the people who send them. Whenever you function as a speechmaker, you need to consider who your listeners are and how to make yourself understood.

Use Appropriate Language

The more appropriate your language, the more inclined your audience will be to understand you. In order to accurately determine what type of language would turn off an audience, you will need to develop your powers of sensitivity and empathy. Dress your speech in words that are suitable for your audience and, at the same time, be certain that the language you use is appropriate to both you and your topic. Just as your words can cause your listeners to become irritated, alienated, or distracted, so your words can make you feel out-of-place or uncomfortable. It is embarrassing to be caught trying to ingratiate yourself with a group by speaking "their language," only to discover that you are speaking it incorrectly. Speakers who use "big words" to impress their audience run the risk of being judged as insincere. Likewise, people who try to talk "just like their listeners" run the risk of having people feel they are being talked down to. This next exercise will help enable you to detect inappropriate language.

SPEECH EXPERIENCE: Oops!

1. Divide the class into groups of four to five students.

2. Place the following list of speech topics in one container and the following list of audiences and occasions in a second container.

    a. *Topics:* The Sexual Revolution, Inflation, Pollution, Unemployment, The Draft, Cheating.

    b. *Audiences and Occasions:* An appeal to a jury, a valedictory address to the senior class and guests, the President's Inaugural speech to the nation, a classroom lecture, a report to stockholders.

3. In turn, a representative from each group is to come to the front of the room and select a card from each container. Group members will then work together to create an example of how language could be used in a way that would be judged *inappropriate* for the selected situation.

4. The entire class should discuss possible causes of inappropriate usage and note how it could be corrected.

It is important to recognize that your language will be judged appropriate if you adapt it to your audience, to the occasion on which you are speaking, and to your own abilities. Understanding how language works will help to improve your ability to communicate with an audience. There are a number of language devices that can further simplify your communication tasks.

Stirring Your Audience's Imagination

If your speech contains words that are forceful and vivid, your listeners not only will be more apt to understand your ideas, but also will remember them as well. Commonly referred to as "figures of speech," the following eight stylistic devices can be used to help hold an audience's attention and add impact to a speech.

Simile

A simile is easily identified because it makes an explicit comparison between two things and, generally, uses either the word *like* or *as*. It simply compares the qualities of one thing to the qualities of another. In describing the way a famed guitarist looked as he played a song, one public speaker said, "He bent over his instrument as a man might bend over a woman he loved." Speakers who want to explain an idea or an image in clear, understandable language, find the simile a useful device.

Metaphor

A metaphor functions like a simile, except that it omits the words *like* or *as*. For example, the metaphorical equivalent of the simile, "That bird looks like a frog," is simply, "That bird is a frog." By relating two hitherto unrelated objects, the public speaker can widen the audience's perception of the subject. Virginia Woolf used a metaphor when she wrote, "Anonymous was a woman." Likewise, Martin Luther King, Jr. expressed the problems of black people by noting,

"The Negro lives on a lonely island of poverty in the midst of a vast ocean of material prosperity."

Personification

Personification is the attributing of human qualities to an inanimate object, an animal, or an idea. Examples of personification include statements such as, "The old train groaned in pain as it chugged up the steep hill," or "The waves danced chaotically, signaling the arrival of the storm." Again, Martin Luther King, Jr. gave truth a human dimension when he said, "We shall overcome because . . . truth crushed to earth shall rise again. . . ."

Hyperbole *gross exageration*

Hyperbole, or overstatement, is the figure of speech which writers and speakers employ when they make exaggerations. For example, "You eat like a bird," or "It's so hot, you could fry an egg on the sidewalk," or "That's the most beautiful baby in the world." These are all examples of hyperbole.

Understatement

Understatement is the opposite of hyperbole. Instead of exaggerating the facts, understatement involves a conservative depiction of them. Like hyperbole, understatement can be used to dramatize a situation. Were you to say, "It's a bit dry outside," while delivering a speech to an audience situated in the middle of Death Valley, you would be using understatement.

Irony

Irony is a language device used to imply the opposite of what you actually say. It is a powerful way of satirizing happenings or illustrating injustices. "With a friend like you, who needs enemies?" is an example of a common ironic statement that has been used in many unsatisfactory interpersonal encounters.

Alliteration

Speakers will sometimes use the same initial consonant sound in a series of words. An alliterative style helps add rhythm and movement to verbal expression. "Naturally, Nathan needs nourishment," and "violent vocal vipers," are examples of alliteration in action.

Imagery

Effective speakers also use words that appeal to our senses. This helps us to experience things as they look, sound, smell, taste, and move. When employing imagery, you may use some of the stylistic devices we have already mentioned. In addition, there are six basic image categories with which the public communicator should be familiar. Images appealing to the senses are: 1) sight—visual images, 2) hearing—acoustic images, (3) taste—gustatory images, (4) smell—olfactory images, (5) touch—tactile images.

Beyond those images which appeal to the five traditional senses, a speaker must also be concerned with those images that appeal to an audience's motor system—those body mechanisms which make physical movement possible. Search out the images used by Edward R. Murrow in his broadcast entitled, "In Search of Light." [3]

April 15, 1945
Permit me to tell you what you would have seen, and heard, had you been with me on Thursday. It will not be pleasant listening. If you are at lunch, or if you have no appetite to hear what Germans have done, now is a good time to switch off the radio, for I propose to tell you of Buchenwald. It is on a small hill about four miles outside Weimar, and it was one of the largest concentration camps in Germany, and it was built to last. As we approached it, we saw about a hundred men in civilian clothes with rifles advancing in open order across the fields. There were a few shops; we stopped to inquire. We were told that some of the prisoners had a couple of SS men cornered in there. We drove on, reached the main gate. The prisoners crowded up behind the wire. We entered.

And now, let me tell this in the first person, for I was the least important person there, as you shall hear. There surged around me an evil-smelling horde. Men and boys reached out to touch me; they were in rags and the remnants of uniform. Death had already marked many of them, but they were smiling with their eyes. I looked out over that mass of men to the green fields beyond where well-fed Germans were ploughing.

A German, Fritz Kersheimer, came up and said, "May I show you round the camp? I've been here ten years." An Englishman stood to attention, saying, "May I introduce myself, delighted to see you, and can you tell me when some of our blokes will be along?" I told him soon and asked to see one of the barracks. It happened to be occupied by Czechoslovakians. When I entered, men crowded around, tried to lift me to their shoulders. They were too weak. Many of them could not get out of bed. I was told that this building had once stabled eighty horses. There were twelve hundred men in it, five to a bunk. The stink was beyond all description.

When I reached the center of the barracks, a man came up and said, "You remember me. I'm Peter Zenkl, one-time mayor of Prague." I remembered him, but did not recognize him . . . there was applause from the men too weak to get out of bed. It sounded like the hand clapping of babies; they were so weak. The doctor's name was Paul Heller. He had been there since 1938.

As we walked out into the courtyard, a man fell dead. Two others—they must have been over sixty—were crawling toward the latrine. I saw it but will not describe it.

In another part of the camp they showed me the children, hundreds of them. Some were only six. One rolled up his sleeve, showed me his number. It was tattooed on his arm. D-6030, it was. The others showed me their numbers; they will carry them till they die.

An elderly man standing beside me said, "The children, enemies of the state." I could see their ribs through their thin shirts. The old man said, "I am Professor Charles Richer of the Sorbonne." The children clung to my hands and stared. We crossed the courtyard. Men kept coming up to speak to me and touch me, professors from Poland, doctors from Vienna, men from all Europe. Men from the countries that made America.

We went to the hospital; it was full. The doctor told me that two hundred had died the day before . . . Dr. Heller pulled back the blankets from a man's feet to show me how swollen they were. The man was dead. Most of the patients could not move . . .

I asked to see the kitchen; it was clean. The German in charge had been a Communist, had been at Buchenwald for nine years, had a picture of his daughter in Hamburg. He hadn't seen her for almost twelve years, and if I got to Hamburg, would I look her up? He showed me the daily ration—one piece of brown bread about as thick as three sticks of chewing gum. That, and a little stew, was what they received every twenty-four hours . . .

Dr. Heller, the Czech, asked if I would care to see the crematorium. He said it wouldn't be very interesting because the Germans had run out of coke some days ago and had taken to dumping the bodies into a great hole nearby. Professor Richer said perhaps I would care to see the small courtyard. I said yes . . . The wall was about eight feet high; it adjoined what had been a stable or garage. We entered. It was floored with concrete. There were two rows of bodies stacked up like cord-wood. They were thin and very white. Some of the bodies were terribly bruised, though there seemed to be little flesh to bruise . . . I tried to count them as best I could and arrived at the conclusion that all that was mortal of more than five hundred men and boys lay there in two neat piles.

There was a German trailer which must have contained another fifty, but it wasn't possible to count them . . . It appeared that most of the men and boys had died of starvation . . . But the manner of death seemed unimportant. Murder had been done at Buchenwald. God alone knows how many men and boys have died there during the last twelve years . . .

As I left that camp, a Frenchman who used to work for Havas in Paris came up to me and said, "You will write something about this, perhaps?" And he added, "To write about this you must have been here at least two years, and after that—you don't want to write any more."

I pray you to believe what I have said about Buchenwald; I have reported what I saw and heard, but only part of it. For most of it I have no words.

Use an Oral Style

Usually, your speech will be heard by any audience only once. Since it is not usual for an audience to receive a copy of your speech in advance, members will be unable to look up unfamiliar words or reread confusing parts. Public speakers, therefore, should seek to design their speeches so that they are intelligible more to the ear than to the eye—that is, achieve an oral style.

A number of characteristics are identified with an oral style. An oral style is more conversational than is a written style. It does not use complicated sentence structures or unfamiliar language. When compared to a written style, an oral style contains more internal summaries, more repetition, and more familiar language.

Summary

In this chapter we try to clarify the nature of language as a symbol system, and the relationship that exists between words, things, and human behavior. We discuss the verbal side of public speaking and indicate how choosing the right words can help you become a more effective speechmaker. We examine certain language problems, and give you guidelines to follow to help insure that your listener will understand and appreciate your presentation.

Putting Your Speech Together[1]

Behavioral Objectives

After reading this chapter, you should have a better understanding of:

- the need to organize your speech.
- what is meant by a "purpose statement."
- how to formulate a purpose statement.
- the functions served by the body of a speech.
- how to use three basic speech formats: chronological, spatial, and topical patterns.
- the nature of an outline.
- how to develop an outline.
- how to use transitional words and phrases effectively.
- how to create an effective introduction.
- how to create an effective conclusion.

[1] This chapter was written by Dr. Michael Gamble, Professor of Speech at New York Institute of Technology.

Introduction

Once you have chosen your speech topic and gathered information on that subject, you need to organize and juggle your ideas until you create a coherent, effectively patterned address.

Why should you organize? Consider the performer who is happily juggling ten bowling pins. At first glance, the juggling process appears to be a random affair with no real sense of order. But is it? What happens if the juggler makes just one error? Where do the bowling pins end up? On the ground? On his head? Juggling is a precise art that requires a great deal of practice and skill. Thus, juggling and public speaking are similar activities. Like the juggler, the public speaker works with a variety of materials and attempts to use them in an organized and effective fashion. Just as a misplaced pin or a poor catch can spell trouble for the juggler, so an illogically placed point or an inappropriate reference can spell disaster for the speechmaker. Yet, like proficient jugglers, accomplished speakers make the process of appearing before others seem natural and almost effortless. How do they do this? Both jugglers and public speakers work with numerous pieces of equipment. However, instead of working with bowling pins, speakers are concerned with ideas. Effective speakers have simply found ways of shaping or organizing the information they gathered into logical and coherent messages.

Organizing your ideas will help you and your audience piece together the bits of information you compiled so that everyone understands how the ideas contained in your talk relate to each other and to your subject as a whole. Organizing your ideas will also help you to remember the key points of your speech, and it will make it easier for the members of your audience to retain the information you deliver.

What is the best way to organize your speech? There is no precise answer to this question, since how you organize your material depends upon your preferences, your topic, and your audience. However, there are some general procedures which will provide you with useful guidelines as you seek to juggle your ideas into a meaningful pattern for your presentation to the audience.

Developing Your Speech

To function properly, the gears in an automobile or a fine watch must mesh smoothly. This same requirement should be made of any speech; if it is to be effective, its various parts must flow smoothly from one into the other. The *introduction* (a preliminary statement of the topic) must neatly generate the *body* of the speech (a development of the topic), and the body, in turn, must give rise to a *conclusion* (a summing up of the speech topic).

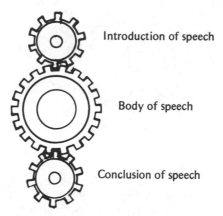

Figure 8–1. Line Drawing of Three Gears Meshing with One Another. (Middle gear is the biggest; the other two equal in size.)

It is impossible to begin organizing the materials of your speech until you determine your reason for speaking. Of course, you may be speaking because it is a requirement. For example, your boss may ask you to give a report, or your instructor may insist that you deliver a certain number of speeches in order to complete your course. Whatever your purpose, it goes well beyond such preliminary obligations. The question, "Why am I here?," is something that every speaker has to face. Your purpose for speaking is something you need to clarify for yourself.

Therefore, we recommend that all speakers develop *purpose statements* for their talks. A purpose statement is a single sentence or phrase that tells precisely what you want the audience to know, believe, or do, as a result of listening to your speech.

An effective sequence scheme to follow when developing your speech is 1) develop your purpose statement, 2) develop the outline of the body of your talk, 3) develop your introduction, and 4) develop your conclusion. As you work through these stages, it may be necessary to revise and replan your ideas. Let us now examine the speech development procedure in detail.

Your Purpose Statement

Assume that you have selected a subject area for your speech, you have researched your topic and have narrowed it down to the allotted time. Occasionally, you may run into this next problem. Although your speech purpose was clear when you began, it subsequently may have become unclear. Perhaps,

Figure 8–2.

as a result of your research, your mind has become cluttered with a number of sub-issues. Perhaps you have become concerned or preoccupied with interesting but extraneous details. In any case, your goal has become fuzzy and you have lost sight of your central purpose. When this happens, you need to re-identify and clarify the purpose of your speech.

A technique to help you define your central purpose is to draw a sketch or doodle that depicts the action or object about which you wish to speak.

SPEECH EXPERIENCE: PURPOSE PICTURES

1. With either a partner or by yourself, generate a list of eight to ten potential speech topics.¨

2. For each topic, draw a sketch of the key subject matter. Place one sketch or doodle on a sheet of paper, 8½" x 11". Although the sketches need not be artistic, they must be large enough so that others can see them clearly.

3. Share your sketches with your classmates. Take turns identifying the speech subject or topic depicted in each sketch.

When you sit down to prepare a speech, you may want to help define your purpose by drawing a sketch, as suggested above; keep it in front of you as you prepare your address. This may help you to limit your comments to your chosen subject area. At this point, it will be necessary for you to define your purpose in more specific terms; that is, to substitute words for pictures. You need to work your central idea into a purpose statement.

Most speeches are designed to achieve one of the following general purposes: to inform, to persuade, or to entertain. Although every speech contains informative, persuasive, and entertaining elements, a speech usually emphasizes one element over the others. For example, your prime aim may be to inform your audience about a particular type of tree or period in history, or to persuade your audience to support the passage of a certain bill in Congress, or to entertain your audience in a manner made famous by talk show hosts or after-dinner speakers. Thus, purpose statements will include the words persuade, inform, explain, convince, motivate and/or entertain. Some examples of a purpose statement are:

1. To explain the operation of a digital clock. (informative)
2. To convince the audience to vote for Candidate X. (persuasive)
3. To motivate audience members to donate blood. (persuasive)
4. To entertain the audience at a class reunion by recalling "the good old days." (entertaining)

Your purpose statement should be specific, contain only one idea, and spell out any limitations, whenever possible. Finally, the purpose statement should be presented in a declarative form, not phrased as a question. As a speechmaker, it is your responsibility to take a stand on a subject or issue. Improve your purpose statement by participating in the following experience.

SPEECH EXPERIENCE: PURPOSE STATEMENT PICTURES

1. Select several sketches from the previous exercise for further work.

2. Again, with either a partner or by yourself, develop as many purpose statements as you can for each sketch.

3. Share what you consider to be the best of your efforts with the class.

4. You may evaluate your purpose statements by asking yourself the following questions:

    a. Is the purpose statement clearly worded?

    b. Is it specific?

    c. Are limitations indicated, where appropriate?

    d. Is it possible to develop a speech on the topic as it is presented in the purpose statement?

If you answered "yes" to each question, you are in good shape and can proceed to the body of your speech.

The Body of Your Speech

Once you have formulated your purpose statement, you are ready to begin work on the body of your speech. Your aim, in this phase, is to create a logical and effective structure upon which to base the main points of your speech. If you think of the listener's mind as a computer, you will understand why it is vital for you to develop an effective organization. In order for the human brain to take in information and store it efficiently, the data must be presented in a logical fashion. Once information has been effectively received (input), it can be understood, stored, and retrieved at a later date. The need for organizing the material you present in the body of your speech will become clearer as you attempt to memorize the following random list of bits or items of information:

shirt

ground beef   ketchup

dresser   telephone

chairs   newspaper

vest

raisins

pickles   apples

telegraph   table

sugar   hats   salad

sandwich

dog

rabbit   serpent

muskrat   shoes   couch

typewriter

bread   magazine

penguins

Your ability to memorize this information could have been simplified if we had pointed out that the information could be divided into categories, or if we had organized the provided material into logical systems of data, as follows:

Food	Animals
ground beef	dog
ketchup	rabbit
bread	serpent
pickles	muskrat
apples	penguin
raisins	
salad	
sugar	
sandwich	

Clothes	Furniture	Forms of Communication
hat	chairs	telephone
suit	couch	telegraph
shirt	dresser	magazine
vest	table	typewriter
shoes		newspaper

As a public communicator, you should not expect your listeners to do your mental homework for you. Audiences must be provided with information that is arranged in a way that permits them to concentrate on the meaning of the ideas being presented. A poorly planned speech body will confuse an audience and will often be ignored. The responsibility for organizing the body of your speech lies with you—the speechmaker.

Although there are many organizational patterns you may use to develop the body of your speech, we will focus on three basic formats: *The Chronological Pattern*, *The Spatial Pattern*, and *The Topical Pattern*. Just as stereo speakers amplify sound so that it can be heard more easily, these organizational patterns allow you, the speaker, to expand upon your initial subject sentence so that it can be more easily understood by your listeners.

The Chronological Pattern

When you choose to explain your topic by listing or describing events according to a time-ordered sequence, you are using a chronological pattern of organization. Increase your understanding of this approach by trying the following:

SPEECH EXPERIENCE: CHRONOLOGICAL AMPLIFICATION

1. Think of all the events that have occurred to you since you awoke this morning.

2. Next, identify four or five of the most important events; i.e., eating breakfast, missing a bus, and so on.

3. Find a partner, and, in turn, dictate each of the identified events to him or her in the order in which they occurred. Use as few words as possible to describe each happening to your partner, without sacrificing clarity. Aim for a high level of understandability; aim to make your thoughts crystal-clear to your partner.

4. Once your list is completed, change roles and have your partner list his or her occurrences to you.

What you have done in each case is to amplify the topic, "What happened to me today." Because you approached the problem in a chronological fashion, each of the lists should have been clear and easy to follow. What would happen, however, if you try this next exercise?

SPEECH EXPERIENCE: CHRONOLOGICAL MUDDLE

1. Tear each of your previous lists into strips so that each item appears on a separate sheet of paper, like this:

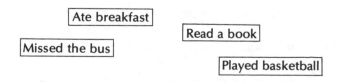

2. When this is completed, place the strips in random order. Tape them onto a sheet of paper and display them to other members of your class.

Questions About "CHRONOLOGICAL MUDDLE"

    1. What happened to each list when the chronology was juggled?
    2. Was your day more difficult to understand? Why?

While the point of this experience may seem obvious, many speakers approach speechmaking in such a disjointed fashion. They jump from point to point, start in the middle, backtrack, jump ahead, and so on instead of following a simple chronology. Listeners find such poorly organized speeches unsettling. When you choose to amplify the body of your speech by using a chronological sequence, make certain to develop your points in a logical manner. Remember, if you order your message in a random manner, you will be introducing static or interference into your listener's system of reception. Always aim to make your speech clear, concise, and static-free.

The Spatial Pattern

Speakers use spatial patterns of organization when the objective is to detail the parts of a whole entity as they exist in space. In other words, you may use a spatial format when your talk describes something which can be seen. Such an arrangement might describe an object from top to bottom, bottom to top, right to left, or left to right.

You might even begin at a central point and work outward. The important thing to keep in mind when using a spatial approach is that you need to devise a systematic way of describing how something looks or functions. It is also important to keep the object, picture, or sketch of the object in front of you as you organize your presentation. A spatial arrangement is designed to help your listeners create pictures in their minds of how something looks, as it exists in space. To clarify the use of the spatial organizational pattern in your own mind, try this:

SPEECH EXPERIENCE: DESCRIBE THAT OBJECT

    1. Divide into groups of four to five students each.
    2. Each student should choose an object about which he would like to speak. Be sure to select an object with which others are familiar such as: a cup, a fence, a car, and so on.
    3. Picture the object in your mind and describe it from top to bottom.

Write your description: _____

_____

_____

_____

4. Read your description to the other members of your group. As you read, your listeners should try to visualize the object.

5. The listeners should point out any descriptive words that are confusing, as well as points where you deviated from your top-to-bottom organizational scheme.

6. Once each group member has had an opportunity to practice spatial organizational techniques by describing something from top to bottom, you may begin a second round by having everyone write and share descriptions of an object as it appears from bottom to top. If time allows, a similar procedure may be utilized to gain experience in describing things from left to right and from right to left.

It is essential that you proceed systematically in your spatial descriptions. Deviating from your pattern will tend to confuse your audience and reduce the effectiveness of your speech.

The Topical Pattern

The third and final type of organization pattern to be described is the topical pattern of idea development. As a speechmaker, you occasionally will have to communicate on subject matters which do not lend themselves to either the chronological or the spatial pattern of development. When challenged by such subjects, you will have to examine your material and devise a series of topics under which all of your important data can be organized. Topical patterns of organization include such schemes as advantages vs. disadvantages, social, political and economic factors, or management, employee, and general public considerations about an issue.

A topical pattern is simply a grouping of themes that are relevant to your topic. The themes you select must be comprehensive enough to cover all the points you need to include in the body of your speech. To develop a clearer understanding of topical organization, try this next exercise.

SPEECH EXPERIENCE: TOPICS–TOPICS–TOPICS

1. Pretend that you have been asked to report on the current status of your school cafeteria. Your task is to report on all phases of its operation. Under what general topics might you organize your research data? Food quality? Costs? Staffing procedures? What additional topics might be worthy of your consideration? Working alone or in small groups, devise an many topical patterns of organization on this subject as you can. Share your topics with your classmates.

2. Choose a topic that is currently in the news or of importance to your school. Working in groups or individually, generate as many topical organizational patterns as you can to cover the relevant points about the chosen subject. Share your topical patterns with other classmates.

To repeat, remember that topical patterns are directly related to the subject matter of your speech. As with other patterns, deviation from your chosen pattern can result in some confusion on the part of the audience. By using an outline, you can help guard against such confusion or misunderstanding.

Outlining

As you develop your speech, it will become necessary for you to write down your information according to the organizational pattern you selected. This will permit you to examine the entire speech picture you are creating. While doing this, we recommend that you utilize the standard outline format, which we will describe. It will provide a structure upon which to build your ideas.

What is an outline? A speech outline is a fairly short, yet complete, sentence representation of your speech. Not only does it aid you in developing the overall body of your speech, it also provides you with a modular structure through which ideas can easily be pulled out, reordered, or eliminated, as necessary. In some ways, an outline is similar to a piece of electronic equipment in which individual circuitry cards or components are pulled out, one by one, tested and replaced without disturbing the remaining pieces of equipment. Similarly, you can pull, repair, and replace the ideas in your speech without disturbing or destroying the overall structure of the speech. Let us examine a speech outline so you may determine how to use the system for your own work.

Write the title of your speech at the top of your outline and, under it, your Purpose Statement:

Title:_____

Purpose Statement:_____

Positioning your purpose statement beneath your title will supply you with a constant reminder of your main reason for speaking. As your outline progresses, you may discover that you need to alter your purpose statement to make it conform with the speech you have created. It is imperative that, in your finished product, your purpose statement and supporting points relate to one another. In time, you will add an introduction and a conclusion to your speech outline. However, for the present, let us concern ourselves with outlining the body of the speech.

As you begin developing your speech, you may find that you have five, ten or even fifteen ideas which, at first glance, seem to be main ideas for your talk. Since it takes time to explain each main point, however, you may see why discussing more than five main points becomes impractical and unmanageable. A five minute speech, with a one minute introduction and a one minute conclusion, leaves only three minutes to develop the main body of your talk. A presentation with more than five main points tends to overload your audience with in-

TITLE

Purpose Statement: _____

BODY

I. [Main Point] _____

    A. [Primary subpoint] _____

        1. [Secondary Subpoint] _____

        2. [Secondary Subpoint] _____

           a. [Tertiary Subpoint] _____

           b. [Tertiary Subpoint] _____

    B. [Primary Subpoint] _____

II. [Main Point] _____

Figure 8-3. Modular Concept of a Speech Outline.

formation. This is inadvisable because, after all, you do want your listeners to remember what you are saying. For this reason, we recommend that you limit your speeches from two to five main points. Our experience has shown that three main points is the average used by most effective student speakers.

Write down each of your main points and under each main point, list the supporting information. Ask yourself how the pieces of information relate to one another. Determine if all the points are of equal importance. Assess how the bits of information can be ordered so that the relationships between them are made clear. In addition, be prepared to show how the materials you have gathered (examples, illustrations, anecdotes, and so on) support your ideas. Few things annoy an audience more than having a speaker say, "Perhaps I should have mentioned this earlier but. . . ." Such a remark prevents a speech from flowing smoothly and causes the speaker to backtrack.

Utilizing too many subpoints to support a major point can be very confusing. To avoid committing this error, we recommended that you adopt the following modular concept of an outline. (See Fig. 8–3)

While the modular outline is difficult to describe, it is easy to picture. The outline clearly indicates which ideas are subordinate to others. Outline entries should consist of complete sentences rather than isolated words or phrases. Each division of the outline—either major or minor—must contain only one idea. Thus, if a speaker were discussing the effects of a storm, the following entry would be inappropriate:

1. Storm damage was heavy and costly to area residents.

It would be better to separate these two ideas, like this:

1. Storm damage was extensive.
2. Storm damage was costly to area residents.

It is worthwhile repeating here the importance of maintaining a solid relationship between your major and minor points. If you were discussing the physical characteristics of a particular breed of dog, it would be confusing to introduce emotional characteristics and then abruptly return to physical characteristics. Test your understanding of this concept by organizing the following materials into a standard outline form.

SPEECH EXPERIENCE: OUT-OF-ORDER OUTLINES

The following elements of the outline are jumbled. Attempt to organize each sentence into a standard outline format. Work alone, in pairs, or small groups. Clearly label both main and subpoints.
1. The Little Red Schoolhouse
   - Learning was slower compared with the modern systems of education.
   - The purpose of this speech is to discuss the advantages and limitations of the Little Red Schoolhouse.
   - It was inefficient in many ways.
   - The Little Red Schoolhouse had many disadvantages.
   - The cost was quite low per pupil.
   - Older students tutored younger ones.
   - Slate tablets eliminated the cost of paper.
   - There were too many students for one teacher.
   - The Little Red Schoolhouse had many advantages.
2. Macbeth
   - Lady Macbeth's desire for advancement is revealed early in the play.
   - Macbeth's downfall is the result of his own ambition, his wife's ambition, and the murder of Duncan.
   - The contributing cause of Macbeth's downfall is his wife's ambition.
   - Duncan's murder is the first of several crimes which turn his followers against Macbeth.
   - The remote cause of Macbeth's downfall is his own ambition.
   - Macbeth's response to the witches' prediction that he will be king indicates his own desire for power.
   - The immediate cause of Macbeth's downfall is the murder of Duncan.

A word of caution should be noted here. The use of complete sentences may lead speakers into the trap of writing out the entire speech, word for word.

This may have an adverse affect on the final presentation. For this reason, we subscribe to the one-third rule. Your outline should contain approximately one-third the number of words that will be used in your final presentation. Inasmuch as we speak at the rate of about 150 words per minute, a five minute speech will contain approximately 750 words. Therefore, your outline for such a speech should contain approximately 250 words. Although this is a rough estimate, it will help you to determine the appropriate length of your outline.

Recognizing the difficulty many students have outlining their speeches, one creative speech teacher drafted a speech entitled, "How to Prepare a Speech." Not only will you find it helpful, you will also find it an example of a lively imagination.[1]

Specific Purpose: To explain the rules of preparing a proper speech outline.
Introduction
    I. Does a speaker need to pay attention to rules of outlining a speech?
    II. My years of experience with beginning speakers has supported the generalization that a good speech starts with a good outline.
    III. Let us look at these rules and show how they give your speech a solid, logical structure.
Body
    I. Use a standard set of symbols.
       A. Main points are usually indicated with Roman numerals.
          (I, II, etc.)
       B. Major subdivisions are indicated with capital letters.
          (A, B, C, etc.)
       C. Minor subheadings are indicated with Arabic numerals.
          (1, 2, 3, etc.)
       D. Further subdivisions are indicated with small letters.
          (a, b, c, etc.)
    II. Use complete sentences for major headings and major subdivisions.
       A. Complete sentences explain the relationship of the main points to the purpose sentence.
       B. When key ideas are written out in full, the speaker will find it easier to follow the next two rules.
    III. Each main point and major subdivision should contain a single idea.
       A. This will assure you that development will be relevant to the point.
       B. You will be able to line up supporting material under the appropriate main point.
       C. Your audience will be better able to see and understand the material.
    IV. Minor points should relate to or support major points.
       A. This principle is called subordination.
       B. This process of subordination acts to reinforce those main ideas which you want your audience to remember.
    V. Main points should be limited to a maximum of five.
       A. An audience has difficulty assimilating a speech with more than five main points.
          1. It's a simple psychological fact that an audience will better remember two main points with four divisions than eight main ones.

---

[1] This speech outline was written by Prof. Silvana Bogin, New York Institute of Technology.

      2. The audience will see and understand the relationship better if it is presented already organized for them.

   B. The fewer the main points, the less cumbersome the material will be for the speaker to handle.

Conclusion

   I. As a beginner, you can save yourself a lot of trouble if you learn to outline as suggested.

   II. If you get used to complying with the rules stated here, you will see that there is a direct relationship between outlining and quality of speech content.

Transitions

After you have completed your speech outline and begin to rehearse it, you will discover that you need to find ways of moving smoothly from point to point. Beginning speakers often have problems making the transitions from various main points. Fortunately, the English language is filled with a number of transitional words and phrases which you may insert to help the audience follow the organization of your speech. Such transitions serve to smooth the rough edges of your speech by eliminating abrupt introductions to new points. To help you in selecting transitional words and phrases, we have provided a representative list, as follows:

1. To Indicate Addition: again, and then, besides, equally important, finally, next, second, secondly, thirdly, lastly, furthermore, in addition, moreover.
2. To Indicate Cause and Effect: accordingly, as a result, consequently, in short, otherwise.
3. To Indicate Comparison: likewise, similarly.
4. To Indicate Concession: after all, although this may be true, at the same time, even though, I admit, naturally.
5. To Indicate Contrast: after all, although true, and yet, at the same time, however, in spite of, on the other hand, yet.

You may wish to increase your understanding of transitional words and phrases by trying the following exercise:

SPEECH EXPERIENCE: MAKE THAT TRANSITION

1. Choose a newspaper or magazine article and circle all of the transitional words and phrases in it. Notice how each is used. Select one or two representative samples to share with your class.

2. In pencil, insert transitional phrases between each of the major ideas of an outline you are preparing. You may wish to make these transitions a part of your speaker's notes to remind you of how you plan to get from one point to another during your presentation.

Transitions are the mark of a highly polished speech. They function as a high gloss wax and provide a shine to your final presentation. Transitions will give your speech a truly professional sound.

The Introduction

Now that we have considered the body of the speech, methods of organization, and the outline, it is time to turn our attention to the introduction. Have you ever watched the first few minutes of a television program and then turned the channel to something else? Certainly! We are all accustomed to selecting what we view from a wide variety of possibilities. If none catch our interest, we may decide to turn off the set and engage in other activities. Television programmers are well aware of this, and they work hard to gain the attention of the audience. During the early years of television, a program began with an announcement of the show's name and the listing of its stars. A series of commercials would then follow. This is seldom the case today. Let us examine the introductory techniques used by present-day television programmers.

SPEECH EXPERIENCE: COMING ATTRACTIONS

Television programs use carefully controlled and planned introductory sequences to gain our attention. They are similar to the "coming attractions" we often associate with motion picture theatres. The main difference is that the announced television programs begins after 120 seconds of commercials. Familiarize yourself with the way television uses the coming attractions by completing the television program log on page 120. NOTE: To do this exercise, it is not necessary to watch an entire program—just the opening segment.

Every audience is equipped with a channel-switching device. Although an audience physically cannot turn you off, it can easily tune you out by daydreaming. Therefore, it is your responsibility to prepare an introduction that will make your listeners want to listen to what you have to say. This is not an easy task. It is one which requires considerable thought. You may decide to change your introduction several times while preparing your speech. Your goal should be to find the most effective way of beginning your address.

Introductions must fulfill several functions. First, they must gain the attention of the audience. Opening phrases; such as, "Well, I have to speak today . . .," or "I really do not want to be here, but . . .," are inappropriate because an audience does not want to listen to a speaker who does not want to talk. Beginning speakers often make the speechmaking process seem like a chore or an assignment which must be done, rather than make their audiences feel that what they have to say is important, interesting, and packed with valuable information.

Program Title: Day: Time:

_____   _____   _____

Introductory Segment Description: _____

_____

_____

_____

_____

_____

Length of Segment: _____

Overall Effectiveness of Segment: _____

_____

Figure 8–4.   Television Program Log.

Second, your introductory comments should provide your audience with background information about your topic. Although your audience may be extremely familiar with some topics on which you choose to speak, other topics will be completely new to them. The latter will require more time to acquaint your listeners with the subject area. For instance, while the continuing rise in prices may be a familiar problem confronting the members of the audience, the need to create a foundation to support research for the obscure disease, *neurofibromatosis*, may be totally foreign to them.

Speechmakers often begin their talks with unusual facts or shocking statistics about their topics. Sometimes they use humorous stories or illustrations to gain attention. Human interest stories also serve as effective introductory pieces. Tales about children, an old person, specific criminals, or your next-door neighbor can be used to introduce your subject area to your audience. In addition, if you chose your topic because you have a personal interest in it, you might want to use a personal anecdote to begin your talk.

Once you have completed the introduction to your speech, a statement containing the subject sentence, which was discussed earlier, should be incorporated. For example, you might say:

1. Today, I would like to discuss some of the alternatives to marriage.
                                    or
2. We must develop ways of controlling crime on our city streets.

The utilization of such a statement will help your audience understand the relevance of your opening remarks. At the same time, it will help to focus their attention and draw them into the main body of your talk.

The function of your introduction is to make people listen to you. It is your task to arouse interest and curiosity in your subject. For practice, try this.

SPEECH EXPERIENCE: CURIOSITY CREATORS

1. The class should be divided into small groups of four to five students.
2. Each group will be assigned one of the following speech topics:
   Clothing Styles
   Hit Recordings
   Strange Animals
   How to Be a Boss
   Halloween Antics
   Vacation Spots
   or a topic of your choice
3. It is the task of each group to write an introduction that will gain immediate audience interest. Introductory comments should be no more than sixty seconds in length. Choose one person in each group to present the introduction to the class.

The Conclusion

The last speech part is the conclusion. Although the comedian, Steve Martin, usually concludes his act by simply saying, "Well, that's all," and David Brenner frequently ends his act by stopping and walking off the stage, we do not recommend that you adopt either of these techniques. Instead, we suggest that you bring your speech to a close in a manner that gives it a sense of completeness. Unlike Martin and Brenner, your goal should be to reinforce the central idea or theme of your presentation. This will be done if you design a well-constructed conclusion.

You may wish to begin your conclusion with a brief summary of the main points presented in the body of the speech. You might say:

1. In conclusion, the three major causes of the recent rise in crime in our city are. . . .

or

2. Remember, when growing tomatoes, you must follow these six procedures. . . .

Your summary statement should not be made to stand alone. You need to create an ending that will heighten the impact of your presentation.

An often used technique is to make reference to your introductory comments. This technique tends to give your speech a sense of unity. If, for example, you are speaking about the murder of seals in Alaska and you began your talk by showing a poster of baby seals being clubbed to death, you might refer to your opening remarks in your conclusion and show the poster again as a means of enlisting the sympathy and support of your audience. Another effective conclusion is a quotation. You may discover useful quotations while conducting your research. For example, if you were speaking about women's rights, a quote by Gloria Steinem, Phyllis Chessler or Bella Abzug could provide you with an excellent conclusion. You may also draw upon your own experiences to help you design an interesting closing statement. Appeals that incorporate personal experiences are commonly used to motivate audiences. We see this in Douglas MacArthur's "Address to Congress" in 1951.

I am closing my fifty-two years of military service. When I joined the Army even before the turn of the century, it was the fulfillment of all my boyish hopes and dreams. The world has turned over many times since I took the oath on the plain at West Point, and the hopes and dreams have long since vanished. But, I still remember the refrain of one of the most popular barrack ballads of that day, which proclaimed most proudly that—
"Old soldiers never die; they just fade away."
And, like the old soldier of that ballad, I now close my military career and just fade away—an old soldier who tried to do his duty as God gave him to see that duty. Goodbye.

Summary

This chapter has described various ways of organizing your speech. We have examined the three major parts of your speech (the introduction, the body, and the conclusion), discussed three common organizational formats (chronological, spatial, and topical), learned how to create an outline, as well as how to design an effective introduction and conclusion. You now have the tools with which to develop an organized, coherent, and effective presentation.

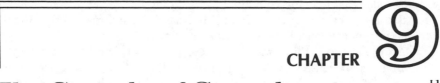

CHAPTER 9

The Sounds of Speech

"Testing . . . 1-2-3 . . ."

Behavioral Objectives

After reading this chapter, you should have a clearer understanding of:

- what goes on inside your body when you speak.
- how your diaphragm makes it possible for you to breathe in and out.
- how the mechanism in your neck (your larnyx) makes sound.
- how the muscles in your face shape sounds into speech.
- why the cavities in your head are so important to your speech.
- the various ways you can alter the way you speak.
- how "lazy speech" can work against you as a speechmaker.

Introduction

On the road to painless public speaking, you have thus far been introduced to a number of speech techniques. It is now time that you also become familiar with the equipment inside your body that makes it possible for you to speak. After reading a description of this equipment, you should have a better understanding of 1) the respirator in your chest, 2) the phonator in your throat, 3) the articulators in your mouth, and 4) the resonators in your head.

An explanation of the organs you need in order to speak is the subject of *paralanguage*. It consists of studying those qualities of your voice which give shape and character to what you say. They are: volume, pitch, rate of speech, articulation and pronunciation, and vocal crutches.

Respirator in Your Chest

To speak, you need air. You get this air from your environment. When you breathe, air passes in and out of your body. Your diaphragm makes this exchange possible. Although you have heard the word *diaphragm* thousands of times, it is quite possible that you cannot accurately locate it in your body. Did you know that the diaphragm is a muscle? Many people are not aware of this fact. How about your trachea and bronchial tubes—can you locate them? While you probably can locate your lungs and know that you have two of them, a knowledge of your trachea and bronchial tubes, along with how your diaphragm operates, may require some clarification. To make sure that you understand how the respirators in your chest work, read the following description.

Within your chest cavity, you have a right and left lung. When you breathe the air goes in and out of them, much like a set of Scottish bagpipes. Going in, the air enters your nose or mouth, passes down a tube in your neck called the *trachea* (or windpipe) into another set of tubes in your chest cavity called *bronchi*. These bronchi or bonchial tubes finally end in tiny air sacs called *alveoli*. The air going out of them takes the same route, but in reverse. In Fig. 9–1, you can see the lungs, trachea, and bronchial tubes.

Diaphragm

Your diaphragm is a large, dome-shaped muscle which separates your chest cavity from your abdominal cavity. Without a diaphragm, you could not breathe. If you had a diaphragm which was not operating properly, you would have trouble breathing. If you have ever seen someone in an iron lung, you have seen someone whose diaphragm is not functioning properly. A disease which could lead to the need of an iron lung would be bulbar poliomyelitis.

In normal breathing, when your diaphragm goes down, air rushes into your lungs, making your chest and abdomen rise upward and outward. To test this action, place both of your hands on your chest and inhale. You should feel your chest move upward and outward. Now, place your hands on your abdomen and breathe in again. You should feel your belly move outward and slightly upward. In both cases, when you breathe out, your diaphragm will go

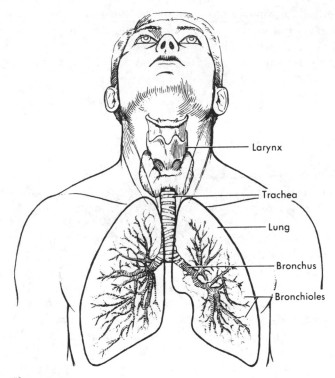

Figure 9–1.

up, push the air of your lungs, and your chest and abdomen should relax. (See Fig. 9–2))

While public speaking experts agree that there is a relationship between breathing and proper voice production, they have been unable to agree on the best method of breathing. Many seem to favor a method called "central breathing" because it uses the gross abdominal muscles in exhalation. King and Di

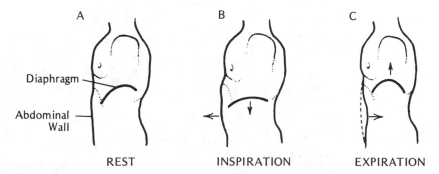

Figure 9–2.

Michael[1] explain that in order to support tone, the breath must be controlled by a strong, steady push by the gross abdominal muscles. Since central breathing seems to keep muscular tension away from the throat region, a phrase to remember might be—in matters concerning the voice, look to the movement of the abdomen.

Phonators in Your Throat

Feel the Adam's apple in your neck. It is part of your larynx, the medical term for voice box. If you can't find it, run your fingers downwards from your chin until you reach a bump in your neck. Don't be alarmed, it is your Adam's apple. (See Fig. 9–3)

Contrary to a popular myth suggesting that only men have an Adam's Apple, women also have them. Perhaps, it should be called an Eve's Apple. The proper name for the Adam's apple is the *thyroid cartilage*, and it forms the front wall of your voice box. For a better view of it, see Figure 9–4.

Since most of the other terms to be found in this figure are for the more advanced student of anatomy, just locate the *thyroid cartilage*, *larynx*, and *trachea*. Your *vocal cords* (also referred to as vocal folds) are located right behind the thyroid cartilage. As air goes past them, they vibrate like the strings of a violin or guitar. When you speak, your larynx or voice box moves up and down. While this is happening, changes in the position and tension of your vocal cords are also taking place. When you raise the pitch of your voice, your larynx moves upward; when the pitch is lowered, the larynx moves downward. The amount of movement of your larynx will depend upon how you speak. If you speak in a monotone, it will display very little movement. If you should speak in a flam-

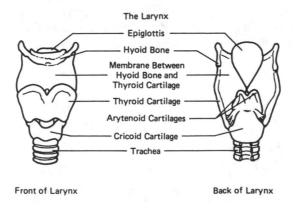

The Larynx

Epiglottis

Hyoid Bone

Membrane Between
Hyoid Bone and
Thyroid Cartilage

Thyroid Cartilage

Arytenoid Cartilages

Cricoid Cartilage

Trachea

Front of Larynx   Back of Larynx

Figure 9–3. Thyroid Cartilage (Adams' Apple).

[1] Robert King, and Eleanor DiMichael, *Articulation and Voice* (New York: Macmillan Publishing Co., Inc., 1978), pp. 355–.

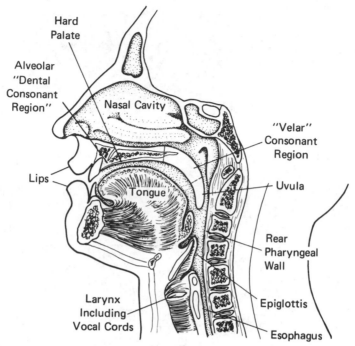

Figure 9–4. Sagittal Section of the Nose, Mouth, Pharynx, and Larynx. (Gray's *Anatomy*, Courtesy of Lea & Febiger, Philadelphia.)

boyant manner, it will be observed to be much more active. To experience the upper and lower ranges of your laryngeal movement, place your fingertips on your Adam's apple (or Eve's Apple) and say the words "hee-haw" several times. To see what a physician sees when he or she looks down your throat, see Figure 9–5. When you have a case of laryngitis and can't speak, your vocal cords have become inflamed and fail to vibrate properly. Notice in the diagram something called the *glottis*. It is the space located between the vocal cords.

Articulators in Your Mouth

The term *articulators* refers to your tongue, lips, jaw, and soft palate. Working together in both simple and complex ways, these articulators in your mouth give shape to consonants and vowels. If you have ever had a shot of novacaine at the dentist that deadened your tongue and lip, you can appreciate how important these muscles are to your speech. The soft palate is easy to locate, if you use a mirror and look into your mouth. At the back, hanging down like a little finger, you will notice something called the *uvula*. It is part of your soft palate. Its

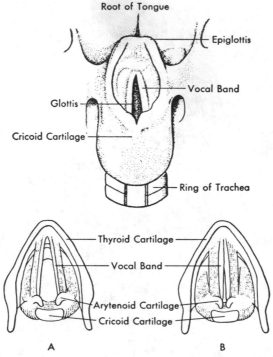

Figure 9-5. The Larynx As Seen by Means of the Laryngoscope in Different Conditions of the Glottis.

function, in addition to shaping sound, is to keep food and fluids from going up instead of down. Remember when someone made you laugh while you had food or fluid in your mouth. What happened? It went up into your nasal passage. This occcurred because your soft palate was not quick enough to block off the passageway leading from your mouth to the back of your nose.

A number of movie and television personalities are recognized by their manner of speech. Impersonators spend a great deal of their time studying not only the tongue, lip, and jaw movements of those they imitate, but also their tone of voice. To more fully appreciate the job your articulators do, try talking with your lips puckered, your mouth open, your teeth clenched, or holding the tip of your tongue.

SPEECH EXPERIENCE: How Many Words in a Breath?

Test your breath control while speaking increasingly longer sentences.

1. This is a competitive exercise to see who has the greatest lung capacity.

2. Five volunteers from the class are to go to the front of the room.

3. Each is handed a slip of paper with the following eight sentences on it.

The teacher will have these slips made up before the exercise begins.

a. A good voice is important.

b. Very few people are good listeners when others speak.

c. People with pleasant voices are often taken to be intelligent.

d. One of the best ways to know yourself better is to meet many different kinds of people.

e. The exact meaning of a word is often missed because the person hearing the word has a different definition for it, based upon another set of experiences.

f. The best kind of movie is the kind that gets you involved so that you forget not only who you are and what you are doing in the theatre, but also the people with whom you came.

g. Many students freeze up when they have to take an examination because they are convinced that the questions will be on material the teacher didn't cover or that they did not study the night before.

h. Many people do not like to argue because they are convinced that arguments not only make enemies, but also create a situation in which they build up an inner emotional storm with which they cannot cope and for which they will one day have to seek professional help.

4. In the first round, each student will read aloud the first sentence, using only one breath. The same thing should be done with the second sentence in the second round, and so on, until they reach the last sentence. If at any time during the rounds, a contestant runs out of breath and fails to complete a sentence, that individual immediately becomes disqualified and must withdraw from the contest.

5. If more than one contestant remains after the eighth sentence has been read, a play-off should consist of reading the following sentence. In the event that no one completes the tie-breaker, the person who goes the farthest is to be declared the winner.

Tie-breaking Sentence:

Communication is an art which most people do not understand or wish to understand because it is made up of many different parts which, in certain situations and under certain circumstances, do not conform to a definite outline or system of parts that a majority of experts in the field strongly argue are not only unnecessary but, to say the least, are contrary to the best interests of the subject itself and which will, in time, destroy both the foundation of communication and all of the principles that have since grown out of it.

Resonators in Your Head

Located above your vocal cords are the tubes and cavities of your throat, mouth, and nose. They act as resonators. Depending upon their size, shape, and condi-

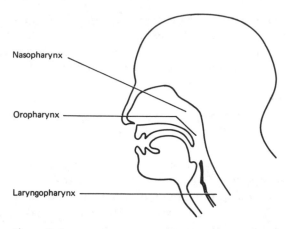

Figure 9–6.

tion, your voice can be made to range anywhere from harsh to beautiful. (See Fig. 9–6)

Having described the respirator in your chest, phonators in your throat, articulators in your mouth, and resonators in your head, you should have some idea of how the organs of speech work in the human body. Let us now move on to what happens to the sounds you make as they leave your mouth.

Paralanguage

The public speaker who possesses a working knowledge of paralanguage has a distinct advantage over the one who doesn't. Audiences are extremely sensitive to how a speaker says something. It is the wise speaker who knows how to get the most meaning out of a word or phrase. Assuming that you are interested in developing this ability, here are some helpful paralinguistic hints.

Volume

As a public speaker, you must learn to control the loudness and softness of your voice. Individuals who cannot may run into difficulty. There are two basic situations with which you will soon have to cope. One involves having to deliver a speech with a microphone; the other, without a microphone. Although the sound level on most public address systems can be adjusted, you must exercise some voice control. Not having a microphone requires even more control.

There are various factors capable of dictating your voice control. These include 1) room size, 2) number and type of people in your audience, 3) speech topic, and 4) a need for emphasis. Your ability to adapt to them will, in part, determine your skill as a speechmaker.

Room Size

Without the aid of a microphone—the larger the room, the louder you will have to speak. If you have the benefit of a microphone, it will usually more than compensate for the need to speak up. What you might have to do, however, is hold the microphone at an appropriate distance from your mouth. This distance usually is determined during a test period before your speech.

Number and Type of People in Your Audience

Except under unusual circumstances, the more people in your audience, the more noise they are inclined to make. Low talking, whispering, coughing, giggling, and ordinary body movements are some of the sounds you will have to overcome. Although a smaller audience might make these noises, the sound generally is proportionate to the number of people present.

The type of people who comprise any audience will often determine its behavior. The mix may range from the crude, vulgar and impolite type to the polished, sophisticated and courteous type. As you might expect, the more noise and restlessness an audience exhibits, the more volume you may have to employ to reach it.

Speech Topic

The topic of your speech should also influence the volume of your voice. Take such subjects as chamber music, macramé, or caring for African violets. Generally, these topics warrant being spoken of in a relatively soft and gentle voice. Conversely, subjects like Saturday night wrestling, disco dancing, and student protest rallies will accommodate a louder and more vigorous vocal delivery.

Another guideline to voice volume is emotionality. The more emotionally charged a subject is, the more fitting an increase in volume is inclined to be. Subjects that are considered to be less emotional in nature or, perhaps controversial generally dictate a decrease in volume.

Emphasis

Just as you use capital letters, underlining, and exclamation marks to emphasize a written word or phrase, you likewise need ways of emphasizing *what* you say. Increasing the volume of your voice is one such way. In addition to emphasizing any given word, you can also emphasize part of a word or phrase. For instance, a sergeant in the military calling a platoon to order will shout, "Attention!" And, to emphasize such an order, he will stress the second half of the word; e.g., "AttenTION! The meaning of anything you say can be altered by the way you emphasize words. Consider the following sentences. Read each of them aloud, placing emphasis on a different word each time.

1. I am the president.
2. Who do you think you are?
3. Please, don't squeeze the bananas.
4. I deserve an "A".

Pitch

There is a difference between volume and pitch. In the preceding section, you were told that volume deals with the loudness or softness of speech. Here, under the heading of pitch, we are talking about the highness or lowness of a voice. Your own voice has a pitch, a basic pitch that is determined by the structure of your larynx (voice box) and how you use it. Because a child's larynx is smaller, it generates a sound that is different from your own. Another difference exists between male and female voices because of the differences in the lengths of their vocal folds. "The vocal folds of the female larynx are generally shorter in length (seven-eights of an inch to one inch in length) than the vocal folds of the male (one to one and one-fourth inches)."[2] This causes the female voice to generally possess a higher pitch than the male.

The pitch of your voice is not fixed. You can change it at will. In a sense, it is the pitch of your voice which gives it its musical quality. The pitch of a speaker's voice is capable of helping or hindering the impact of a speech. If the pitch is irritating or too variable, the audience may react negatively. Another way the impact of your speech can be hampered is through overly emotional changes in the pitch of your voice. Dramatic mood changes can elevate or lower your pitch. When some people get angry, their voices go up. With others, their voices go down. Too emotional a pitch in a speaker's voice can tire and annoy an audience.

Be careful of what the pitch of your voice is revealing to the audience. If, while delivering a speech, your pitch should rise, it could mean that you are in doubt about something, hesitant, not sure of yourself, or slightly confused. If your pitch should fall, it could suggest that you are self-confident and know exactly where you are going with your ideas. Should your pitch remain unchanged or unvaried, it will earn the label of being *monotonous*—a coffin nail to any speech.

Ideally, you should find the pitch level which your voice produces with the greatest amount of ease and at which it resonates most effectively. Generally, you will find it about one-fourth of the way up your total range. Once you have

---

[2] Ibid., p. 412.

found this most comfortable pitch, you will discover that your speaking voice will be more persuasive, healthier-sounding, and noticeably more energetic.

Rate

In a matter of moments, every audience becomes aware of a speaker's speech-speed. This speed varies not only from person to person, but also from place to place. Language, climate, personality, emotions, circumstances, and topic can all affect how rapidly or slowly someone speaks. The average number of words spoken per minute by an average speaker ranges between 100 and 130. More broadly, the range extends from 90 to 230 wpm.

Do you have any special feeling about people who speak quickly? Do you have any difficulty following what they say? A myth that has been around for years states that it is more difficult to understand someone who speaks rapidly than one who speaks slowly. While this may be true, if the slow talker mispronounces words, leaves out syllables, and employs sloppy speech, he or she may be less clear than a rapid talker.

Rapid but clear speech is the goal of *compressed speech*. This is a special process by which speech is shortened so that the number of words spoken per minute can be increased without raising the pitch of the speaker's voice. This technique makes it possible for someone to listen to a speech at accelerated speeds (up to 250 wpm) and still understand what was said. Naturally, such things as topic interest, unfamiliar words, and a speaker's voice quality can affect the level of a listener's comprehension.

Since there is a significant difference between the average speech-speed (100 to 130 wpm) and the average thought-speed (400 to 600 wpm), audiences are often placed at a disadvantage. Because of the difference between the two speeds, members of an audience have time to take psychological side trips while waiting for a speaker to catch up with their thoughts. This increases the possibility of decreased listening levels, reduced concentration, and delayed reaction to expressed ideas. In short, the slower the speaker's speech-speed, the more sluggish an audience might become. A speech-speed that moves along at a lively rate (provided the speaker speaks clearly) tends to keep most audiences interested and alert.

Articulation and Pronunciation

The terms "articulation" and "pronunciation" overlap somewhat in their meanings. Whereas *articulation* has to do with the way you form sounds, *pronuncia-*

tion is concerned with the way you select, produce, and join individual speech sounds to produce words that can be recognized. Both, however, are vital to the process of issuing understandable speech. To achieve effective articulation and pronunciation, you must be able to coordinate reliably the movements of your lips, tongue, and jaws. The lazier these movements are, the poorer your speech will be. The "mumbler" is a typical example of someone whose articulation and pronunciation is poor. If you mumble, your audience may think you a careless speaker—and perhaps a careless thinker as well. Mumbling conveys a lack of self-confidence and lack of desire to communicate with others.

Two other symptoms of faulty articulation and pronunciation are *slurring* and *overprecision*. You slur when you run syllables together that should remain separate. Instead of saying, "What are you doing tonight?," you simply say, "Whutchadoontnight?" Or, instead of, "Do you want a Good Humor," you say, "Wannahgoodhumah?" And, finally, instead of "Give me the garage key," "Gimmedahgahratchke." Running words together like this is nothing more than a bad habit. With less effort than you imagine, it can be corrected.

Overprecision occurs when a speaker is overly conscious of his or her enunciation. You have probably encountered people who enunciate every word as though it were freshly minted by the United States Treasury. It is one thing to speak distinctly, but quite another to overdo it. That is what happens with overprecision.

Mispronouncing a word that you are expected to pronounce properly is seldom excused by a discriminating audience. If you are introduced as an automotive engineer and, during the course of your speech, you happen to say "ca-BOOR-i-tor" instead of "carburetor," your credibility is apt to decline. Or, if you are speaking as a speech pathologist and say, "larnix" rather than "larynx," the same fate may befall you. No doubt you too can think of a number of words that are frequently mispronounced by speakers in all fields, such as "liberry" for "library." Regardless of how much care is taken, public speakers make errors in pronunciation from time to time. This is especially so with technical words and foreign names. The best defense you can have against this happening to you is to check out a questionable word or name beforehand. If it is a technical term, in addition to looking up in a field-related dictionary, check with some knowledgeable person in the field. Bear in mind, always, that audiences are inclined to pay little or no attention to the words you pronounce correctly, but make a big fuss over the one word you happen to mispronounce.

For the fun of it, test your ability to pronounce the following words correctly; which pronunciation is correct?

HO-tel	ho-TEL
com-PAIR-a-ble	com-par-a-ble
DYE-rect	dir-RECT
PO-lice	po-LICE
EE-vent	ee-VENT

Here are some of the more commonly mispronounced words in our language. How do you pronounce them.[3]

veterinarian	veteran
remunerate	athlete
diaper	prescription
vanilla	ophthalmologist
mischievous	salmon
sophomore	almond
coupon	obstetrician

Vocal Crutches

The technical name for vocal crutches is *vocal segregates*. Regardless of which term you prefer, the meaning remains the same. Vocal crutches are sounds such as "uh's," "ah's," "mmmm's" or silences which appear between the articulation of words.[4] While calm speakers often deliberately use periods of silence to add impact to what they say, nervous and insecure speakers fall into uncontrollable periods of silence which immediately betray them to their audience.

Since public speaking has the reputation of being the Number One Phobia in this country, those who must speak before an audience reveal their anxiety in many ways. Using vocal crutches is one of them. Some speakers cannot begin a new thought without saying, "ah" or "er" first. They do it so often that they don't realize they have made these vocalizations. While it may not bother them, it surely is annoying to an audience. In certain cases, vocal crutches go beyond silences and intrusive sounds and crop up as words or phrases which convey no meaning. Wedged in between sentences, they occur in the form of "O.K., right", and "you know what I mean." Although these expressions have meaning in some contexts, overuse destroys such meaning.

To find out whether or not you employ vocal crutches, record some ordinary conversation on the tape recorder. Also ask the people with whom you communicate every day. You will discover quickly not only whether you use vocal crutches, but also how much you use them. It is only after you make this discovery that you can begin retraining yourself to weed them out of your speech.

Summary

When dealing with a mechanism of any kind, there are those people who must know how the mechanism operates, in order to do a good job. There are others

---

[3] Look up the acceptable pronunciation of these words in a reliable dictionary.

[4] Abné M. Eisenberg, and Ralph Smith, *Nonverbal Communication*, (Indianapolis: The Bobbs-Merrill Co., Inc., 1971), p. 24.

who care less about how something works, as long as it works. Your authors tend to side with those who want to know how things operate. Therefore, as a public speaker, you have been supplied with an explanation of the speech mechanism and of those factors which give character and shape to what you say. Armed with such knowledge, you will surely get greater mileage out of the words you speak.

CHAPTER 10

The Silent Side of Public Speaking

"Hmm . . . no fever . . ."

Behavioral Objectives

After reading this chapter, you should have a clearer understanding of:

- the role nonverbal communication (body language) plays in relation to public speaking.
- the nonverbal messages you may be sending to your audience without knowing it.
- what your clothes would say if they could talk.
- the relationship between what you say and how you say it.
- what body rhythm means to a public speaker.
- the ways to improve your own body rhythm.
- how the quality of a speaker's eye contact with an audience could make the difference between success and failure.
- some practical ways to improve your eye contact.
- the difference between "purposeful" and "purposeless" gestures.
- how to use time and space to your advantage as a speechmaker.

Introduction

As you may have discovered already, there is more to making a good speech than simply speaking words. There is also the question of how you look and act in front of your audience. Imagine a speaker whose topic is, "Better Health Through Proper Nutrition." Further, imagine that such a speaker has a pot belly, bald head, dark circles beneath his eyes, and trembling hands. Would you believe someone who looked like this? Probably not. Although, such an individual might have little control over how he looks and has a thorough knowledge of the subject, you would have some difficulty believing that his notions of proper nutrition were correct.

Most people who find themselves in the position of having to deliver a speech spend far too much of their time on its verbal parts—that is, what they are going to say. As they become more experienced, they come to realize that the silent side of a speech can often make the difference between its success and failure. Such things as clothing, posture, body rhythm, eye contact, gestures, space, and time take on added importance. Each of these factors, together and separately, fall under the heading of nonverbal communication; i.e., how a speaker looks and behaves in front of an audience.

Something essential to be remembered is that successful speakers seldom depend upon one aspect of a speech entirely. They always try to execute a careful blending of verbal and nonverbal elements. Why? Because neither words nor actions, by themselves, can earn an audience's applause. Thus, a winning formula is to bring both words and actions to bear on a common cause with equal strength. Use both to get your audience to think, feel, and act more positively toward your position. To assist you in reaching such a goal, this chapter will provide you with ways of reinforcing your words with a variety of persuasive silent messages.

A sensible point from which to begin this process is YOU. How clear a picture of yourself do you have? What nonverbal messages do you think you transmit to an audience by merely standing before it without saying a word? For example, if your clothes could speak, what do you think they would say about you to an audience? To find this out, and more, try the following exercise.

SPEECH EXPERIENCE: DISCOVERING YOUR BODY LANGUAGE

In addition to getting you to think in nonverbal terms, this exercise will give you some idea of how the members of your audience perceive the way you are dressed, your posture, your body rhythm, eye contact, gestures, facial expressions, and how you manage space.

Step 1. Each member of the class will be called to the front of the room by the instructor and asked to deliver a two minute impromptu speech. The topic will be: "Something I love to do, and something I can't stand doing."

Step 2. While each member of the class is speaking at the front of the room, members of the audience should make up a list of their impressions of the speaker, listing the items mentioned in the introduction to this exercise. For example, did the speaker's facial expression convey the impression of fear, confidence, shyness, or apathy to members of the audience?

Step 3. When a speaker is finished, he or she may ask any member of the audience, or several members, for their impressions. In addition, those members of the audience who would like to volunteer their impressions may do so without being asked.

Step 4. After all members of the class have had their turns, a general discussion (led by the instructor) follows. The object of the discussion is to compare various speakers' impressions of themselves with those expressed by their audience. Members of the class will be asked to comment on the relationship between how speakers think of themselves (their self-image) and their nonverbal behavior before an audience.

Clothes

We are the only creatures on the planet Earth who wear clothes. Perhaps because we are jealous of the body coverings Mother Nature has provided other living things, we have chosen to adorn ourselves with animal skins, furs, and feathers, as well as dozens of synthetic materials. Basically, there are four reasons why we wear clothes: 1) to protect us from the elements, 2) as a means of identification, 3) to impress others, and 4) to conceal certain parts of our body. A psychiatrist named Jean Rosenbaum [1] suggests that when we choose clothing, we are selecting a kind of substitute body. Wearing a shirt with buttons or without buttons, shoes or sneakers, boots or sandals, dungarees or a dress, bright or drab colors, tells others about your personality and philosophy of life. Dr. Rosenbaum also suggests that people who wear loose and comfortable clothes tend to have a sense of security about themselves; those who wear tight and uncomfortable clothing are likely to have feelings of anxiety, tension, and even inferiority. Dressing to feel important is called a "costume approach," and those who employ it probably feel insignificant. If their clothes could talk, they would probably say, "I want to be important; please look at me." Do your clothes say the same thing as your words?

In addition to wearing clothes for protection, we wear them to correspond with the events of the day. We own clothes for work and play, formal and informal occasions. If we were genetically shortchanged in certain areas of our bodies, we might wear types of clothing that compensate for that deficiency.

In the late fifties, when John Malloy was an instructor at a Connecticut prep school, he discovered that the way a teacher dressed could affect student performance. He talks about two teachers who taught the same class in separate half-day sessions. One always wore loafers and the other, lace-up shoes. On the

[1] *Long Island* (N.Y.) *Press*, October 22, 1973, p. 11.

basis of this and similar observations, Malloy went into business of telling people how to dress to get desired results. People from all walks of life began seeking Malloy's advice on how to become more effective in their particular business or profession. This led to Malloy becoming America's first wardrobe engineer.

What all this talk about clothes means is that you can definitely influence your audience by the way you dress. To a greater extent than you presently may believe, you advertise who and what you are by the way you dress. This is particularly true in the case of speechmaking. Members of your audience gathered together for a specific purpose—to hear you speak on a specific topic. This means that their expectations are somewhat more defined than those of people simply passing you on the street. Furthermore, a speechmaker's point of view is generally known to an audience beforehand. This tends to add an even greater definiteness to their expectations as to a speaker's appearance. In short, you can either grant or deny an audience's expectations by the way you dress. It is essential that you look believable. If you are talking about how to invest money or how to run a successful business, poor and sloppy dress will discredit what you say, in most people's eyes. Conversely, being dressed like a millionaire and claiming to be poor will also discredit you. Your verbal messages must agree with their nonverbal counterparts. You must look like whatever you say you are.

In most business situations, an employee's dress acts as a symbol of rank. In some retail stores, the owner may be observed wearing a business suit, the clerks in their shirtsleeves, and the stockboys wearing brown or blue work jackets. In certain automobile service centers, dress will vary according to an individual's position. The service manager wears a long white smock, the mechanics, full-length jumpers, and the cleanup people, overalls. At a glance, customers can see that their rank and functions are not the same.

One student at a West Coast university proved to himself how one's clothes can act as a label. For a week, he hitchhiked back and forth from San Diego to Los Angeles. Every other day, he would change the way he dressed, On Monday, Wednesday, and Friday, he wore old levis, sneakers and a T-shirt with the picture of a rock group on it. On Tuesday, Thursday, and Saturday, he wore a clean sport shirt open at the neck, a pair of neatly pressed slacks, and well-shined loafers. Nothing in his routine was changed except his clothes. In his own words, here is what happened:

It was incredible! On my three grubby days, I got rides from people who looked just like I did. Two of them drove old VW buses, and the third had a '55 Ford pickup truck. They all wore levis, boots, etc., and all had pretty much the same life style. On the days when I dressed up, I got rides in shiny new Oldsmobiles and Cadillacs from people who were completely opposite from the ones I had driven with the day before. The very first thing one guy said after picking me up was how nice it was to see a young person who wasn't one of those "hippie types."[2]

[2] Ron Adler, and Neil Towne, *Looking Out/Looking In* (New York: Holt, Rinehart and Winston, 1975), pp. 232–3.

If you are still not convinced that the way you dress can influence an audience, perform your own experiments. Dress differently for various classes. Observe how your teachers and classmates behave toward you. Notice in which situations you feel more or less comfortable. Regard every verbal encounter you have with people on campus as a mini-speech. Treat others as your audience. Experiment freely.

Some suggestions when dressing for a speech are:
1. When in doubt, dress conservatively.
2. Wear clothes that will agree with your audience's prior experience.
3. Do not wear excessive jewelery or ornamentation.
4. Be sure that your clothes fit you properly.
5. If possible, attempt to emulate the manner of dress your audience associates with a successful person speaking on your subject.
6. Avoid wearing anything that will distract your audience unnecessarily (e.g., an outlandish hat, weird glasses)
7. Make sure that your clothes are properly color-coordinated.

Posture

Most people think that posture refers only to how a person stands. This is not true. There is also your sitting posture and walking posture. All three reveal something about you. Have you ever heard the expression, "Flexion is sadness, extension is happiness?" The word *flexion* refers to bending something. In terms of one's posture, it means a bending of the arms, legs, or torso. Think of someone who is very sad sitting on the edge of a bed. In your mind, see how such a person's body might be positioned. The head would probably be pitched forward, the arms bent at the elbows, the fingers folded inward, and the legs bent at the knees. Now, think of a very happy person sitting on the edge of a bed. The trunk of the body would probably be erect, the head held high with the arms and legs extended. Without doubt, posture can be taken as a definite clue to a speaker's emotional state.

Spot check your own posture the next time someone, for no apparent reason, asks, "What's the matter?" You probably will discover yourself in a state of flexion rather than extension. Though you might find this difficult to believe, an enormous number of people have either a vague conception of their own posture, or a distorted picture of how others see them. For example, notice how many of the people you encounter every day fail to hold their heads straight. Observe how many of them fail to stand with their weight equally distributed on both feet. Their weight frequently is displaced to one side or the other. The tendency to displace weight to one side causes hips and shoulders to appear uneven. It is the exceptional individual who holds himself or herself in a straight and balanced posture.

Unless there is some mental or physical disability over which an individual has no control, postural habits are largely learned behaviors. Many are acquired through the process of imitation—by emulating other members of one's family, movie and television idols, members of a peer group, and so on. People act as mirrors for their inner selves because they tend to select images that compliment their psychological needs.

In classroom situations, teachers have been known to make judgments about their students on the basis of posture. For instance some teachers believe that students who slump in their seats seem to lack interest, earn lower grades, and tend to present behavioral problems. In contrast, they believe that those students who sit erect in their seats pay closer attention, earn higher grades, and present fewer behavioral problems. While it is clearly improper to make such assumptions about students, teachers, like everyone else, are influenced by appearances. A speechmaker must be aware of the possibility of being judged, at least in part, on a postural basis.

To heighten your awareness of differences in posture and their effects upon people, try this personal experiment tomorrow. Walk through the halls at school with your arms hanging loosely at your sides and your head bent forward. At another time, walk erectly with your head held high, your arms swinging vigorously to and fro, and your eyes looking straight ahead. On still another day, practice sitting differently in some of your classes. In some sit erectly, in others slump in your seat. Notice how these changes in your posture make you feel and how they make others behave toward you. The question to ask yourself is, "Did varying my posture influence my communication with others?" If so, how?

Let us now direct our attention more specifically to posture and speechmaking. Will holding yourself a certain way really affect your audience? The answer is a qualified, "Yes." The extent of such influence will depend, of course, upon a number of other factors. Successful speechmaking, in addition to the skillful blending of verbal and nonverbal messages, is also influenced by such things as topic, audience mood, composition of audience, time, place, circumstances, and so on. While any one of these elements could make a significant difference in the outcome of your speech, the importance of your posture should not be underestimated. Trained actors and actresses are fully aware of how much even a slight change in a character's posture can shift audience attitude. Notice, for example, how some of our famous impressionists use posture to capture a particular personality. For James Cagney, the shoulders are hunched, hands hang limply with the wrists held against the front of the abdomen; for Burt Lancaster, the head is held high and cocked slightly to one side and the open hands are held out front as if to clap; for Alfred Hitchcock, a profile is assumed, abdomen thrust forward, chin drawn in and lips pursed; and, finally, for John Wayne, arms are held akimbo, torso is turned slightly sideways, and an overbalanced gait is displayed. Without these stereotypical postures, a great deal of the impression would be sacrificed.

Before being called upon to speak, most speakers sit on a dais (a raised platform or the front part of a stage with chairs on it). On some occasions, there are several speakers to be introduced; on others, there is only one speaker. In either case, there usually is a period of time during which the audience is given an opportunity to observe the speaker sitting down. As you have been told already, sitting posture communicates as does standing posture.

In the United States, men generally sit differently from women. Part of this difference is due to their anatomical construction; the other part to training. Most of the difference in sitting posture involves the lower part of the body. Men sit with their legs spread apart; women, with legs close together. This sitting posture has been modified somewhat since more women wear pants, slacks, and dungarees. Men more frequently cross their legs so as to form a number "4." Women, if they are wearing a dress or skirt, more frequently cross their legs at the knees or ankles. If a woman is wearing pants, she might be inclined to cross her legs in a more casual manner; i.e., more like a man. There is something commonly recognized as a typically "male" and "female" standing posture, also. In the upright posture the American male is commonly pictured to look like this: thighs ten to fifteen degrees apart, pelvis rolled back, and arms slightly akimbo. The American female posture is commonly pictured as legs close together, pelvis tipped forward, and arms close to the body.

Both male and female speakers must familiarize themselves with the more established and traditional ways of sitting and getting up to approach the lectern. The ideal sitting posture consists of (a) sitting squarely in the seat, (b) feet placed flat on the floor directly beneath the knees, (c) hands folded in lap. Whereas feet may be discreetly crossed at the ankles, this action should be avoided if possible. Some other actions to avoid include hooking one or both feet around a leg of the chair, folding arms across the chest, placing hands in pockets, or draping one or both arms on the chair to the right and/or left.

There is also a proper and improper way to get up from a chair. The wrong way is to bend forward as if you were going to bow, straighten up, and step forward. The right way to rise is to place one foot slightly in front of the other, keep your back reasonably erect, rock forward and, using your thigh muscles, stand up. Remember also while getting up to keep your eyes on either the audience or the chairperson who introduced you. Do not look down at the floor! Remind yourself that audiences can frequently detect whether a speaker is confident, alert, arrogant, humble, nervous, shy, authoritative, friendly, interested, energetic or listless by the way he or she sits or stands. Make every effort to start winning over your audience before you open your mouth to speak.

Something else you should know about the silent side of public speaking is called the *pseudoaffective stance*. It is said to occur when your posture conflicts with what you are saying. For example, if your speech should deal with being forceful or assertive, you should not be standing with your weight heavily shifted onto one foot, the other knee slightly bent, and one hand placed on your hip. By the same token, if your topic is humility, standing in an arrogant stance with your arms folded across your chest, your head high, shoulders back, and your feet placed on a broad base would be completely out of order. Thus, to avoid being guilty of displaying a pseudoaffective stance, be absolutely sure that the posture you assume is appropriate to your topic.

An excellent way of becoming more aware of your postural personality is to notice other people's posture. For instance, can you tell the difference between a new and an experienced teacher by how he or she stands in front of a class? Do you, generally, pay closer attention to a teacher who delivers a lecture sitting or standing, moving around, or remaining in one place? Are you more apt to believe a teacher who stands erect or who slumps? Think about posture—experiment with your own body; stand in front of a mirror at home and assume various postures and sense how they make you feel. Back up to a wall each day and have a "postural fix." By standing against the wall with your head, back, buttocks, and heels touching it for thirty seconds (with your eyes closed), you will condition yourself to experience good posture. You will be surprised how many people think they are standing up straight, but aren't. Good posture, in addition to being a physical experience, is also a mental state.

General Tips on Posture and Public Speaking

1. Avoid extremes in posture.
2. Vary your posture during a speech.
3. Avoid appearing as if your shoes were nailed to one spot.
4. Look comfortable, but not limp.
5. Do not put your hands in your pockets.
6. Do not hold your speech in your hands while speaking. Put it down on the lectern before you.
7. Try not to mimic other people's postures. Discover your own.
8. Stand with your weight equally distributed on both feet.
9. Look down at your speech with your eyes, not by repeatedly bowing your head.
10. Make yourself more visible by facing your audience directly. Do not angle your body to one side of your audience or the other.

Body Rhythm

Although a speechmaker may stand in one spot while talking, body movements are a part of any speech. In this section, the body rhythm of the speaker shall be looked at in three dimensions: *activity, intensity* and *range.*

Activity

There are some speakers who fidget and fuss while delivering a speech. Others just stand there like statues. Neither extreme is desirable. What is called for is an appropriate amount of body movement consistent with both the speaker's personality and the topic of the speech. Unfortunately, deciding what is appropriate in any given situation is not always an easy task. Audiences generally make that decision on the basis of past experience and existing circumstances.

To most audiences, the amount of body movement displayed by a speaker indicates level of energy. The more movement a speaker exhibits, the more energy he or she is thought to possess. Even though the movement may be a result of nervousness or speech fright, it is nevertheless viewed as an expression of energy. Conversely, a speech delivered in an almost motionless manner is perceived as lacking in energy. However, amount of movement must fit a speaker's topic. Take the case of a speaker whose topic is, "The Art of Relaxation." Imagine such a person standing up there in a perpetual state of motion—shuffling papers, toying with a pen or pencil, rocking the lectern back and forth. A hyperactive body rhythm like that is certain to nullify any attempt by the speaker to impress members of the audience with the importance of relaxation. From another direction, picture a speaker whose topic deals with aggressiveness and asssertiveness, standing before an audience as still as a store-window dummy. How effective do you think either of these speakers would be?

Those who have studied body rhythms, use two labels to apply to most people: *lark* and *owl*. They represent two different energy patterns. The lark is a "day person" who goes to sleep early and gets up early. On arising in the morning, larks are full of energy. They do their best work early and tire early. Owls have a hard time getting up in the morning but come to life in the afternoon, and continue on energetically until the wee hours. They are "night people."

This distinction between the lark and the owl clearly applies to public speakers. Consider how effective an owl speechmaker would be delivering a speech at 8:30 A.M. or a lark speechmaker talking at midnight. Both would consider such scheduling a hardship, and the opportunity to switch times, a pleasure.

Also related to body rhythm activity are the terms *tortoise* and *hare*. The speechmaker who is labeled a tortoise does everything slowly—turns the pages of the speech as if they were made out of the fragile papyrus of the Dead Sea Scrolls and moves like a character in a slow motion film. The hare speechmaker moves fast, talks fast, and appears to be going to a fire. The speech is often over before an audience knows what hit them.

If you are able to admit you are a lark or an owl, a tortoise or a hare, it is possible for you to do something about it. You may not be able to or want to change your character and temperament, but you can modify your speech making habits in order to be a better speaker. Just how much you change will depend upon your motivation—your drive to improve.

The first step to changing your body rhythm is to become clearly aware of how you are currently behaving. You can do this by observing yourself on videotape or movie film, listening to the commentary of teachers and friends whom you respect, and delivering speeches in front of a full-length mirror. After deciding what it is you want to correct, you are ready to begin retraining yourself.

For the Hare Speechmaker
- Get a wristwatch with a sweep second hand.
- Select a speech of moderate length. Read it and time it.
- Read it again at half speed.
- Extend the time it takes to eat your meals by ten minutes.
- Mark your speeches with the word PAUSE at various intervals.
- Whenever you get dressed or undressed, pretend that your clothes are soaking wet.
- Think of yourself as the star of a slow-motion film.

For the Tortoise Speechmaker
- Get a wristwatch with a sweep second hand.
- Select a speech of moderate length. Read it and time it.
- Read it again at double speed.
- Constantly think of yourself as being late for wherever you're going.
- Take up a sport or hobby which requires great speed.
- Associate with people who are fast talkers and walkers.

Intensity

In addition to how much physical activity a speaker displays, audiences also react to the level of intensity. A classic example of a highly intense speechmaker was the fanatic Adolph Hitler. Films of his speeches to the German people during World War II show him with his body rigid, arms hysterically snapping back and forth from the Nazi salute to a defiantly crossed position on his chest, and rigid head, neck, and face. The intensity of this man's nonverbal behavior was so unmistakable that a blind person could feel the electricity it generated.

Although most speakers accurately perceive the intensity within their muscular systems, there are some who misread their own body state. People who are usually intense will notice comparatively little difference in themselves when delivering a speech. However, speakers who are normally relaxed will be more aware of the contrast of intensity in speechmaking. It is amazing how many intense people fancy themselves calm. Fewer in number are those quiet people who imagine themselves intense. The point being made here is that intensity, whether real or imagined, is clearly a matter of perception on the part of both the speaker and the audience.

Whether a given speech calls for more or less intensity, the trained speechmaker must be prepared to deliver it. To do this, the speaker must develop a more reliable sense of body control. This can be accomplished by learning something about muscle control. It involves acquiring the ability to contract and relax most of the major muscles of the body at will. This means practice—a great deal of practice. For the interested speaker, here is a basic routine which might be used effectively to control nervousness before a speech.

Learning to Control Speaker's Body Intensity
- Make a tight fist with both hands (hold for 5 seconds). Relax both hands.
- Flex both biceps (hold for 5 seconds). Allow both arms to hang limply at your sides.
- Draw both shoulders up toward ears (hold for 5 seconds). Allow both shoulders to relax.
- Fold arms across chest and tighten chest muscles (hold for 5 seconds). With arms still across chest, relax arm and chest muscles.
- Draw abdomen in and hold both arms outstretched to the sides as though they were made of iron (hold for 5 seconds). Let abdomen relax and arms drop to sides.
- Tighten buttocks (hold for 5 seconds). Relax buttocks.
- Tighten both thighs (hold for 5 seconds). Relax thighs.
- Tighten calf and feet muscles (hold for 5 seconds). Relax calf and feet muscles.

Range

Just as handwriting varies from person to person, so does the range of motion vary among speechmakers. Some make very small hand and arm movements, others paint pictures in the air using sweeping hand and arm gestures. If you were making a speech, and had to speak the following lines, what kind of gestures would you use? Read these statements and actually make whatever gestures you feel are appropriate to them.

1. "He was a very little boy."
2. "The fish I caught was a whopper. It was about this big."
3. "The people in the parade were really marching. They looked like this."
4. "Suddenly, his mind snapped. He went completely berserk."

Notice the range of your gestures in comparison with others. Were they smaller or larger? Did you use other parts of your body in addition to your hands and arms? Do not get the impression from what is being said here that the bigger your gestures, the better. More important is the intent and appropriateness of a gesture. Although it is permissible for the size of a speaker's gestures to be slightly greater on the platform than in usual conversation, be careful not to overdo it.

Eye Contact

Poor eye contact with an audience is unforgivable. More speakers fail when it comes to good eye contact than any other aspect of public speaking technique. Perhaps it is because people think that engaging an audience's eyes carries with it greater psychological risk. When speakers exchange glances with members of their audience, they are nonverbally acknowledging their existence and accepting the responsibility of delivering a meaningful message. To look away from an audience—that is, to ignore them, is to renounce such a responsibility.

Unlike many of the other nonverbal characteristics assigned to speakers in this chapter, eye contact is the most intimately linked with the inner self. It betrays a substantial part of an individual's personality, character, and emotional equilibrium. More than likely, a person with poor eye contact in a one-to-one conversation will be doubly poor from the speaker's platform. Why? Because the perceived threat is often proportionate to the number of eyes looking at a speaker.

Good eye contact accomplishes many positive things. It informs an audience that a speaker is self-confident, assertive, and desires to be heard. However good a speaker, a lack of eye contact can easily spell failure. Strong and purposeful eye contact, however, can compensate for a number of other shortcomings.

Improving your eye contact will probably require more effort than any other attempt at self-improvement. But, it can most definitely be done. Here, again, are some helpful hints:

Improving Your Eye Contact
- Visit a neighborhood playground and practice your eye contact with children.
- Visit a neighborhood senior citizen's center and practice your eye contact with older people.
- Whenever you eat in a restaurant, look at the waiter or waitress while ordering you meal.
- Walk up to strangers, maintaining good eye contact, ask for directions to a nearby place.
- Stand on a busy streetcorner and watch the people go by. Try to trade eye contact with as many of them as possible for two seconds each. Do the same thing at another time, wearing dark glasses.
- Maintain good eye contact with your teachers when you ask or answer questions in class.

For centuries, writers and artists have been fascinated by human eyes. Like traffic lights, eyes direct people engaged in communication. Without making a sound, eyes can often outspeak mouths.

According to recent research in body language, we maintain better eye contact with people we like than those we dislike. Also, those who seek to exert control over others tend to exercise greater eye contact. Check these findings out on your own. Notice, among your friends and co-workers, which ones look at you directly when they talk and which ones look away. Do those who need your cooperation and help, establish better eye contact than those who do not? Become more sensitive to the role your eyes play in communication. Use them with more purpose. By bringing your eyes under the control of your will, they will better serve your needs as a speechmaker. Tell people what you want of them with your eyes, and you will be pleasantly surprised at the results.

Gestures

We respond to gestures with an extreme alertness and, one might say, in accordance with an elaborate and secret code that is written nowhere, known by none and understood by all.[3]

An anthropologist made this observation several decades ago and it remains as accurate today as it was then. Moreover, it was probably equally accurate thousands of years ago. Gestures predate spoken language. All societies use gestures such as pointing fingers, smiling, raising eyebrows and sticking out tongues.

As a public speaker, you should know that gestures can add to or take away from what you are saying. Gestures can be *purposeful* or *purposeless*. If you are talking about sewing a button on a shirt and, while doing so, simulate the process with your hands, you are creating a purposeful gesture. But, if you pull on your earlobe and drum your fingers on the lectern while talking about picking lettuce in the San Fernando Valley, your gestures are to be considered purposeless. They have nothing whatever to do with your topic.

A curious thing happens with purposeless gestures. After you have been performing them habitually for some time, you become unaware of their existence. Take the simple act of holding your hands in your pockets, playing with your keys, or pushing a strand of hair back from your face. After a while, these gestures become unconscious. And, when someone brings them to your attention, you snap back with, "I'm doing what?"

Consider something as innocent as showing your tongue. Have you noticed how many people, while threading a needle, extend their tongues slightly between their lips? Others, while doing arithmetic in their heads, turning a screwdriver, maneuvering a bicycle, or putting on mascara, also protrude their tongues a little. Under what circumstances is your tongue visable without your realizing it? When it is out, are you aware of it? One professor at the University of Pennsylvania spent five years studying why people show their tongues. He discovered that when most people showed their tongues, they were under some kind of stress. A distinction must be made between a partial showing of the tongue while performing one of the tasks just mentioned and the deliberate act of "sticking out one's tongue." The first act is purposeless and often unconscious. The second act is not only conscious but deliberate and purposeful. In the United States, people stick out their tongues to show contempt, annoyance, ridicule, or hostility toward others. In Tibet, the same act is considered a sign of politeness and respect. In New Caledonia, the protruded tongues of ancestors

---

[3] Edward Sapir, "The Unconscious Patterning of Behavior in Society," *Selected Writings of Edward Sapir in Language, Culture and Personality*, ed. by David Mandelbaum (Berkeley: University of California Press, 1949), p. 556.

carved on wooden statues signify wisdom and vigor. It is interesting how the same gesture can have different meanings in other parts of the world.

Smiling is another peculiar facial gesture. Expert on body language, Professor Ray Birdwhistell cautions us that a smile in one society might portray friendliness; in another, embarrassment; and in still another, warn that hostility and attack are imminent. His research tells us that in New England, there is more smiling among familiars and less with strangers. Southerners think they are friendlier because they smile and New Englanders think they are more reserved because they don't. Although there is a temptation to categorize people on the basis of their smiles, it can be misleading. Again, the warning: neither speech nor speaker should ever be judged on the basis of a solitary gesture.

Another classification of gestures signifies whether they are formal or informal. An example of a formal gestural system is the sign language of the deaf.

Among the more familiar informal gestures are handwringing, nail-biting, chin-stroking, knuckle-cracking, head-nodding, toe-tapping, to name a few. Are any of these informal gestures part of your own body language? Are you always aware that you are doing them? If you should want to get rid of them, you must bring them up to a conscious level.

At best, speaking before an audience is a stressful experience. This is especially true when a speaker has never done it before. According to psychological literature, the more stress a person is under, the more likely these informal tension-reducing gestures are to appear. Although there is a natural desire to eliminate these distracting gestures, a better strategy would be to try to convert them. All gestures, whether they are purposeful or purposeless, formal or informal, represent bound energy—energy capable of doing work or being converted into other forms. This means that you have it in your power to convert a purposeless gesture into a purposeful one.

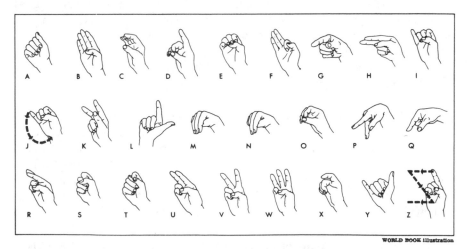

WORLD BOOK Illustration

Figure 10–1. Sign Language of the Deaf. (From *The World Book Encyclopedia*. © 1980 World Book-Childcraft International, Inc.)

Space

The study of how meaning communicates through the use of space is called *proxemics*. In public speaking, it deals with such things as 1) how near or far a speaker stands from the audience, 2) an audience's seating arrangement, and 3) a speaker's relationship to a lectern. By altering any one of these spatial factors, it is possible to affect the course, character and outcome of a speech.

Speaker-Audience Distance

The further you are from your audience, the less distinctly its members will be able to see and hear you. Although a good public address system can easily compensate for the aural part of your speech, it cannot do so for the visual part. Those sitting in the front part of an audience experience a speaker differently from those in the back. Up front, people are able to see a speaker sweat, blush, tremble, and display a variety of facial expressions. It is these nonverbal messages which are able to make the difference between getting and not getting an audience's approval. Then, there is the question, as stressed earlier, of words and actions agreeing with one another. Words reinforced by appropriate actions increase the impact of a message; whereas words reinforced by inappropriate actions tend to lessen their impact.

To become an effective speaker, you must learn how to adapt to increases in distance from your audience. For example, you must not only use a great number of appropriate gestures, but also increase their dimensions. If you make reference to a high mountain range, use both arms fully, so that they can be seen easily by those in the rear of the room. People are more moved by an animated speaker than by one who looks like a store window dummy. The larger the audience, the more body language you must use.

With a smaller audience and a lesser distance between you and its members, you need not employ such dramatic gesturing. It would be both excessive and quite unnatural. While maintaining the richness of your body language, scale it down in relation to the closeness of your audience.

Seating Arrangement

At the beginning of this century, chairs in schoolrooms across the nation were neatly arranged in rows with the teacher's desk at the front facing them. All the students at the rear saw of their classmates were the backs of their heads. If a student in the middle of the room was asked a question, only the teacher had the benefit of the student's facial expressions and eye contact. Except for some side views of one another, the students were clearly at a disadvantage from the standpoint of communication. It has been said that the reason for the neatly arranged rows was that the janitors could clean the classrooms more easily and the arrangement allowed for a maximum amount of sunlight.

As classroom lighting improved, teachers began to question the traditional arrangement of students in rows. They experimented with circles and discovered several things. Most important of all was the fact that allowing each student to have direct eye contact with both the teacher and every other student greatly improved their communication. Being able to clearly see the person with whom they were talking caused them to listen better. Listening, in turn, helped make them more responsive to what was actually said. Another benefit to be derived by sitting in a circle was that everyone sat in full view of everyone else. Unlike the partial concealment of half the body when seated in rows, circular seating allowed for greater communication through body language. And finally, circular seating seemed to create a greater feeling of togetherness and participation among the students—a sense of informality and openness which also led to improved interpersonal communication.

The lesson to be learned here with regard to the seating arrangement of your audience is rather straightforward. Whenever at all possible, try to have the members of your audience seated in a circle. If this is not possible, try for a semicircle. Although this is obviously impossible with larger audiences, it is workable with smaller ones.

So as to avoid unnecessary audience annoyance with rearranging chairs, try to have the chairs in the room in which you will be speaking prearranged by the custodian or some organizational aides.

Speaker and Lectern

It is a great temptation for many speakers to use a lectern as a crutch, a blockade, or an extension of themselves. To shield yourself from your audience with a lectern is to conceal the lower half of your body from view. To lean on a lectern is to convey to your audience, not only an impression of anxiety and insecurity, but also a deficiency in nonverbal assertiveness. Only successful speechmakers have the courage to come out from behind a lectern and openly confront their audience. They rarely permit themselves to become glued to a lectern. At no time are they seen rocking it back and forth, embracing it, or holding on to it for dear life. While experienced speakers can, if they so desire, hold an audience in the palm of their hand without leaving a lectern, it is generally utilized as a speech-holding device.

Good advice for a public speaker is to place the speech on a lectern and, using it as home base, strive to create a sense of aliveness and freedom before the audience. Neither stand in one place behind the lectern nor move about incessantly. Avoid the extreme in either case.

Time

Without using a wristwatch, how closely can you judge the passage of ten minutes? If you were to ask a dozen public speakers to make such a judgment, you would be surprised at how many miss the mark. Some would run overtime, others undertime, and only a few would hit the ten-minute mark on the nose. Young children between the ages of four and six occasionally display an extreme distortion of time. For example, five minutes after being told by a parent that the family is going on a picnic next week, they will ask, "Is it next week yet, Mommie?"

No experienced speechmaker would ever give a speech without an accurate watch. Since whoever is chairing a program will almost always provide a speaker with a time limit, it is the speaker's ethical responsibility to respect that time allotment. A long-winded speaker will not only offend an audience, but also other speakers on the program by cutting into their time allowance. Regardless of how good a speaker is, misjudging time is a luxury one cannot afford.

Beyond the importance of accurately judging the length of your speech, you must also be able to judge how long its parts—introduction, body, and conclusion—run. A too long introduction or conclusion could easily crowd the body of your speech and by so doing, cause you to run overtime. It would therefore be a good idea to time each part of your speech as well as the whole.

Summary

You read in this chapter about the silent side of public speaking—how you dress yourself, posture yourself, move, gesture, maintain eye contact, and manage space and time before an audience can help you become a more effective speechmaker. Words and actions must be brought to bear on a common theme with equal strength. Lack of appropriate actions will deprive any worthwhile speech from achieving its full potential. Verbal elements must be carefully merged with nonverbal elements so that each exerts a positive influence upon the other. In short, when delivering any speech, your silent messages should ring loud and clear.

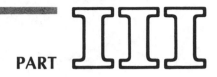

PART III

Taking the Pain Out of Presentation

If You Are Worried About Having to Give a Speech, Read This

Behavioral Objectives

After reading this chapter, you should have a clearer understanding of:

- the myths associated with speech anxiety.
- the various ways speech anxiety can manifest itself in a speechmaker.
- the kinds of fears a great many speakers experience.
- the more common causes of speech anxiety.
- how to determine your own degree of speech anxiety.
- some of the more effective ways of combatting speech anxiety.

Introduction

Whether your fear of getting up in front of an audience is slight or extreme, you may have been told that you suffer from *stage fright*. Actually, the term is misleading. Feelings such as fear or fright are emotional reactions to external causes—things outside of your body. They might include a fear of fire, drowning, suffocation, major surgery, or an airplane crash. In each of these cases, the cause exists outside the body. By comparison, the emotional reaction you get from having to deliver a speech comes from within the body and, more properly, should be labeled as apprehension or anxiety.

Speech assignments, by themselves, are quite harmless. It is highly unlikely that speech anxiety has ever been listed as the cause of death. What is likely, however, is that certain speechmakers have been known to overreact to the thought of making a speech. It is while working themselves up into preparing to make a speech that many people begin to suffer from anxiety or apprehension. The difference between someone who gets unduly upset and someone who takes a new experience in stride is A–T–T–I–T–U–D–E or, in fancier language—PERSPECTIVE.

Making a speech is easy. It is simply talking to people. You have been talking to people almost all of your life. Take a moment to realize that it isn't the speech that is the problem, but rather your *attitude* toward speaking. Having an improper attitude toward something, whether it be money, marriage, or making a speech, can make all of the difference. You might bear in mind that clever saying, "I have met the enemy and it is me." With speech anxiety, you not only have a problem, you are also part of that problem.

SPEECH EXPERIENCE: TALKING TO THE WALL

　　1. All members of the class should rise, stand one foot from the wall, and distribute themselves evenly around the room.

　　2. At a signal from the instructor, all students should begin talking to the wall in front of them about anything that comes to mind; that is, things they love a great deal, things they can't stand, and so on.

　　3. One by one, the instructor will tap students on their shoulder. When tapped, the student should turn around, face the center of the room, take three steps forward, and continue talking.

　　4. In turn, at another signal from the instructor, half of the students will stop talking and act as listeners.

　　5. Class members should then discuss their reactions to the speech experience.

　　　　a. How did you feel talking to the wall?
　　　　b. How did you feel talking to the entire class?
　　　　c. How did you feel talking to a group of listeners?

We take a close look at speech anxiety, or speech apprehension, in this chapter. Our purpose will be to discuss what causes it, some of its signs and symptoms, and how to deal with it.

Myths

Starting right now, you must realize that it is normal to have some speech anxiety. You must also take into account the fact that a great many very famous people confess that before a game or performance, they have a terrible time. Paul Lynde, star of stage, screen, and television, admits, "I have never gotten over being terrified in front of an audience. Oh, I know most performers get the jitters before they go on. My reaction is more like nervous collapse." [1] Even Cicero, twenty centuries ago said, "I turn pale at the outset of a speech and quake in every limb."

From coast to coast, an incredible number of highly successful people in the business and professional world describe the most peculiar symptoms associated with speech anxiety. Experts seem to agree that, within normal limits, speech anxiety is nothing to be ashamed of. It has been claimed that a certain amount of apprehension is necessary for effective speechmaking. It is only when it is uncontrollable that it warrants professional help. Fortunately, this is the exception rather than the rule.

Signs and Symptoms

When faced with the prospect of addressing an audience, most of us exhibit certain signs and symptoms of speech anxiety. These may be sweating, irregular breathing, weakness in the knees, a need to visit the bathroom, faintness, headaches, nausea, forgetfulness, and overall restlessness. In addition to these physiological signs and symptoms, there may also be such psychological states as insecurity, alienation, intimidation, self-pity and embarrassment.

The extent to which any of these physical or emotional states occur will depend upon the type of individual. It is important to also mention here that speech anxiety is not prejudiced; it has absolutely no regard for a person's race, color, or creed. It fully respects the constitutional guarantee that all men and women are created equal.

---

[1] B. Thomas, "Hollywood Helps Comedian Enjoy Himself," *Richmond (Va.) News Leader*, July 17, 1962, p. 15.

Speech Anxiety Quotient

Just how frightened are you of making a speech? Because self-evaluations are often deceiving, it is difficult to determine just how anxious or apprehensive you are. Here is a simple quiz that will supply you with additional insight. *Instructions*—Circle 0 if you are not at all anxious, *1* if you are mildly anxious, *2* if you are anxious, *3* if you are really getting uptight, *4* if you are approaching panic, and *5* if you are panic-stricken.

1. I am afraid that my mind will go blank.

    (0) 1 2 3 4 5

2. I will be asked questions I cannot answer.

    0 1 (2) 3 4 5

3. People in the audience will laugh at me.

    (0) 1 2 3 4 5

4. My speech will be boring.

    0 1 (2) 3 4 5

5. Someone in the audience will cross-examine me.

    0 (1) 2 3 4 5

6. People will walk out.

    0 (1) 2 3 4 5

7. My teacher will embarrass or humiliate me in front of the class.

    0 1 2 (3) 4 5

8. People will make fun of how I look.

    (0) 1 2 3 4 5

9. My voice will quiver or I will stutter.

    0 (1) 2 3 4 5

10. I won't know what to do with my hands.

    0 1 (2) 3 4 5

11. People will think that I am stupid.

    (0) 1 2 3 4 5

12. Everyone will stare at me.

    0 (1) 2 3 4 5

Score yourself by adding up the numbers you have circled. It will represent your Speech Anxiety Quotient. *Terrified*: 60–56; *Very Frightened*: 55–41; *Apprehensive*: 40–26; *Casual*: 25–16; *Unconcerned*: 15–0.

Although this quiz is by no means a purely scientific indicator of your anxiety as a speaker, it should provide you with some idea as to what disturbs you about speaking publically.

Causes of Speech Anxiety

There are two ways you can deal with your speech anxiety. Either attempt to discover what is causing it or treat the symptoms it produces. Since most speech experts agree that speech anxiety can seldom be traced to a single cause, you would be better off dealing with its symptoms. Searching for that *one* thing that is causing you to be afraid may, in the long run, create more anxiety than it is worth. In a sense, it is like having a skin allergy and going from one allergy specialist to another, hoping to find "the answer." It is not uncommon to learn that you are allergic to more things than you bargained for and must be willing to settle for a little relief rather than a cure.

Another reason for treating symptoms rather than their cause is *time*. If you are taking a course this semester requiring that you deliver one or more speeches, there may not be enough time to figure out why you get so nervous and upset. What you need is an immediate remedy rather than a permanent cure. Unfortunately there is no miracle drug currently available to eliminate speech anxiety. Your best bet is to attempt to get a clearer understanding of its multiple causes, plus an expanded awareness of the techniques you can use to reduce the symptoms mentioned previously. Let us begin by citing some of the more common causes that have been associated with speech anxiety.

Fear of the Unknown

Whether it involves moving to a new neighborhood, across the country, to a new job, to a new school, or changing your major, most people experience varying degrees of anxiety or apprehension. Having to deal with new situations or the unexpected is a chore few people relish. They would much rather contend with the old and familiar situation, where they can make fairly reliable predictions as to its outcome. Most individuals perceive giving a speech as threatening because of its unknown quality and, consequently, seek to avoid speechmaking whenever possible. Although they are intellectually aware of what can or cannot happen in front of an audience, their emotions seem to take charge and cause them to behave irrationally.

Feeling Inadequate

If feeling adequate is a state in which an individual feels capable of coping with a given situation, feeling inadequate means just the opposite; i.e., feeling incapable of coping with a given situation. Psychologists tell us that an extraordinary number of people have difficulty making decisions in both their private and public lives. One of the explanations for such indecision is related to something called risk-taking. Again, as with fearing the unknown, people are also afraid of taking risks. In addition to saying or doing something that is socially frowned upon or even thinking certain things, they prefer to play things safe by going along with the crowd.

David Reisman, the sociologist, tells us that there are *inner* and *other*-directed people. The inner-directed types think and do whatever they personally feel is right. Other-directed types are preoccupied with how others will respond to their behavior. Anyone who has studied human psychology must have noted that there are more other-directed people than inner-directed. All too frequently, children are made fully aware of their shortcomings and only rarely aware of their talents. Is it any wonder that so many adults feel inadequate when they are asked to stand up and deliver a speech? Standing up in front of an audience appears to demand an enormous amount of personal risk. And, as such, a speaker's adequacy (or feeling of adequacy) is really put to the test.

Fear of Being Judged

As you read about each of these possible causes of speech anxiety you should be noticing how they feed into one another. Here we are dealing with the opinions of others. Just how sensitive are you to being judged? Do you believe that everything an audience says about you is necessarily true? If you do, this may well be part of your problem. People who have been judged negatively by others most of their lives stand a good chance of losing their psychological balance; that is, their psychological perspective. If this has happened, their desire to survive may cause them to avoid situations in which they will be judged on any account. Public speaking is one such situation.

Inability to Face Consequences

In the extreme, two things may result from giving a speech. The audience either may like it or dislike it. More simply, it may either be a success or a failure. And, with each outcome, there is usually some consequence. In the classroom situation, an unsatisfactory speech might earn a failing mark; in a business situation, it could result in losing an account. Whatever the result, a speaker must be prepared to cope with consequences. This, to some people, constitutes a threat. With a failing grade for a speech, there is the chance that the entire course will be failed. If the speech is a smashing success, there is a chance that it will be held up as a model for other students to emulate. Each outcome imposes a responsibility upon the speaker. How an individual handles these responsibilities will influence future events.

Transparency

As unreasonable as it may seem, there are people who dread public speaking because they honestly believe that members of an audience can see through them. No matter how you confront them with evidence to the contrary, they will insist that audience members have X-ray vision and are able to read minds. Upon first hearing someone put forth such a belief, there is a strong tendency to think they might be psychologically disturbed. Except in an extreme case, this conclusion is not necessarily true. Perfectly normal and rational people have been known to entertain some pretty abnormal and irrational ideas when it comes to speechmaking. Why the thought of having to deliver a speech brings out such strange notions in people continues to remain an unsolved mystery. All we do know, for certain, is that how an individual believes has the capacity to strongly influence his or her behavior.

Language Barriers

With our world getting smaller, people who speak different languages are being brought into closer contact with one another. As if speakers and audiences who share a common tongue do not have enough communication problems, a multilingual audience adds additional confusion. In many colleges and universities, students from many backgrounds and areas are lumped together in classrooms. Whereas lecture classes rarely present any problems, those in which speechmaking is required often cause panic in the hearts and minds of students whose native language is not English. Unless you have gone through such an ordeal personally, you cannot fully appreciate the degree of anxiety and apprehension someone without an adequate command of the English language experiences when asked to give a speech. Students who are knowledgeable and articulate in their native languages may suddenly be made aware of the limitations of their English. Even individuals who speak well, by American standards, have serious difficulty. Characteristically, there is an inherent fear of making mistakes and, by so doing, making a fool of oneself. This idea is compounded by the popular belief that the longer you have been in the United States, the better you should be able to speak English. Although such an assumption sounds logical, it is not a reliable barometer of someone's speaking skill. For example, you cannot know just how much English an individual speaks outside of class, the quality of that English, or their motivation to speak English. Add to such a language barrier an assortment of emotional factors and you are likely to be confronted by a full-blown case of speech anxiety.

Negative Past Experiences

It is almost impossible to erase an unpleasant public speaking experience from a person's memory. The damage is even worse if it is repeated several times. All that one can ever justifiably do to make things right is to overlay them with positive speaking experiences. Certain cases of stuttering have been traced back to traumatic speaking experiences involving such things as physical abuse, continually interrupted speech, and excessive criticism. Whatever the nature of one's prior speaking experience, if it was perceived to be negative, there is a chance that it will constitute a basis for speech anxiety.

Ignorance

The word *ignorance* is being used here to indicate that an individual who is expected to deliver a speech simply lacks information. It is not intended to suggest stupidity. There are speakers who, for instance, develop varying degrees of speech anxiety because they do not know 1) what constitutes a good speech, and 2) what an audience expects of them. Without such information, no speaker can expect to achieve success. Speakers without clearly defined goals wander aimlessly and are destined to fail. Like a traveler without a map, or an architect without a blueprint, speakers who are ignorant of what constitutes a good or successful speech place themselves at a disadvantage.

Though there are certainly other causes of speech anxiety, those which tend to be the most common are fearing the unknown, feeling inadequate, a fear of being judged, an inability to face consequences, transparency, language barriers, negative past experiences, and ignorance. Use the space provided to list, to the best of your ability, those things which cause speech anxiety in you.

Having done this, you are now ready to consider the best possible remedy for your speech anxiety and apprehension.

Suggested Remedies for Combatting Speech Anxiety

Face Up to Speech Anxiety

From the beginning of this chapter, you were told that beginners as well as experienced speakers run the risk of suffering from speech anxiety. Accept the fact that speech anxiety is *not* an affliction which strikes only those who are lacking in intelligence, emotional stability, courage, or motivation. Realize that whatever symptoms you experience, they can be brought under your control with a respectable amount of effort. You must come to grips with the fact that speech anxiety is not some mysterious demon which enters your body prior to giving a speech. It is nothing more than your normal mental and physical energies thrown into a state of imbalance. And, by facing up to this fact, you can exercise the control necessary to bring them back into a state of balance. In short, say to yourself, "I am nervous, anxious, weak in the knees, and scared to death of making this speech. It is a perfectly normal set of reactions which I shall work through. I am in complete control of my mind and body. I am dealing with these feelings in a positive way. This attitude will enable me to succeed."

Perspective

The word *perspective* refers to the way you look at something. A recent article in a local newspaper made this point nicely. It dealt with why certain executives in large corporations suffered high blood pressure, strokes, nervous breakdowns and heart attacks, and others did not. The conclusion reached in the article zeroed in on a particular executive's perspective. Those who viewed their jobs as their life, rather than merely a part of their life, suffered a higher incidence of ill health. The difference was to be found in their perspective; that is, their attitude toward their job in relation to other aspects of their lives.

This same principle of perspective should be brought into play with regard to speech anxiety and speechmaking. It is highly unlikely that the outcome of any one speech will cause your entire life to crumble. If you mentally step far enough away from any speech, your attitude toward its importance may be altered. Treating any speech as a means rather than an end will also make a noticeable difference in your perspective. To the reasonable person, every speech should be looked upon as a learning experience, a basis for the speeches that lie ahead.

Think "Audience"

Before and during any speech, you have two options. You can *think "self"* or you can *think "audience."* With very few exceptions, the more you think "self," the more you are inviting the symptoms of speech anxiety. As mountain climbers increase their chances of falling by looking down, speakers, likewise, must not think entirely of themselves but of their audiences. The speechmaker, like the mountain climber, must constantly keep his target or goal in sight.

Contrary to what you may now believe, audiences want speakers to succeed. When speakers fail, what do audiences gain? Little or nothing. They come away either annoyed or angry, disappointed or disillusioned. If speakers succeed, audiences come away feeling good, satisfied with the superior judgment and fine taste that prompted them to attend. Being aware that your audience wants you to succeed is a truth to be continuously borne in mind. In every audience, there is the raw material from which any speaker can construct a successful speech.

By thinking "audience," do not get the impression that you are to ignore yourself as a speaker. It is more a matter of emphasis, not choice. Dwell not on what you are doing, but rather on *why* you are doing it in terms of your audience. Almost every audience can be persuaded. All audience members need is the appropriate information with which to arrive at a particular set of conclusions. Thus, you must think of your audience members and supply them with such information. Speakers are the means; audience reactions, the end.

Be Yourself

While imitation may be the highest form of flattery, it hardly applies in speech-making. The moment you attempt to imitate someone else, something essential in you runs the risk of being lost. Although psychologists tell us that a great deal of our behavior results from imitating others, there is still resident in each of us a core or essence which is entirely our own. That which we borrow from others represents little more than frills or window-dressing. Your greatest success as a speaker will be realized when you capitalize fully upon your own resources, not the resources of others.

This suggestion, like many others being made here, is not to be taken as an absolute. There can be little wrong with emulating successful speakers. Surely, learning and applying what you have learned by watching and listening to eminent speakers can be valuable. It is only dangerous when you sacrifice your own identity in the process.

Pick Topics You Like

When a speaker is bored with a topic, you can be sure that the speaker's audience will also be bored. By picking a topic you like, you increase your chances of being perceived as enthusiastic. Enthusiasm in a speaker lessens speech anxiety. The more interested you are in your topic, the less stress is placed upon your nervous system. This is extremely important because your nervous system regulates your other systems; e.g., circulatory, muscular, digestive, respiratory, genito-urinary, and endocrine. When your nervous system's balance is upset, it creates other states of imbalance often evidenced in speech anxiety.

Another benefit to be derived from picking a topic you like, or with which you are familiar, is that it puts you one step ahead of your audience. Knowing that you know more about a subject than your audience should arm you with additional reassurance and self-confidence. If you successfully convey this advantage to your audience, the feedback you receive from them may result in an even greater defense against speech anxiety. Audiences, as a rule, are more receptive to and respectful of speakers whom they realize know what they are talking about.

If you are put into a situation in which you are required to speak on a topic about which you know very little, you will have to work a little harder. In a situation like this, try to anchor the unfamiliar aspects of your speech to people, places, and events with which you are familiar. Imagine that you are assigned to give a speech on soccer, a game about which you know practically nothing. Further, imagine that you are very familiar with both baseball and football. Find out what you can about the rules governing soccer and proceed to compare them with the rules governing baseball and football. Whether you are talking about politics, sports, education, or travel, there is always a way of engaging in comparisons; hence, it is a way of bridging the gap between what you don't know and what you do know.

Still another advantage to be gained by picking a topic you like is that you have the benefit of hindsight. If you are like most of us, chances are that you have talked about your topic with others previously. As a result, you have pretested your ideas on the subject and, with a reasonable amount of assurance, know how people will react. This type of insight can have a calming effect upon most speakers. The absence of such insight will tend to have just the opposite effect—a state of nervous tension and uncertainty.

Prepare Your Speech Adequately

There is no substitute for adequate preparation. But, how much is adequate? This will vary from speaker to speaker and from situation to situation. A general rule of thumb suggests that you are ready to give your speech when you can say, "yes," to the following questions: 1) Have you researched your topic thoroughly? 2) Have you organized your speech so that it flows smoothly and intelligently from point to point? 3) Have you made an intensive audience analysis? 4) Have you pretested your speech on someone and carefully established its running time? 5) Have you made a list of the possible questions your audience might ask you and how you would answer them? If you can honestly answer, "yes," to each of these questions, you are ready!

Use Props

Aside from you and your words, everything else is to be regarded as a prop. The way you are dressed, any emblems you might be wearing, or your environment as a speaker constitutes a prop. Picture a speaker in a local school auditorium. Traditionally, there is an American flag on the stage. While this prop might go unnoticed and take on little importance during an average, uncontroversial speech, it could take on special importance if the speaker's topic is patriotic in nature.

Props, whether audio or visual, serve to divide an audience's attention. Your average stage magician depends upon such a division of attention. Without it, his illusions wouldn't have a chance of succeeding. You, too, can take advantage of dividing an audience's attention. The more intensely your audience focuses its attention entirely upon you, the more inclined you are to experience speech anxiety. For some reason, having an entire audience look at you and you alone, makes you feel like a bug on the slide of an experimenter's microscope. You can combat this feeling by getting members of your audience to focus on something else related to your topic. If your speech is on the life of Jesus, you might want to hold a Bible; if it is on records in sports, carry the *Guinness Book of Records*. For every topic, you should be able to think of something your audience can see, touch, hear, or smell. If you are talking about how deaf people communicate, you might have a large chart displaying the language of the deaf available for your audience; if your topic concerns how sightless people read, arrange to have samples of Braille distributed and let them experience how Braille feels.

Here are several random topics. List one or two props you might use in connection with each of them:

1. Capital punishment_____

2. Diabetes_____

3. Marijuana _____

4. Pollution of our waterways _____

5. Terrorism_____

6. Nuclear power_____

7. U.F.O's _____

8. Dangers of smoking_____

9. Gun control_____

10. Cloning_____

Don't Hold Your Speech

A surefire way of making yourself more nervous than you already are is to hold your speech in your hands while you are speaking. This illustrates a form of *biofeedback*—a process by which people receive information from themselves. For example, there is a gadget used in biofeedback techniques which registers a person's physiological responses to certain thoughts. The subject is connected to the instrument. When they think upsetting or aggravating thoughts, the needle moves sharply to the right. When the subject thinks peaceful and tranquil thoughts, the needle moves to the left. What the biofeedback instrument does is enable subjects to monitor their own anxiety states; i.e., when the needle goes up, they can bring it back down by thinking soothing thoughts.

Holding your speech in your hands acts much like one of those biofeedback mechanisms. When you are nervous, the papers in your hands will shake. As you settle down, they will shake less or remain motionless. There is only one problem. No matter how relaxed you are, the simple act of holding your arms out in front of you creates a normal tension which will cause your papers to tremble. So, rather than risk having your trembling papers give you the kind of feedback which produces speech anxiety, put them down on the lectern or table before you.

If Your Mind Goes Blank

Fearing that your mind will go blank is one of the more realistic fears associated with speech anxiety. Minds occasionally do switch off. Rather than apologize to your audience or beginning your speech again, there are certain things you can do and, if you are fortunate, carry on with your speech without having too many people be the wiser.

The moment your mind goes blank, immediately go to a reviewing point. In most cases, you will have covered certain material before your mind goes blank. Go back to some aspect of that material and stress its importance or relevance to your topic. If this does not work, single out some term you have used and redefine it or, perhaps you might want to reclarify or restate a point made earlier. Whatever you do, don't say to your audience, "I can't go on!"

Another trio of strategies you might wish to employ involve pouring and drinking a glass of water, distributing relevant material, or asking your audience for questions. While these ploys will not give you much time, they often do supply you with enough time to gather your thoughts and press on with your speech. You might also avoid rushing your speech because rushing frequently increases the probability of a mind going blank. Inasmuch as thought-speed exceeds speech-speed by approximately four or five to one, your speech often has a difficult time keeping up with your thoughts. Increase the pressure upon this normal differential between thought and word speed by rushing, and you increase your chances of losing your place.

Summary

Having taken the aforementioned suggested remedies for combatting speech anxiety seriously and applied them diligently, you have decreased your fear of speech anxiety and increased your understanding of the dynamic factors which cause it. By facing up to speech anxiety as a normal phenomenon needing to be understood and dealt with rather than avoided, by placing it in a realistic perspective, thinking "audience" rather than "self," being *you* rather than imitating others, picking topics with which you are familiar, preparing your speech adequately, using props effectively, putting your speech down on the lectern so that your hands don't tremble, and knowing what to do when your mind goes blank, you will have taken a giant step toward bringing it under your control.

If you are still worried about having to give a speech, it might help to read this chapter again.

CHAPTER **12**

Is Anyone Listening?

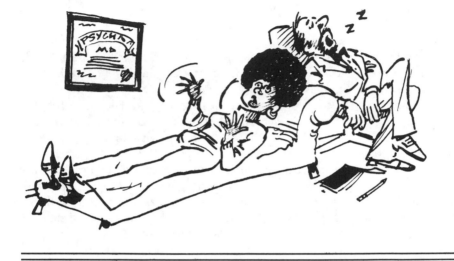

I know that you believe you understand what you think I said, but I am not sure you realize that what you heard is not what I meant.

R. D. Laing

Behavioral Objectives

After reading this chapter, you should have a clearer understanding of:

- the concept that there is more to listening than meets the ear.
- some of the things about listening that many people believe which are not true.
- the things that prompt people to listen.
- why the ability to concentrate is such an important aspect of the listening process.
- the things you can do to make your audience listen to you.
- what a person must do to be considered a good listener.
- what factors discourage people from listening.

Introduction

Though it may sound peculiar, becoming a good speaker requires becoming a good listener. But, what does listening have to do with speaking? Aren't they two separate and distinct arts? The answer is an emphatic, "NO!" As you shall soon see, speaking and listening are two sides of the same coin. In the deeper sense, you cannot have one without the other. While preparing your speech, you must listen to yourself carefully. The process by which you come up with what you are going to say in your speech involves mentally testing new knowledge against old knowledge. Thus, inside your head, you are both listening and speaking continuously to yourself—in search of those words best suited to the meaning you wish to convey to your audience. In short, listening takes place between your ears as well as through them.

If you plan to become a successful speaker, you must learn to listen to yourself as well as to your audience. It never ceases to be a source of amazement that many people speak before clearly thinking out what they want to communicate to others. Proof of this phenomenon is the fact that many, when asked what they just said, are either unable to accurately recapture the ideas they just expressed or unable to clearly explain what they meant. Not only are people frequently inclined to be fuzzy communicators, but fuzzy listeners as well. So, speaking and listening go hand in hand. Although it is quite possible for someone to be a good listener and a poor speaker, the reverse is comparatively rare; i.e., a good speaker is seldom a poor listener. Many politicians, for example, lose sight of this point. Because they are often preoccupied with what they are going to say at a particular rally or meeting, they fail to listen carefully to the questions they are asked by members of their audience. Naturally, this would not apply to those who deliberately, for political reasons, sidestep the issues. The best speakers are the responsive speakers—the ones who listen attentively to what the audience asks or says.

By studying the art of listening, you will accomplish two things. One is the ability to "tune in" to yourself and, by so doing, better manage your mind. The other benefit you will derive is the ability to more clearly understand where your audience is coming from at any given time. Listening, like a compass, keeps a speaker on course.

Unfortunately, most of us come from a speech-centered society. As children, we were not told that speech is silver, silence is golden. We were told that learning to "speak up" would increase our chances of surviving in a competitive society. Never, or hardly ever, were we taught how to listen effectively. At best, we were told that, if we kept quiet and paid attention, we would learn whatever we needed to know. Throughout the United States, relatively few schools have listening programs or laboratories—places where students could be trained in the art of listening. Although a great many educators are aware of the importance that listening plays in effective communication, this awareness is seldom observed in practice. Convince yourself of this truth by answering these questions:

- What are ten things a good listener must do?
- What are ten common barriers to effective listening?
- What are some common misconceptions about listening?

Misconceptions About Listening

On the surface, the term *listening* seems to have a very clear meaning to most people. This conception is quickly overturned when you discover how many definitions for listening exist in the field of communication. Surely, if its meaning were so crystal-clear, why are there so many different definitions? Here are some of the more popular definitions of listening:

The perceptual process by which verbal and nonverbal communications (including mechanical sounds) from some source or sources are selectively received, recognized, and interpreted by a receiver or receivers in relation to the perceptual fields of the parties to the process.[1]

In a sense, it is a combination of what we hear, what we understand, and what we remember.[2]

When a human organism receives data orally.[3]

A conscious or unconscious process by which internal (intrapersonal) and external (interpersonal) vocal stimuli are translated into conscious and unconscious verbal and nonverbal responses ("nonverbal" includes changes in blood pressure, muscle tension, heart rate, and so on).[4]

A complex and unique function of perception and attention which involves both auditory and visual capacities of a listener.[5]

These are, by no means, all of the definitions you would encounter if you were to do a research paper on the subject of listening. There are many others. They do, however, represent the core of what experts in the field consider to be the process of listening. Now, without getting too technical, let us look at some of the misconceptions many speakers have about listening.

---

[1] Martin P. Anderson, E. Ray Nichols, Jr., and Herbert W. Booth, *The Speaker and His Audience*, 2nd ed. (New York: Harper & Row, Publishers, 1974), p. 230, 231.
[2] Ralph G. Nichols, and Thomas R. Lewis, *Listening and Speaking*, (Dubuque, Iowa: William C. Brown Company, Publishers, 1954), p. 1.
[3] Carl H. Weaver, *Human Listening* (Indianapolis: The Bobbs-Merrill Co., Inc., 1972), p. 5.
[4] Abné M. Eisenberg, *Living Communication* (Englewood Cliffs, N.J.: Prentice-Hall, Inc., 1975), pp. 281–2.
[5] John W. Keltner, *Interpersonal Speech-Communication* (Belmont, Calif.: Wadsworth Publishing Co., Inc., 1970), p. 130.

Listening and Hearing Are the Same Thing

Although, whenever you are listening, you are automatically hearing, the same is not the case the other way around; i.e., when you are hearing, you are not necessarily listening. Hearing is the process by which sound from your environment is conveyed to your brain; listening is the process by which such sound is assigned meaning. Still better, think of listening as an emotional and intellectual process by which you translate what you hear into meaningful units of thought.

From both sides of a lectern, you may encounter hearing without listening. Audiences have been known to *hear* a speaker's words without intellectually understanding what they had been designed to mean. Conversely, speakers have been known to speak words without intellectually comprehending their meaning. Given these shortcomings, you may conceivably find yourself in a situation in which, while both speaker and audience are hearing what is being said, neither is listening to the other.

Good Listeners Are Born, Not Made

While there may be some inherent quality in certain individuals causing them to become good hearers, they may not be good listeners. Merely having the ability to sit quietly while someone talks does not automatically denote a good listener. Who knows where such a person's mind may wander while sitting there, not saying a word. It is only an assumption that quiet people are listening. In order for such people to be labeled good listeners, we must find out what they do psychologically with what they hear. Without this information, we may be making an unfounded assumption about them.

There is no evidence to support the belief that good listeners are born. There is, however, some evidence to show that good listeners can be developed through special listening-training programs. Professor Charles Irvin, at Michigan State College, tested 1,400 freshmen before and after listening training. There was a definite difference—a nine to twelve percent difference over those students who were not given any listening training.

We Talk More Than We Listen

Unless someone talks for a living (salesperson, teacher, telephone operator, tour guide), most people listen more than they talk in an average day. This conclusion was proven to be accurate by several studies. Generally, the percentage of communication activities are as follows: *writing—9%*; *reading—16%*; *talking—30%*; and *listening—45%*. Think for a moment about an average day in your own life. If such things as television, radio, tapes, theatre, concerts, and going to school all demand a great deal of listening, how much of your time do you spend with each of them? In all probability, you will discover that you listen considerably more than you thought you did.

Listening Is Easy

A gut reaction might prompt you to say that listening is much easier than talking. Such a reaction is especially attractive when you think in terms of the kind of talking associated with giving a speech. But, in the more conventional, non-stress affairs of everyday activity, there are those who would argue that it is listening that is more difficult.

Have you ever wondered during the course of a typical day while speaking with your parents, friends, and teachers, which of them actually cares two pins about what you have to say? Is there anyone out there listening? If you are inclined to agree with the indictment that not too many people with whom you come into contact do much listening, you must also be wondering why. The answer is to be drawn from the title of this section—listening is easy. Well, listening isn't easy! It requires a great deal more attention and concentration than most people are willing to expend. The seemingly simple act of keeping one's mind from wandering requires an enormous amount of mental energy.

Like thinking, listening adheres to well-established patterns and moves in familiar directions. The moment your thinking or listening is confronted by an unfamiliar or threatening set of circumstances, it tends to pull back and revert to safe and familiar psychological territory. Developing the discipline needed to counter such a reaction requires three essential elements: patience, perserverance and motivation. These are perhaps, some of the major reasons why most people find listening difficult and, as a result, something they consciously or unconsciously do poorly.

Listening Automatically Yields Understanding

Knowing the letters of the alphabet does not mean you can spell nor does knowing a great many words mean that you can write. Likewise, understanding the language being spoken to you is no guarantee that you are listening to what is being said. There is more to the art of listening than meets the ear. Listening involves taking all of those bits of information you hear and, through a very complex neurological process, translating them into meaningful units of thought. Certainly you have had the experience of sitting in class, listening attentively to a professor, and coming away with as little understanding as when you entered. Why should that be? You understood the language spoken, you listened carefully, but why didn't you understand the lecture? Obviously, the ability to listen, by itself, is not enough. What is required is a deeper insight into the listening process, as a whole.

A Listening Philosophy

Basically, there are two ways you can think of listening: as a speaker-centered or an audience-centered phenomenon. If you choose the latter, you will be obliged to examine all of those factors capable of influencing how and why an audience listens. Should you choose the former, you must examine the same topics with regard to yourself as the speaker. Whichever route you select, you will notice rather quickly that both speaker and audience share a great many characteristics in common. It is becoming familiar with such common ground that will most benefit you as a speaker. For example, the quality of patience in an audience tends to increase its willingness to listen. Impatient audiences rarely listen well. Members are restless in their seats, prejudge a speaker's purpose or intent, talk among themselves, ask inappropriate questions, and transmit a variety of negative nonverbal signals to the speaker. Impatient speakers often transmit similar negative signals when they are impatient; i.e., restless movements, prejudging an audience's intent or purpose, rushing through a speech or making inappropriate references to time. In addition to patience, a person with a listening philosophy should also possess such qualities as selfishness, involvement, and the ability to think "listening."

Selfishness

Although the word selfishness has a negative connotation, it has its positive side. While you are speaking, say to yourself, "What I have to say is important. If I think it is important for my audience to listen, why shouldn't I extend the same courtesy to myself? As a concerned speaker, why shouldn't I hope for a selfish audience—one which will become annoyed if they cannot catch my every word, one that will say to itself, "I am going to pay strict attention to this speaker. Nothing will distract me. I will glean as much as I can from this lecture." Such selfishness will benefit everyone concerned.

Involvement

An archenemy of listening is the attitude conveyed by the popular saying, "I don't want to get involved." People subscribing to it must have special filters in their brains which prevent certain information from getting through. It is a defense mechanism which, from their point of view, has survival value. Unfortunately, unless someone is a hermit who lives in a cave on top of a mountain, remaining uninvolved is almost impossible. We are social animals and, as such, share a great deal in common with one another. Consequently, whenever you open your mouth as a speaker, you automatically become involved with your fellow human beings. By sharing a common biology, you cannot *not* become involved. As a speechmaker, this is an extremely important point. Almost anything you might choose to say about yourself, in all probability, will be confirmed by some member of your audience. This is particularly true with regard to such characteristically human traits as love, pride, pain, and the need to communicate.

People, wherever they are, reach out for other people. Although some may fear the consequences, they still want to become involved to some degree. As a speaker, you must capitalize on this tendency. Offer audience members involvement and they will listen. They will interpret such behavior as a sincere gesture of caring and sharing.

Think "Listening"

Living in a speech-centered society makes it easy to understand why the majority of inexperienced speakers think "speaking" rather than think "listening." Somehow, they convince themselves that if they can get through the speaking portion of their speech, everything will be alright. While such reasoning may hold up with the average run-of-the-mill speech, it rarely applies to the extraordinary speech. Outstanding speakers are vitally interested in the way their audiences will respond to their words—that is, how and to what they will listen.

Speakers who think "listening" are keenly aware of the fact that the best speech in the world will fall flat on its face if the audience to which it is directed fails to listen. Norbert Weiner, the father of cybernetics, captures the importance of this point when he states, "Speech is a joint game between the talker and the listener against the forces of confusion." It is, therefore, the solemn responsibility of all speakers to think "listening" and, by so doing, help their audiences more accurately grasp their meaning.

No communication occurs until there is a listener. It follows, then, that people feel a need for other people to listen to them. In certain states, to accommodate this need for someone to listen, listening services called "dial-a-counselor" and "dial-a-friend" have sprung up. On the West Coast, a coffee house provides its customers with listening services; for an hourly charge, a patron can drink coffee and have the undivided attention of a paid professional listener. Rapidly, more and more people are becoming aware of the fact that listening is the key to more effective communication.

Why People Listen

For a more rounded understanding of listening, you must know why people listen. They listen for a wide variety of reasons. Sometimes, they do it consciously; other times, unconsciously. We pick up considerably more information than we realize every day. Even while asleep, some of us continue to listen. In some instances, we can recall entire conversations. Seldom are our listening circuits completely switched off. After completing the following exercise, compare the reasons you gave for listening with our reasons in this chapter.

SPEECH EXPERIENCE: WHY DO YOU LISTEN?

Prepare a list of reasons why you listen in each of the following situations:

At home: _____

At work: _____

At school: _____

At a party: _____

To Find Things Out

Since we are living in an age of discovery, the mass media has seen fit to provide us with an overload of information. Television programming supplies us daily with information on such subjects as education, politics, ecology, religion, entertainment, meterology, philosophy, business, international affairs, child-rearing, yoga, physical fitness—the list seems endless. And, because people's interests differ, each subject soon finds its audience.

The desire "to know things" seems to dominate the listening habits of many individuals. Like moths, they are drawn to information of every description; i.e., how various machines operate, how to care for and prevent certain illnesses, how to build things, how to succeed in practically every occupation or profession, how to earn high grades, and so on. For those who listen to find out about things, *listening facilitates learning*.

To Be Courteous

In a civilized world, children are often taught to listen even though they are not interested in what is being said to them. This is particularly true when the person being listened to is an adult and the listener is a child or young adult. A staggering number of people, at this very moment, are being listened to in this manner—out of politeness or common courtesy. While such listening is, at best, only superficial in nature, it does pass as listening in most circles.

To Impress Others

What better way is there to impress others than with a show of knowledge or skill? And what better way is there of acquiring such knowledge or skill than listening? People who have a need to impress others listen for a different reason than those who listen in order to grow intellectually. Take something as simple as a streetcorner argument or a classroom disagreement. There are certain individuals who will listen intently to what is being said for only one reason—to seize upon an opportunity to impress others by repeating or expanding upon something that was already said. Or perhaps they listen for a mistake to be made which they can exploit. Whatever their listening intent, its expressed purpose is to impress or take advantage of others. This type of listening has little or nothing to do with learning.

For Profit

A number of professionals listen for profit; (e.g., grade advisors, guidance counselors, psychologists, psychiatrists, marriage counselors, and so on). Then there are those individuals who, on a social plane, profit from their ability and willingness to listen. A number of people are highly sought after because of their listening skills. While they may not profit in dollars and cents, they do profit in other ways. The advantages include social acceptance, feelings of special importance, peer group recognition, and identification and approval as someone who cares. While good listening appears to be endangered by compulsive talking, the psychological profits to be derived from listening must not be underestimated.

Out of Fear

We all know what it means to listen out of fear. The classroom situation is a classic example. If we don't listen, we run the risk of failing the course or at least receiving a poor grade. Then there is listening on the job. Supervisors, managers, and employers all must be listened to, regardless of whether what they say makes sense. In short, if you want to keep your job, you listen! And finally, on a more personal level, there are those who demand to be listened to. A failure to extend them an opportunity to talk with a minimum of interruptions may easily constitute a short-lived relationship. This phenomenon can also be found in some marriages where husbands or wives insist that their spouse listen or be criticized as uncaring. Thus, whether in a classroom, on the job, on a date, or in the home, there are people who listen out of fear.

To Compare Ideas and Thoughts

People have ideas on practically every subject. Some of them are popular, others are unpopular. Whatever type of ideas they are, individuals are prone to seek out others with similar ideas. This is particularly true with the unpopular ideas. The more unpopular the idea, the greater is the need to have that idea shared. We all walk around with our antennas up—listening about for ideas that match our own. If they do not come easily, some of us will actually go out of our way to seek them out. Listening to ideas which compliment our own is a well-known source of psychological comfort.

Recall how good it felt to have one of your teachers put forth an idea which you, yourself, held. Similar opinions, somehow, have an affinity for one another. Thus, without being fully conscious of it, many of us spend our days tuned into thoughts and feelings that reflect our own. We do this by listening selectively.

Whether you listen to *find things out, to be courteous, to impress others, for profit, out of fear,* or to *compare notes,* you listen for a reason. Knowing why a person listens makes for an excellent baseline from which to begin formulating a public speaking strategy. Gain a greater insight into your own reasons for listening by giving one example from your own life for each of the following:

- Listening to find things out_____
- Listening to be courteous_____
- Listening to impress others_____
- Listening for profit_____
- Listening out of fear_____
- Listening to compare notes_____

Concentration

Whether you are delivering a speech or sitting in an audience, an ability to concentrate is essential. Briefly, concentration may be described as exercising control over the subject matter at hand, and the direction in which your thoughts move. Deprived of either control or direction, all forms of communication run the risk of being misunderstood.

Practically everywhere we go, people insist that we pay attention, concentrate! They make this demand because inattention and a lack of concentration are two of the most common barriers to effective listening. One clever college student, realizing this tendency, came up with an extremely interesting scheme. On the day of her speech, she calmly walked to the front of the room, opened a gold locket which hung from her neck, and sprinkled the ashes it contained at the feet of the students in the front row. She then announced, "The title of my speech is CREMATION. These ashes are all that remain of my boyfriend, Larry." Rest assured, she had the undivided attention of every student in the room. Now, all that remained was for her to *hold* their attention.

Despite what most people might think, attention spans are very short. One expert suggests that the average attention span of an adult for a single act only lasts from 3 to 24 seconds. Take the act of listening—one's attention wanders constantly and decreases in strength. As a rule, we can cope with four to five objects at a time through our sense of sight, and five to eight through our sense of hearing. To illustrate this, pretend you are sitting in a class in geography and the teacher is tracing the routes taken by such explorers as Vasco de Gama or Magellan. On a large map, your teacher points to each step of a particular explorer's voyage and briefly explains its significance. It is expected that you have been paying close attention at all times and concentrating on what was being said. Unless your teacher is exceptionally gifted, your attention and concentration were seriously strained. Consider how many things in a typical classroom continuously bid for a student's attention; i.e., street noises, room temperature, preoccupation with an examination to be given the next period, hall noises, weather conditions visible through room windows, and the activity of other students. Only by exercising strict control over the subject at hand and the directions in which your thoughts would like to move will you be able to maintain your concentration. Only this will make it possible for you to pay the kind of close attention that is necessary for effective listening.

When a speaker or audience member pays close attention, it makes certain things possible. It enables them to *perceive, conceive, distinguish,* and *remember* elements central to the subject at hand. When you perceive something, you are made aware of it through your senses (seeing, hearing, tasting, touching and smelling). When you take whatever it is that you have become aware of and formulate it in your mind, you have conceived it. You are distinguishing such thoughts by comparing them with the information you have already acquired. And, lastly, the ability to recall what you have payed attention to in the past is called *remembering*. Successful listening incorporates the combined benefits of perceiving, conceiving, distinguishing, and remembering the substance of any given text. Additional aids to concentration include: 1) putting yourself in either the speaker's or the audience's place, 2) being on the alert for interesting statements, 3) becoming seriously involved with what you are saying or hearing, 4) disposing of any internal or external distractions, and 5) anticipating any upcoming sources of possible confusion.

As a means of determining how well you can concentrate, try this:

SPEECH EXPERIENCE: "IF I'M NOT MISTAKEN, YOU SAID . . ."

Step 1. All members of the class are to sit in a circle.

Step 2. All students are to participate in an open discussion using one of the following topics:

unisex clothes	compulsory education
federal health insurance	censorship in T.V.
teenage marriage	legalized prostitution
sexism in sports	value of the electoral college
racism in society	

Step 3. After a signal to begin has been given by the teacher, all participating members of the discussion group must adhere to this rule: Before anyone can speak, he or she must first repeat, in reasonably accurate terms, what the preceding speaker said. That individual must then agree that the interpretation was correct. The discussion should not be permitted to continue until the meaning intended by one speaker is accurately restated by the

next speaker. Naturally, the opening statement will not be a restatement. It should be kept in mind throughout this speech experience that a restatement of what a prior speaker is thought to have said need not be a word for word repetition. Paraphrase is a perfectly acceptable form. *Time Limit:* Approximately 15 minutes.

Step 4. A general discussion should now take place in which all participants are expected to volunteer their opinions of the experience and its relevance to real life listening situations.

A classroom experience like this puts listening to the test. If done properly, it should illustrate how people, accidentally and intentionally, listen badly. Quite innocently, without knowing that they are doing it, people twist what others say into knots. Basically, such individuals fall into three classes: 1) Additive listeners—those who expand or exaggerate what they hear. *Example:* If an accident involved five cars, the additive listener would say that it involved ten or twelve. 2) Subtractive listener—those who make less out of what they hear. *Example:* If there were ten cars in an accident, the subtractive listener would report there being only five cars involved. 3) Distortive listener—those who alter what they hear so that it differs significantly from what was originally said. *Example:* They would report as a minor automobile accident one in which several cars went out of control, drove off a bridge, and plunged helplessly into a raging river below.

Each of these listeners, as a result of inattention or spotty concentration, altered the messages they sincerely believed they heard. Though we all, at some time or another, have taken certain listening liberties with what others have said, it is the degree to which we have done it that makes a difference.

You Are What You Remember

Concentration involves attention. It also involves memory. Both theory and practice show that the more effectively one listens, the more one has to remember; the more one remembers, the more effectively one is able to listen. Whereas, remembering (an activated memory) is a different process from listening, the two are inseparably linked by the need to listen first. Perhaps, the single greatest obstacle to remembering is the failure to listen.

Inasmuch as we spend a good part of our lives collecting information (particularly during our years of formal education), we spend precious little time learning how to manage such information; that is, to manage our minds and memories.

The instant you stand up before an audience, unless you are going to mechanically read your speech as it is written, you will have to rely heavily upon your memory banks for information. You will be judged, to a great extent, upon what comes out of your mouth. This reinforces the notion that you are what you remember.

Since a speaker's fate depends largely upon a good memory, it seems fitting here to offer some advice about a concept called *familiarization.* It is founded on the premise that the basis of all learning lies in connecting what is new to us with something we already know. This is a basic technique of memorization. The ideas we have do not exist in isolation, but are connected with other ideas. When we memorize, we must link an old and a new idea.

Here is how memory expert, Ernest E. Wood, in his book, *Mind and Memory Training,* suggests you proceed:

Let an unfilled circle ◯ represent an idea. When this idea is familiar, in-

dicate it by darkening the entire circle, thus ● . But if the idea is not familiar

to you, denote it by a circle with an "X" in its center, in this manner ⊗ . You

may then symbolically say your problem is that of converting a ⊗ to a ● .

This you must do before attempting to memorize the ⊗ idea.

Memory problems can be reduced to the following degrees of difficulty:

- 1st Degree of Difficulty: ●──→● It is the easiest to deal with and

requires only linking the familiar to the familiar.

- 2nd Degree of Difficulty: Here you see an unfamiliar idea

which must be linked to a familiar one so that it can be associated in your

memory with what already exists there.

- 3rd Degree of Difficulty: Here we have two unfamiliar

ideas that need to be remembered. Each new idea must be tied to a familiar

one. Then, it is simply a matter of relating the two familiar ideas to one

another.

While all this connecting up of little symbols might be very interesting, it doesn't mean much until you, yourself, can see how it would work with an actual speechmaking situation. Let us apply these principles right now.

You are scheduled to deliver a speech in class tomorrow. Your subject is "the jury system." You want to make sure not to forget two things rated as 3rd Degree of Difficulty. You need to remember two Latin terms with which you are unfamiliar: *prima facie* and *sequester*. A *prima facie* case, in law, refers to one that is logically taken at face value—a case that is self-evident. *Sequester* means to separate, remove, or to closet; hence, after a case has been heard, the jury is asked to leave the courtroom and be sequestered (locked up) until it has reached a verdict. What you must do now in order to remember these terms is to link each of them with something familiar to you. For example, you might want to link *prima facie* with the Prime Minister of England. With the word *sequester*, you may prefer to link it with the thought of twelve jurors locked in a closet. The trick, no matter what images you use, is to link the unfamiliar with the familiar.

Encouraging Your Audience to Listen

Nothing could be more important to a speaker than having an audience pay attention, concentrate, and listen to what he or she is saying. Here are some valuable safeguards against your audience not paying attention, not concentrating, and not listening to what you have to say.

Clean Up Your Speech

Sloppy speech discourages listening. Contributing to sloppy speech are the mispronounciation of familiar words, an accent which interferes with understandability, dropping the endings of words, speaking in a monotone, and awkward phrasing. It might be a good idea for you to have your speech evaluated by a speech therapist so that you will know exactly what you must do to make it more listenable.

Pick an Interesting Topic

It is just as easy to pick an interesting topic as it is to pick an uninteresting one. Give some serious thought to your speech topic. Ask several people, whose opinion you respect, to choose a topic from a list you have compiled. And, for your own future reference, try to find out why they chose a particular topic.

Avoid Excessive Detail

Audiences generally dislike being put under pressure. In all likelihood, should your speech topic require a great deal of mental gymnastics, it will turn off your audience. They simply won't listen or, if they do, it will be a kind of token listening. If your speech does happen to contain certain unavoidable detail, try to make it as brief and simple as possible.

Don't Filibuster

It has been said that an audience's ability to tolerate a speech is proportional to how much their bottoms can endure—how long they can sit. A filibuster is a particularly long-winded speech in the Senate, issued by someone wanting to obstruct the passage of a bill. Audiences, whether in government or the private sector, dislike speakers who talk too much. Brevity is always in order and in good taste. To avoid going on longer than you should, time your speech carefully beforehand, and know exactly when to sum up your speech. Have the point at which you wish to wind down clearly marked in your notes.

Humor Is Not Always a Laughing Matter

Though humor in a speech can be a dynamic asset, it could also backfire. A careful audience analysis should indicate what your audience will and won't find laughable. A good rule to guide your judgment is: *When in doubt, leave it out.* Because many speakers are somewhat unsure of themselves, they think that making their audiences laugh will make their audiences like them. While audience laughter can be an excellent means of reducing tension, it is a risky business. They could easily be laughing at you, with you, or about something foolish that you said. Weigh your attempts at humor with extreme care.

Maintain Good Eye Contact

Not looking at your audience when you speak is unforgivable. Your eyes, like a television camera, must search out those to whom you are speaking. People who are being looked at tend to listen much more attentively than those who are not. Work your audience with your eyes—survey the audience from right to left and front to back. Insist with your eyes that everyone in your audience listen.

Organize Your Material

Few things will be tolerated less by any discriminating audience than a poorly organized speech—one that jumps around without any rhyme or reason. A responsible speaker is expected to organize his or her speech so that it flows easily from thought to thought, from section to section. Audiences resent having to pull a speech together in their minds—having to provide the necessary organization which should have been supplied by the speaker. Release your audience from having to do this by organizing your speech thoroughly. See to it that your material moves along in such a way as to make your audience comfortable, both mentally and physically. Remember, disorganization invites disinterest, and disinterest means poor listening.

Be Sensitive to Nonverbal Cues

Audiences, if carefully observed, give off a great deal of information. Speakers who are aware of this fact can maintain, like radar screens, a constant sense of their audience's mood. When an audience ceases to listen, it communicates this to the speaker in a number of ways. Most of these signals are nonverbal in nature. They will break eye contact with the speaker, become restless, seek out personal reading matter, visit the lavatories, or simply get up and leave. Facial expressions are also an excellent source of information. When members of an audience have ceased to listen, they often wear bored, disappointed, annoyed, apathetic and unhappy expressions on their faces. In no uncertain terms, such facial expressions are indications that the speaker has lost the ball and has been denied the audience's willingness to listen.

The speaker who is sensitive to these signs can use them to his or her advantage. Before becoming any further alienated from the audience, the speaker must make efforts to recapture their interest. By being unaware of these signs, the speaker forfeits any chance of compensating for the decline in listening.

Keep an Open Mind

In the moment that your audience discovers your mind to be closed on an important issue, it will tend to tune you out. This is especially true if the point of view to which your mind is closed happens to be that held by the audience. Audiences have the reputation of perking up their ears when the speaker supports their opinion on a particular subject and of shutting them down when the opinion is one of disagreement.

SPEECH EXPERIENCE: Getting Your Audience's Attention and Holding It.[6]

Step 1. Have two good talkers go to the front of the room and, facing the audience, stand next to one another inside of imaginary circles two feet in diameter, with three feet between the circles.

Step 2. Both speakers are to talk on any subject which interests them for one or two minutes without interruption.

---

[6] Abné M. Eisenberg, *Understanding Communication in Business and the Professions* (New York: Macmillan Publishing Co., 1978), p. 230.

Step 3. At a signal from the teacher, both speakers, each remaining within their own circle, are to begin talking at the same time. They should both strive to get and hold their audience's attention and interest. They should make every effort to draw the audience's attention away from the other speaker. To accomplish this, they may use such devices as vocal tones, colorful gestures, body movements and facial expressions, or an exciting topic. At all times, they are to ignore the other speaker.

Step 4. After the teacher has signaled the pair of speakers to stop, the entire class should be invited into a group discussion of what happened during this listening experience. Members of the class should advance as many reasons as possible to explain why they listened to one speaker and not the other at any given time. Also, if their attention shifted back and forth between speakers, they must explain why they think it happened.

Most of you have not had the experience of listening to two speakers at the same time, at least not from the same speaker's platform. The closest you may have come to this type of experience is when a couple of friends talk to you on a streetcorner or at a party. At first, it feels a bit strange, and you wish one of them would stop while the other one spoke. However, after a while (if they continue to speak at the same time), you begin to divide your attention between them. The questions raised by this speech experience is, "What determines to which speaker you will listen at any given moment?" Here, arranged in a scrambled order, are the most common things to which members of an audience generally pay attention. Rearrange them according to your evaluation of their relative importance.

1. Topic   1. _____
2. Charisma   2. _____
3. Loudness   3. _____
4. Clothing   4. _____
5. Eye Contact   5. _____
6. Voice Rhythm   6. _____
7. Vocabulary   7. _____
8. Enthusiasm   8. _____
9. Posture   9. _____
10. Gestures   10. _____

Summary

Having come this far, you should appreciate the fact that both audiences and speakers need to listen to each other if public communication is to be effective. And, to make you more aware of the critical role played by listening, this chapter has taken a multidimensional approach to the subject which includes: a) placing listening into a workable perspective, b) presenting current listening myths, c) advancing a listening philosophy, d) listing reasons why people listen, e) spelling out the importance of concentration and memory training, and, lastly, f) advising the speaker how to encourage his or her audience to listen.

CHAPTER 13

The Informer

Behavioral Objectives

After reading this chapter, you should have a better understanding of:

- how to use informative discourse in your daily life.
- the kinds of informative messages you send and receive daily.
- the basic types of informational messages including messages of explanation, description, and definition.
- the purpose of the informational message.
- how to increase audience retention by relating your speech to the lives and experiences of your listeners.
- how to analyze an informative speech.
- how to prepare, rehearse, and deliver an informative speech.

Introduction

The next three chapters provide you with an opportunity to use the skills and techniques we have discussed and rehearsed thus far. The emphasis in this particular chapter is on presenting information. The skills you gained while studying the chapters on choosing a topic, listening, audiences, verbal and nonverbal communication, support, and organization are all relevant to the work you will now be asked to do.

SPEECH EXPERIENCE: INFORMATION, PLEASE.

1. Make a list of all the informative messages you receive during the next 24 hours. For each message, identify the source of the message, the medium through which it is communicated, the type of information that was transferred, and whether you initially understood the message as the speaker intended.

2. Compile a second list of the informative messages you sent to other people during this same time period. For each message, note the type of information contained in it, the medium through which you sent it, and your receiver's reaction to it; i.e., whether it was understood as you intended.

3. Be prepared to make a three-minute presentation to the class in which you report your findings. Identify the different types of informative messages you send and receive regularly, and explain how sender and receiver behaviors can contribute to the success or failure of a message. Use examples and illustrations to support your conclusions.

Analyzing your experiences with informational messages as well as sharing the experiences of others can help you achieve your informative speaking goals and refine your informative speaking skills. Let us now identify the main types of informative speaking we engage in regularly, the communicative purposes served by the delivery of these messages, and the strategies that can be used to improve the chance for success of each message.

Types of Informational Messages

We send and receive information every day. Through this exchange, senders and receivers develop shared meanings and understandings. Thus, whenever you send an informational message, your purpose is to present the information contained in that communication in such a way that it will be understood and retained by your listeners. Whether your goal is to explain how glass is blown into shapes, to describe the appearance of the Great Pyramid, to introduce a new club policy to members, to discuss research findings on the effectiveness of laetrile, or to list the reasons why earthquakes occur, your ultimate purpose is to encourage listener comprehension. Informative speeches commonly deal with people, places, things, concepts, occurrences, processes and problems. The list of potential informative speech topics is virtually endless. Keeping this in mind, let us examine a number of representative informative speech formats.

Messages of Explanation

At its simplest level, the informative presentation may be considered to be an explanatory speech, or a how-to speech: how to prepare chili con carne, how to operate a CB radio, how to stain wood, how to use mouth-to-mouth resuscitation, how to change a flat tire. Sometimes, the explanatory speech lends itself to humor or satire, as when a speaker appears to transmit information no one really wants to learn: how to develop high blood pressure, how to fail a course, how to have a car accident. It should be noted, however, that in addition to utilizing humor, such speeches also serve serious informational purposes by subtly telling an audience how such problems may be avoided. As we saw in an earlier chapter, delivering clear, understandable, and easy to follow instructions makes as many, if not more, demands on the speaker as listening to such directions makes on the listener.

Variations on the explanatory speech include: how not to do something, how something operates, or how it was developed. Each of these forms of delivery requires a slightly different arrangement of the information being presented.

Messages of Description

Speakers who deliver descriptive speeches seek to help their listeners construct mental closeups of people, places, or things. You can achieve such a goal by finding ways to describe the size, shape, weight, color, age, and/or condition of your subject. A major characteristic of the descriptive speech is its reliance on imagery. An image is a group of words that trigger the senses. Thus, descriptions function to fill in the qualities of a person, place, or object by telling how it looks, sounds, smells, tastes, feels, or moves. Sample topics for descriptive speeches include: "The Grand Canyon," "An Ant Hill," "The Old Scientist," "The Mona Lisa" and "King Arthur's Castle."

Messages of Definition

A definition can also serve as the basis for an informative speech. During such a speech, the speaker would discuss the meaning of particular words and phrases. In fact, among the best topics for definitional talks are general or abstract terms such as fear, freedom, socialism, obscenity, morality, jealousy, expressionism, and prejudice. Also worthwhile topics are controversial terms like women's liberation, free speech, the sexual revolution, common labels such as "a good teacher," "the ideal job," "good citizenship," and "the perfect friend." How a speech of definition is organized depends on the purpose of the speaker.

Speeches of definition can compare and contrast. For example, you might compare and contrast a good teacher's behavior with a poor teacher's behavior. Definitional speeches can also classify; that is, break a concept into smaller parts. Thus, the concept of jazz could be divided into subsections: improvisation, syncopated rhythms, and so on. Speeches of definition can also trace processes. A speaker delivering a talk on the topic of lung cancer could make the illness more understandable to the audience by detailing the step-by-step process of the disease from its first symptoms to its full development.

Achieving the Purpose of Your Informational Message

The purpose of each of these types of informative speeches is to provide the members of an audience with a learning experience. If you want your listeners to be receptive, to comprehend and retain your message, you must employ certain principles of motivation and reinforcement to help them learn. You need to make your listeners aware of the importance of the information you bring them. You can do this by relating your ideas to their experiences and by finding ways to help them recall and apply the information you give them. Use these guidelines to help you accomplish these goals.

The More a Speaker's Information Relates to the Lives and Experiences of an Audience, the More Readily That Information Will Be Received

Audience members automatically find information relating to life and death issues more relevant. Such crucial topics are, however, relatively limited in number. As a result, you really have to work hard to make your information relevant. You can do this by directing your comments to perceived audience needs. Recognize that for a topic to be considered relevant by your listeners, you have to establish what it has to do with their lives.

SPEECH EXPERIENCE: RELEVANCY RESEARCHERS

1. Select any piece of information from a resource such as *Ripley's Believe It or Not, The Guinness Book of Records,* a textbook, an encyclopedia, or other reference works.

2. Working individually or in groups, devise as many ways as possible to

make the information relevant to each of the following groups: the class, the people in your neighborhood, a business luncheon, the police force.

3. Present your ideas to the class in a two to three minute informative speech.

Audience members seek out and retain information which they believe relates to them. How does this excerpt from the work of psychiatrist Karl Menninger reflect this fact?

My first observation is that mental illness is something that may occur in the lives of any of us. It always develops rather unexpectedly. Nobody plans to get mentally ill, you know, and nobody expects to get mentally ill. We all expect we may get pneumonia or we may get a bad cold next winter. We expect physical illnesses of certain kinds. But no one expects a mental illness.

Nevertheless, mental illness does come; it strikes down friends and acquaintances, the prominent and the lowly, rich victims and poor ones. It is no respector of persons. It may come to any one of us.[1]

Presenting Startling Information Helps Improve the Information Reception and Retention of an Audience

Dr. Thomas Elmendorf recognized this when he spoke these words before a Congressional committee investigating the effects of television.

By the time a child is 18 years old, he has spent more hours in front of a television set than he has in school. Over TV he will have witnessed by that time some 18,000 murders and countless highly detailed incidents of robbery, arson, bombings, shootings, beatings, forgery, smuggling, and torture—averaging approximately one per minute in the standard television cartoon for children under the age of 10.[2]

Presenting Humorous Information Serves to Increase the Willingness of an Audience to Listen

You can hold the attention of your audience by making listening to your message more enjoyable. James Lavenson, a business executive, realized this when he said:

Frankly, I think the hotel business has been one of the most backward in the world. There's been very little change in the attitude of room clerks in the 2000 years since Joseph arrived in Bethlehem and was told they'd lost his reservation.[3]

[1] Karl Menninger, "Healthier than Healthy," *A Psychiatrist's World*, (New York: The Viking Press, Inc., 1959), p. 635.

[2] Thomas Elmendorf, "Violence on TV," *Vital Speeches of the Day* **42** (October 1, 1976) pp. 764–767.

[3] James Lavenson, "Think Strawberries," *Vital Speeches of the Day*, **40**: 346 (March 15, 1974).

If these guidelines are buttressed with good support, coherent organization, and effective delivery, the odds in favor of your audience displaying greater receptivity, comprehension, and retention will be markedly increased.

Now that we have enumerated certain principles of informative speaking, let us see how they work in practice. Read the following informative speeches. Make a special effort to discover as many of the techniques used by the speakers as possible. Try to imagine what you might have done differently in each case.

Can't Nobody Here Use This Language? [4]

I learned last May you have to be careful in speaking to a group of professional communicators. After I conducted a writer's workshop at the Toronto Conference of the International Association of Business Communicators, Janine Lichacz wrote me to speak here tonight and used the communication techniques I had recommended. She even included a footnote citing my lecture. I am susceptible to good communication—and to flattery—so I am pleased to be with you to discuss your topic for the evening, "The Use of Language in the Art of Speechwriting."

I suppose we must begin by shaking our heads woefully over the sad state of language today, whether in formal speeches, casual conversation, or in writing. Most of us in this room no doubt agree with the generally negative tone of *Time Magazine*'s year-end assessment of 1978 which claims "our language has been besieged by vulgarities." But to preserve our sanity as professionals in communication, most of us would probably join *Time* in optimistically expecting English somehow to survive and even to prosper.

On the negative side, if I may use a vulgarity to criticize vulgarity. I am often moved in my own profession to paraphrase Casey Stengel and ask, "Can't nobody here use this language?"

To generalize about the language ability of students, I would say far too many of them can't express themselves well, and they don't seem to care. The most significant hollow verbalization among students today is not "y'know." It is "needless to say."

I have a respectful appreciation of the rules of the classical rhetoricians, and on occasion I have discussed in class the stylistic device of antithesis. One of my students, quite unconsciously I am sure, gave the technique a try in a speech on physical fitness and said, "A well-rounded body makes for a well-rounded mind." We've come a long way down from *mens sana in corpore sano*.

Faculty members are often worse. Some time back I attended a conference on setting standards for language competence in Virginia's schools. In one presentation a professor from a distinguished university repeatedly used the expression "scribal language." I finally turned to someone to ask what the devil that meant and was told the term was a fancy synonym for "writing". I wrote a letter to the professor suggesting a requirement for a report on competence in language should be competence in language. He did not take it well.

One of my colleagues wrote a lengthy document on the proper use of classrooms and stated forthrightly, "It is necessary to employ characteristics of uniqueness where uniqueness is held to be important. The idea of flexibility should be placed in a balanced way with other particular instructional and design needs to achieve a maximized learning atmosphere. In some instances, degrees of flexibility may have to give way to other equally creative and significant dimensions of a classroom environment."

I happen to know what that means, and I will be happy to provide a translation at

[4] Jerry Tarver, "Can't Nobody Here Use This Language?", *Vital Speeches of the Day*, 45: 420–3 (May 1, 1979).

twenty cents a word. If you want the answer, send your dollar to me at the University of Richmond.

A certain church group which supports many colleges throughout the South regularly sends me a publication which purports to be educational. Leaders of this group use up a goodly portion of the alphabet with the impressive degrees they attach to their names and employ this publication to increase the size of the audience for their various pronouncements. The quality of the writing is so gloriously and innocently bad that the entire magazine could easily pass as a satire written by a clever member of a high school debating team. One of the speeches from a couple of months ago contained the striking statement, "Drifting causes a loss of direction." That was one of the major points in the speech which incidently was delivered at the inauguration of a college president.

On the positive side, *Time* finds our language "enriched by vigorous phrases and terms" from such sources as CB radio and situation comedies. The major bright spots I see are the writing in advertising and on the bathroom wall. Let me quickly add that the *worst* writing also appears in these two places. Some of the most crude and senseless tripe I have encountered has appeared in ads or graffiti. But when they are good, they are very, very good. Both the writer and the graffiti artist must work within a small compass. They must be concise. To the point. And each is moved, urgently moved, to communicate. Unfortunately for the motivation of the advertiser, I am one of those people who can enjoy the sizzle and forego the steak. I don't smoke cigars, and I don't even remember the brand involved, but who can forget the classical commercial in which Edie Adams used to urge, "Why don't you pick one up and smoke it sometime?" I admit I don't have a Texaco credit card, but the little I read of modern academic poetry moves me as much as the soothing jingle, "You can trust your car to the man who wears the star."

My favorite graffiti is the plaintive sort. A poor soul eloquently crying out to be understood. In the men's room just down from my office, someone in apparent anguish wrote with painstaking care in the grout between the tiles, "What in the hell am I doing here?" Weeks passed before someone undertook a reply. Whether done in a spirit of helpfulness or malice, I cannot say, but finally in different handwriting, there appeared, "If this is an existential question, contact Dr. Hall in the Philosophy Department. If this is a theological question, contact Dr. Allen in the Religion Department. If this is a biological question, take a look."

Years ago I saw a quotation printed on a little gummed paper strip which had been attached to the wall of a men's room off the New Jersey Turnpike. It offered a simple Biblical text and had apparently come to the attention of a tired truck driver. The quotation asked the question, "If God be for us, who can be against us?" No doubt in despair, the truck driver had replied underneath, "the dispatcher."

How can we capture the vitality of the best of grafitti and advertising in our own writing and speaking? Perhaps some of you would agree with a sociologist friend of mine, Dr. James Sartain. Whenever Jim is offered a chance to improve his teaching, he says, "I already know how to teach better than I do." I suspect this is true for most of us. So, we may not be discovering tonight as much as reminding.

But there could be some ground for controversy. Let me first of all attempt to play down the current emphasis on correctness. Grammar—much like spelling—is one of the manual skills of expression. Almost any fool can learn to make a subject agree with a verb according to the standard rules of English.

I think the pseudo-objectivity of correctness attracts many followers. But grammatical systems are, after all, themselves arbitrary. We could change the rules if we wanted to. Our failure to alter our grammar to include a sexless pronoun can hardly be blamed on the sanctity of the rules. If you wish to attack the sentence, "He done done it," you can't attack it by claiming it does not follow a rigid set of rules. It just doesn't follow the system most widely taught.

I'm not suggesting you break rules at random. Just don't be too proud of yourself for not using "very unique" or "hopefully, it will rain." And remember George Orwell's advice that you should break any rule rather than "say anything outright barbarous."

My desk dictionary includes among its definitions of the word function, "The action for which . . . a thing is specially fitted or used or for which a thing exists. The concept of function reminds us that words act upon people.

Let me give you an example of a piece of communication which illustrates function. You may recall in *Catch 22* Lt. Milo Minderbinder at one point instituted an elaborate procedure for going through chow line. It involved signing a loyalty oath, reciting the pledge of allegiance and singing "The Star Spangled Banner." But the entire system was destroyed one day when Major de Coverly returned from a trip and cut through the red tape with two words: "Gimme eat."

That simple, and quite ungrammatical, phrase shows language in action. Words at work. Expression that eliminates the unnecessary gets down to cases.

A grasp of function causes a writer to think of results. Impact. Effect. Audience becomes important. Who will read or listen? Why? Function calls for the communicator to examine the reason for the existence of a given communication and to choose words that will be a means of expression and not an end.

Next, as I said, we must be sensitive to quality. I know of no objective way to determine quality. But I agree with Robert Pirsig who insists in *Zen and the Art of Motorcycle Maintenance* that most people intuitively know quality in language when they encounter it.

Most of us have written material we knew was merely adequate. No errors. All the intended ideas in place. No complaints from the boss or the editor. But deep down inside we knew we had done a pedestrian job.

I use a chill bump test for quality. For poor writing or speaking I get one type of chill bumps. For good language, a better brand of chill bumps. For most of the mediocre stuff in between, no chill bumps at all.

Quality does not mean fancy. When General McAuliffe reportedly answered a Nazi surrender ultimatum with the words "nuts," his language had no less quality than the declaration of the Indian Chief Joseph. "From where the sun now stands, I will fight no more forever," Either of my examples would probably not fare well in a classroom exercise in English composition. But anyone who used such language in that situation would be guilty of ignoring the concept of function.

Only after we agree that we must be concerned about function and quality can we properly turn our attention to rules. I offer the following ten guidelines for the speech writer. Some of the guidelines apply primarily to the language of speeches; some apply primarily to the language of writing. I do not consider my list exhaustive, and I should point out that the items on it are not mutually exclusive.

Guideline Number One. Be simple. Tend toward conversational language. Earlier this month I conducted speaker training for a corporation which distributed a speech manuscript containing such expressions as "difficult to ascertain" and "management audits attest." There's nothing wrong with these phrases in print, but I wouldn't say "ascertain" or "attest" out loud in front of the Rotary Club. "Find out" and "show" would sound more natural.

Guideline Number Two. Be expansive. Speeches use more words per square thought than well-written essays or reports. The next time you get a speech writing assignment, see if you can't talk your boss into throwing out two-thirds of the content and expanding the remainder into a fully developed expression of a limited topic. I realize gobbledygook is wordy, but I assume none of us will be writing gobbledygook. And I don't know of anyone who has suggested that Martin Luther King's "I Have a Dream" speech suffered from excessive repetition.

Guideline Number Three. Be concrete. Specific terms limit a listener's chances to misunderstand. Back in November, Combined Communications Corporation President, Karl Eller, gave a speech out in Phoenix in which he used a glass of milk to describe our free enterprise system. He said, "Some farmer bred and raised the cow. Some farmer owned and tended the land it grazed on. He bought special feed from someone. Some farmer milked the cow or cows and sold the milk to someone else who processed it, pasteurized it and packaged it. He sold it to a wholesaler who sold it to a retailer. And all along the line the produce was either made better or its distribution was simplified and narrowed, and a lot of people had jobs. Wealth was created." I have quoted less than a fifth of Eller's description. I'm convinced nobody left his speech confused.

Guideline Number Four. Be vivid. Appeal to the senses. President Carter's speech writers attempted to paint a word picture in the state of the union address when they wrote of the power of nuclear weapons "towering over all this volatile changing world, like a thundercloud in a summery sky." I am reminded of Mark Twain's distinction between the lightning and the lightning bug. The Carter image fails to stir the imagination. But vivid language can be effective.

In demonstrating the point that his company's nuclear plants are safe, Ontario Hydro Board Chairman Robert Taylor told members of the Kiwanis Club of Ottawa, "You could sit naked, if you had a mind to, at the boundary fence around the Pickering nuclear station for a year, drink the water and eat the fish from nearby Lake Ontario, and you would pick up a total of five units of radiation. That's less than you would get from natural sources such as rocks, good air and cosmic rays. A single chest x-ray would give you eight times that exposure."

Guideline Number Five. Be personal. Use the personal pronoun. Don't be afraid of making a speaker sound egotistical. Ego springs from attitude, not language. A modest speaker can say "I know" and "I did" and "I was" with no problem. But I know a fellow who is so egotistical he can say "Good morning" and seem to take credit for it. Still, it's hard to imagine Caesar saying, "One comes, one sees, one conquers."

Guideline Number Six. Be smooth. Speech demands uncluttered rhythm. Avoid clauses which interrupt your idea. It's a bit awkward for a speaker to say, "William Safire, former Nixon speech writer," but "former Nixon speech writer William Safire" flows a bit better. If you must add a clause, make a big deal out of it. For example, you might say, "Jogging—which can have a fantastically positive effect on your sex life—may clear up minor sinus problems."

Feel free to use contractions if they help the flow of the speech. In conversation the absence of contractions often becomes a device for emphasis. If you don't use contractions in speaking, you risk overemphasis.

In writing jokes into a speech, be sure to put the "they saids" *before* the quoted material, especially in punch lines. Observe the effect of reading: "Why does a chicken cross the road?" she asked. "To get to the other side," he answered.

Guideline Number Seven. Be aggressive. Don't use the loaded language on your enemies. Let me get my prejudice clearly before you. As a consumer, I deeply resent the careless use of the term "consumer advocate." As a breather of air and drinker of water and observer of sunsets, I resent the haphazard application of the term, "environmentalist" to anyone who can gather six friends in a living room to organize a Snailshell Defiance. My sympathy goes out to the engineer who finds it all but impossible to explain how fish like warm water without describing the fish as victims of thermal pollution.

I do not assume that American business and industry always have in mind the best interests of consumers, the environment, and fish, but we need to avoid one-sided language if we are to have an honest discussion of issues. I would prefer to keep away from loaded words or to qualify them with "so-called" or "self-styled."

Guideline Number Eight. Be purposeful. Meaning is assigned to words by listeners; your intent is less important than your listener's perception. The controversy over sexism and racism in language can be settled if we remember words are symbols which listeners interpret. I will not use the phrase "girls in the office" because a significant number of people who hear me will react negatively. For the same reason, avoid "a black day" on the market, in favor of a bleak day or a bad day. We need not resort to awkward constructions. You might not want to say "unmanned boat," but this does not mean you must blunder along with "unpeopled boat." What about "a boat with no one aboard."

Guideline Number Nine. Be eloquent. Use an occasional rhetorical device to enhance your expression of an idea. Indulge at times in a little light alliteration. Balance a pair of phrases: "Ask not what the country can do for General Motors, ask what General Motors can do for the country."

Guideline Number Ten. Be adaptable. Write to suit your speaker. A speech writer for Phillips Petroleum once described his role as being that of a clone. A writer must know the speaker's feelings and the speaker's style. And remember your speaker may need a tersely worded speech one week and a flowery one the next.

My guidelines are far easier to express than to execute. Writing a good speech requires talent, brains, and effort. If you write for others, add to the requirements a self-effacing attitude and a thick skin.

Our language will not be saved by the exhortations of evangelists in the Church of the Fundamental Grammar. It can be saved by writers and speakers with a grasp of function and a sense of quality. We should be proud of your parent organization's contribution; IABC enrolls and nurtures communicators who use language well.

Think Strawberries [5]

I came from the balcony of the hotel business. For ten years as a corporate director of Sonesta Hotels with no line responsibility, I had my office in a little building next door to The Plaza. I went to the hotel every day for lunch and often stayed overnight. I was a professional guest. You know nobody knows more about how to run a hotel than a guest. Last year, I suddenly fell out of the corporate balcony and had to put my efforts in the restaurants where my mouth had been, and in the rooms and night club and theater into which I'd been putting my two cents.

In my ten years of kibitzing, all I had really learned about the hotel business was how to use a guest room toilet without removing the strip of paper that's printed "Sanitized for Your Protection." When the hotel staff found out I'd spent my life as a salesman and that I'd never been a hotelier, never been to Cornell Hotel School, and that I wasn't even the son of a waiter, they were in a state of shock. And Paul Sonnabend, President of Sonesta, didn't help their apprehension much when he introduced me to my executive staff with the following kind words: "The Plaza has been losing money the last several years and we've had the best management in the business. Now we're going to try the worst."

Frankly, I think the hotel business has been one of the most backward in the world. There's been very little change in the attitude of room clerks in the 2,000 years since Joseph arrived in Bethlehem and was told they'd lost his reservation. Why is it that a sales clerk at Woolworth asks your wife, who points to the pantyhose if she wants three or six pairs—and your wife is all by herself—but the maître d' asks you and your wife, the only human being within a mile of the restaurant, "How many are you?"

Hotel salesmanship is retailing at its worst. But at the risk of inflicting cardiac arrest on our guests at The Plaza when they first hear shocking expressions like "Good Morning" and "Please" and "Thank you for coming," we started a year ago to see if it

[5] James Lavenson, op. cit., p. 346–8.

was possible to make the 1;400 employees of The Plaza into genuine hosts and hostesses. Or should I say "salesmen?"

A tape recorder attached to my phone proved how far we had to go. "What's the difference between your $85 suite and your $125 suite?" I'd ask our reservationist, disguising my voice over the phone. You guessed it: "$40!"

"What's going on in the Persian Room tonight?" I asked the Bell Captain. "Some singer" was his answer. "Man or woman?" I persisted. "I'm not sure" he said, "which made me wonder if I'd even be safe going there.

Why is it, I wondered, that the staff of a hotel doesn't act like a family playing hosts to guests whom they've invited to their house? It didn't take too long after becoming a member of the family myself, to understand one of the basic problems. Our 1,400 family members didn't even know each other! With that large a staff, working over eighteen floors, six restaurants, a night club, a theater, and three levels of subbasement, including a kitchen, a carpentry shop, plumbing and electrical shops, a full commercial laundry—how would they ever know who was working there, and who was a guest or just a purveyor passing through? Even the old-timers who might recognize a face after a couple of years would have no idea of the name connected to it. It struck me that if our own people couldn't call each other by name, smile at each other's familiar face, say good morning *to each other*, how could they be expected to say amazing things like "Good Morning, Mr. Jones" to a guest? A year ago The Plaza name tag was born. The delivery took place on my lapel. And it's now been on 1,400 lapels for over a year. Everyone, from dishwashers to the General Manager, wears his name where every other employee, and of course every guest, can see it. Believe it or not, our people say hello to each other—by name—when they pass in the halls and the offices. At first our regular guests thought The Plaza was entertaining some gigantic convention, but now even the old-time Plaza regulars are able to call our bellmen and maids by name. We've begun to build an atmosphere of welcome with the most precious commodity in the world— our names. *And* our guests' names.

A number of years ago, I heard Dr. Ernest Dichter, head of the Institute of Motivational Research, talk about restaurant service. He had reached a classic conclusion; when people come to a fine restaurant, they are hungrier for *recognition* than they are for food. It's true. If the maître d' says "We have your table ready, Mr. Lavenson," then as far as I'm concerned the chef can burn the steak and I'll still be happy.

When someone calls you by name and you don't know his, a strange feeling of discomfort comes over you. When he does it twice you *have* to find out *his* name. This we see happening with our Plaza name tags. When a guest calls a waiter by name, the waiter wants to call the guest by name. It will drive him nuts if he doesn't know. He'll ask the maître d', and if he doesn't know he'll ask the bellman, who will ask the front desk . . . calling the guests by name has a big payoff. It's called a *tip*.

At first there was resistance to name tags—mostly from the oldtime, formally trained European hoteliers. I secretly suspect they liked being incognito when faced with a guest complaint. We only had one staff member who said he'd resign before having his dignity destroyed with a name tag. For sixteen years he'd worn a rosebud in his lapel and that, he said, was his trademark and everyone knew him by it. His resignation was accepted along with that of the rosebud. Frankly, there are moments when I regret the whole idea myself. When I get on a Plaza elevator and all the passengers see my name tag, they know I work there. Suddenly, I'm the official elevator pilot, the host. I can't hide, so I smile at everybody, say "good morning" to perfect strangers I'd ordinarily ignore. The ones that don't go into shock, smile back. Actually, they seem to mind less the fact that a trip on a Plaza elevator, built in 1907, is the equivalent of commuting to Manhattan from Greenwich.

There are 600 Spanish-speaking employees at The Plaza. They speak Spanish. They don't read English. The employee house magazine was in English. So was the employee bulletin board. So were the signs over the urinals in the locker rooms that suggest cigarette butts don't flush too well. It was a clue as to why some of management's messages weren't getting through. The employee house magazine is now printed one side in English, the other in Spanish. The bulletin board and other staff instructions are in two languages. We have free classes in both languages for departmental supervisors. It's been helping.

With 1,400 people all labeled and smiling we were about ready last June to make salesmen out of them. There was just one more obstacle to overcome before we started suggesting they "ask for the order." They had no idea what the product was they would be selling. Not only didn't they know who was playing in the Persian Room, they didn't know we had movies—full-length feature films without commercials—on the closed-circuit TV in the bedrooms. As a matter of fact, most of them didn't know what a guest room looked like, unless they happened to be a maid or a bellman.

The reason the reservationists thought $40 was the difference between two suites was because they'd never been in one, much less actually slept there. To say our would-be salesmen lacked product knowledge would be as much an understatement as the line credited to President Nixon if he had been the Captain of the Titanic. My son told me that if Nixon had been Captain of the Titanic, he probably would have announced to the passengers there was no cause for alarm—they were just stopping to pick up ice.

Today, if you ask a Plaza bellman who's playing in the Persian Room he'll tell you Ednita Nazzaro. He'll tell you because he's seen her. In the contract of every Persian Room performer, there's now a clause requiring him to first perform for our employees in the cafeteria before he opens in the Persian Room. Our employees see the star first, before the guests.

And if you ask a room clerk or a telephone operator what's on the TV movies, they'll tell you because they've seen it—on the TV sets running the movies continuously in the employees' cafeteria.

Believe me, if you are having your lunch in our cafeteria and watch "Female Response" or "Swedish Fly Girls" on the TV set, you won't forget the film. You might, however, suspect the chef has put Spanish fly in your spaghetti.

Our new room clerks now have a week of orientation. It includes spending a night in the hotel and a tour of our 1,000 guest rooms. They can look out the windows and see the $40 difference in suites, since a view of the Park doesn't even closely resemble the back of the Avon building.

As I mentioned, about six months ago, we decided it was time to take a hard look at our sales effort. I couldn't find it. The Plaza had three men with the title "salesman"—and they were good men. But they were really sales*service* people who took the orders for functions or groups who came through the doors and sought us out. Nobody, but nobody, ever left the palace, crossed the moat at Fifth Avenue, and went looking for business. We had no one knocking on doors, no one asking for the order. The Plaza was so dignified it seemed demeaning to admit we needed business. If you didn't ask us you wouldn't ask you. So there! Our three sales-service people were terrific once you voluntarily stepped inside our arena. You had to ring our doorbell. We weren't ringing yours or anyone else's.

This condition wasn't unique to our official Sales Department. It seemed to be a philosophy shared by our entire staff—potentially larger sales staff of waiters, room clerks, bellmen, cashiers, and doormen. If you wanted a second drink in the Oak Bar, you got it by tripping the waiter. You asked for it. If you wanted a room you were quoted the minimum rate. If you wanted something better or larger, you had to ask for it. If you wanted to stay at the hotel an extra night, you had to ask. You were never invited. Sometimes I think there's a secret pack among hotelmen. It's a secret oath you take when you graduate from hotel school. It goes like this: "I promise I will never ask for the order."

When you're faced with as old and ingrained tradition as that, halfway countermeasures don't work. We started a program with all our guest contact people using a new secret oath: "Everybody sells!" And we meant everybody—maids, cashiers, waiters, bellmen—the works. We talked to the maids about suggesting room service, to the door-men about mentioning dinner in our restaurants, to cashiers about suggesting return reservations to departing guests. And we talked to waiters about strawberries.

A waiter at The Plaza makes anywhere from $10,000 to $20,000 a year. The difference between those two figures is, of course, tips. When I was in the advertising agency business, I thought I was fast at computing 15 percent. I'm a moron compared to a waiter. Our suggestions for selling strawberries fell on responsive ears when we described a part of the Everybody Sells program for our Oyster Bar restaurant. We figured, with just the same number of customers in the Oyster Bar, that if the waiters would ask every customer if he'd like a second drink, wine, or beer with the meal, and then dessert—given only one out of four takers we'd increase our sales volume by $364,000 a year. The waiters were way ahead of the lecture—they'd already figured out that was another $50,000 in tips! And since there are ten waiters in the Oyster Bar, even I could figure out it meant five grand more per man in tips. It was at that point I had my toughest decision to make since I've been in this job. I had to choose between staying on as President or becoming an Oyster Bar waiter.

But, while the waiters appreciated this automatic raise in theory, they were quick to call out the traditional negatives. "Nobody eats dessert anymore. Everyone's on a diet. If we served our chocolate cheesecake to everybody in the restaurant, half of them would be dead in a week."

"So sell 'em strawberries!" we said. "But sell 'em." And then we wheeled out our answer to gasoline shortages, the dessert cart. We widened the aisles between the tables and had the waiters wheel the cart up to each and every table at dessert time. Not daunted by the diet protestations of the customer, the waiter then went into raptures about the bowl of fresh strawberries. There was even a bowl of whipped cream for the slightly wicked. By the time our waiters finished extolling the virtues of our fresh strawberries flown in that morning from California, or wherever he thinks strawberries come from, you not only have had an abdominal orgasm but one out of two of you order them. In the last six months we show our waiters every week what's happening to strawberry sales. This month they have doubled again. So have second martinis. And believe me, when you get a customer for a second martini you've got a sitting duck for strawberries—with whipped cream. Our waiters are asking for the order.

"Think Strawberries" is The Plaza's new secret weapon. Our reservationists now think strawberries and suggest you'll like a suite overlooking Central Park rather than a twin-bedded room. Our bellmen are thinking strawberries. Each bellman has his own reservation cards, with his name printed as the return addressee, and he asks if you'd like him to make your return reservation as he's checking you out and into your taxi. Our Room Service order takers are thinking strawberries. They suggest the closed-circuit movie on TV ($3.00 will appear on your bill) as long as you're going to eat in your room. Our telephone operators are even thinking strawberries. They suggest a morning Flying Tray breakfast when you ask for a wake-up call. You just want a light breakfast, no ham and eggs? How about some strawberries?

We figure we've added about three hundred salesmen to the three sales-service team we had before. But most important, of course, is that we've added five pure sales people to our Sales Department. Four of them are out on the street calling—mostly cold—on the prospects to whom they're ready to sell anything from a cocktail in the Oak Bar to a Corporate Directors meeting to a Bar Mitzvah. The chewing gum people sell new customers by sampling on street corners. The Plaza has chewing gum licked a mile. Our sales people on the street have one simple objective; get the prospect into the hotel to sample the product. With The Plaza as our product, it isn't too difficult. And once you taste The Plaza, frankly, you're hooked.

In analyzing our business at the hotel we found, much to my surprise, that functions—parties, weddings, charity balls, and the like—are just about three times more profitable than all our six restaurants put together. And functions are twice as profitable as selling all 1000 of our rooms. Before we had this analysis, we were spending all our advertising money on restaurants, our nightclub, and our guest rooms. This year we're spending 80 percent of our advertising money to get function business—weddings instead of honeymoons, banquets instead of meals, annual corporate meetings instead of a clandestine romantic rendezvous for two. We've added a fulltime Bridal Consultant who can talk wedding language to nervous brides and talk turkey to their mothers. Retailers like Saks and Bonwit's and Bergdorf's have had bridal consultants for years. Hotels have Banquet Managers. Banquet Managers sell wedding dinners. Bridal Consultants sell strawberries—everything from the bridal shower, the pictures, the ceremony, the reception, the wedding night, to the honeymoon, to the first anniversary.

When you fight a habit as long standing as the hotel inside salesman, you don't just wave a wand and say "Presto: now we have four outside salesmen." We want our new salespeople to know how serious we are about going out after business. We started an Executive Sales Call program as part of our "Everybody Sells" philosophy. About forty of our top and middle-management executives, ones who traditionally don't ever see a prospect, are assigned days on which they make outside calls with our regular salesmen. People like our Personnel Director, our Executive Housekeeper, our Purchasing Director, and our General Manager are on the street every day making calls. Our prospects seem to like it. Our salesmen love it. And our nonsales "salesmen" are getting an education about what's going on in the real world—the one outside the hotel.

As a matter of fact, that's why I'm here today. I made a sales call myself with one of our salespeople. We called on your program chairman and tried to sell him strawberries. He promised that if I showed you a strawberry he'd book your next luncheon at The Plaza. I'm looking forward to waiting on you myself. Thank you very much.

SPEECH EXPERIENCE: The Informer

Your goal is to plan, rehearse, and present a five to ten minute extemporaneous speech in which your general purpose is to inform your listeners. On the day you are to speak, hand in:
   a. a brief analysis of the techniques you will use to enhance audience interest and attention, and
   b. an outline and bibliography.

The Persuader

Behavioral Objectives

After reading this chapter, you should have a better understanding of:

- the persuasive process.
- the number of persuasive messages you actually send and receive each day.
- a proposition.
- how to phrase propositions of fact, value, and policy.
- how to orient your speech to neutral, supportive, or resistant audiences.
- how to use persuasive materials.
- how to use persuasive appeals.
- how to analyze a persuasive appeal.
- how to analyze a persuasive speech.
- how to prepare, rehearse, and deliver a speech to persuade.

Introduction

Persuasive messages bombard us every day. Friends, family, the media, salespersons, and advertisers are always trying to persuade us to think, do, or believe one thing or another. Likewise, we try to persuade others. What is persuasion? It is a process by which a source attempts to affect the thinking and/or behavior of a receiver. We use persuasion every day, not just in public communication events.

SPEECH EXPERIENCE: PICK A PERSUADER

Step 1. Make a list of the persuasive messages you receive during the next 24 hours. For each message, note the source of the message, the medium through which it was communicated and your response to it.

Step 2. Compile a second list of the persuasive messages you sent to other people during this same time period. For each message, note the receiver of your message, the medium through which you sent it, and your receiver's response to it.

Step 3. Be prepared to deliver a three minute presentation to the class during which you report your findings. Specifically, identify a persuasive message sent to you that met with success, and a persuasive message sent to you that met with failure. Likewise, identify a persuasive message you sent to a receiver that was responded to favorably, and a persuasive message you sent that was responded to negatively. Attempt to explain the differences between the successful and unsuccessful persuasive messages.

Analyzing your experiences with persuasion should make it easier for you to achieve your persuasive goals in both the interpersonal and public communication arenas. We are often unaware of the many persuasive messages we send and receive each day; in fact, most of our person-to-person attempts at persuasion occur quite unintentionally, frequently without preplanning, and usually without practice. This is not so with the persuasive public communications we send. For the most part, speaking persuasively in public is an intentional activity that is carefully planned, charted, and rehearsed. Let us now take a closer look at persuasion.

The Persuasive Goal

The first task of any persuader is to decide on a persuasive goal. No successful public communicator begins to work without having a clearly stated persuasive purpose in mind. Your persuasive purpose is often referred to as your *proposition*. It contains a precise description of what you want your listeners to do, feel, or believe. Put another way, the proposition indicates whether you want audience members to replace, modify or add a behavior, extinguish, reinforce, or alter a belief.

There are three basic kinds of propositions: propositions of fact, value, and policy. A proposition of fact is a statement regarding the truth or falsity of a supposed fact. Thus, *the assassination of President Kennedy was a Communist plot*, *National Health Insurance would reduce America's health costs*, and *price controls feed inflation*, are examples of propositions of fact. In each case, the speaker seeks audience acceptance of the alleged fact being presented. A proposition of value is a statement concerning a value judgment. *Smoking pot is morally wrong*, *FDR was our best president*, and *the movement to impeach the President is unjustified* are propositions of value. Hence, propositions of value are concerned with the rightness or wrongness, justice or injustice, goodness or badness of ideas. Lastly, propositions of policy advocate the acceptance of a particular course of action. For this reason, such statements as, *capital punishment should be abolished*, *property taxes should be lowered*, and *all Americans should be guaranteed a minimum wage* are to be considered propositions of policy. Each is characterized by asking that something be done.[1]

Regardless of the type, every proposition should be expressed as a simple sentence, phrased in clear, unbiased language, and contain one and only one idea.

SPEECH EXPERIENCE: PROPOSITION PROBERS

Step 1. Divide the class into teams.

Step 2. The goal of each team is to identify the problems with each of the following propositions.

Step 3. Team members are to rewrite each corrected proposition in the spaces provided.

a. The Federal Government should pass laws prohibiting the utilization of animals for medical experimentation.

_____

_____

_____

b. There is too much violence in the media.

_____

[1] For further information on propositions, see: Abné M. Eisenberg, and Joseph A. Ilardo, *Argument: A Guide to Formal and Informal Debate*, 2nd ed. (Englewood Cliffs, N.J.: Prentice-Hall, Inc., 1980), pp. 30–8.

c. You should be immunized against measles because your immunization will prevent you from getting an unnecessary disease. Measles is also said to be more dangerous for adults than for children.

d. Bird-brained politicians who are sympathetic to Communism should be banned from serving in Congress.

Know Your Audience

Knowing your audience can help you determine and achieve your persuasive goal. Unless you know what you want your listeners to think or feel and how you want them to behave, you may not be able to realize your objective. In part, the nature of your persuasive task is related to the extent of change you expect in your audience. It will simplify your job to have some idea where your listeners fall on an agreement–disagreement scale with regard to your proposition.

willing to take action against	strongly oppose	mildly oppose	neutral	mildly agree	strongly support	willing to take action for
−15	−10	−5	0	+5	+10	+15

Once you determine how much of a shift in listener intensity you require to achieve your purpose, you can begin arming yourself with the proof necessary to realize that goal. To a large extent, your success will hinge on the kind of audience you are addressing. This means knowing whether audience members favor your proposition and how much they favor it. While it may be difficult to determine your audience's exact stand on an issue through either polls or demographic[2] information, you can usually place your audience into one of the following general classifications: no opinion, support, or oppose.

No Opinion

On certain propositions, you will encounter audience members who will have formed no opinions. Frequently, this is due to a lack of knowledge of the subject. For example, suppose you seek to persuade your listeners to accept this proposition: *Laetrille should be distributed to all cancer patients*. You are not sure whether your listeners ever heard of laetrille. Thus, your first task would be to explain what laetrille is and how it works. Obviously, no persuasion can occur if your audience doesn't know what you are talking about. On the other hand, apathy rather than ignorance may be responsible for an audience's neutrality on an issue. Here, you would be required to motivate as well as educate your listeners.

Support

You may be fortunate to find that, at times, your audience will already favor your proposition. This does not mean that your task as a speechmaker is finished. It just means that your job is made a trifle easier. While you need not repeat familiar reasons for supporting the proposal, you do need to build upon existing audience beliefs in an effort to motivate people into action. With a supportive audience, see your goal as one of rededication and commitment.

Opposed

Audience members who oppose your proposition are the third type of group to be considered. Do not automatically write this group off as a lost cause. By using arguments that make sense to this audience, you can sometimes persuade them to modify or alter their previous conclusions.

Finally, consider those individuals falling into a neutral camp who are capable of swinging the rest of your audience to their favor. Their open minds can be made to work to your advantage. This should not, however, be taken to mean that those who oppose or who are in favor of your proposition are to be neglected. You must take care to guard against two temptations: 1) taking your supporters for granted, and 2) disregarding your opponents. Supporters can be encouraged to turn agreement into active support and the hostility of the op-

---

[2] *Demography:* The statistical science dealing with the distribution, density, and vital statistics of populations.

posed can be tempered with solid arguments. Thus, in any persuasive encounter, your goal is to keep the loyal, win the undecided, and soften the opposed. To do this, speech materials and an organizational format need to be carefully chosen; also necessary, is a carefully rehearsed delivery.

SPEECH EXPERIENCE: PERSUADE ME, IF YOU CAN

Pretend you want to persuade various groups of people to support the following proposition: *The death penalty should be abolished.* How might you vary the persuasive message you deliver to each of the following audiences:

a. A supportive audience of college students

_____

_____

b. An opposed audience of senior citizens

_____

_____

c. A group of neutral audience members from the business world.

_____

_____

Materials for Persuasion

Many of the materials you will incorporate into your persuasive speech are the same as the ones used in informative presentations, after dinner addresses and are identical with the forms of support we mentioned in Chapter 6. Thus, definitions, examples, and illustrations. statistics, testimony, comparisons and contrasts, repetitions or restatements and humor all have a place in your persuasive message. It is also important for you to realize that delivering a speech to persuade does not automatically exclude the fact that you may inform and entertain the audience at the same time. The difference between the materials used in informative and persuasive speaking lies not in their types but in the way they are used. Whereas the supporting materials of an informative speech are used to 1) explain, 2) clarify or 3) increase comprehension; and the supporting materials of an entertainment address are used to 1) provide enjoyment, 2) generate amusement, or 3) stimulate laughter, the supporting materials of a persuasive speech are used to 1) change beliefs, 2) motivate the audience to respond, or 3) move them to action.

Additionally, like informative speakers, persuasive speakers need to consider what the people they are trying to persuade think of them, of their materials, and whether they believe they have a stake in what the speaker is proposing to them. Let us consider these aspects.

Persuasive Appeals

Speakers persuade us more readily if we respect them personally, are impressed by their arguments, and if we stand to derive some benefit from adhering to their proposals. In other words, effective speakers know how to use personal appeals (ethos), logical appeals (logos), and psychological appeals (pathos) in order to achieve their goal.

Personal Appeals   *credobelty = believobelty*

A speaker's personal appeal is to a large extent, determined by his or her credibility. *Credibility* is what an audience thinks of a speaker. Thus, credibility exists in listeners, not in speakers. For example, suppose I am a speaker and you are one of my receivers. If you see me as an honest, forthright, competent, and trustworthy human being, the fact that I am really dishonest, incompetent, devious and untrustworthy is irrelevant. We are dealing with your perception of me, not with what I really am.

Credibility has three dimensions: *character, competence,* and *dynamism.* A speaker's competence or an audience's perception of a speaker's qualifications to speak on a specific topic is critical. Audiences tend to believe and respond to people who are "experts" on an issue. Consequently, speakers often take it upon themselves to remind their audiences of their qualifications. They do this by mentioning their awards, titles, publications, research, and relevant life experiences. Audiences also value a speaker's trustworthiness. If an audience believes a speaker to be lying, manipulating information, or deceiving them in a way they will be disinclined to accept what the speaker has to say. Listeners also respond to dynamic speakers. A dynamic speaker is perceived to be friendly, highly personable, and vibrant.

If your audience accepts you as a credible source, your ideas have a good chance of receiving a fair and equitable hearing.

SPEECH EXPERIENCE: CREDIBILITY RESEARCH

1. As an indicator of your own credibility, use the following scales. Depending upon how you feel about yourself in relation to the speech topic

you are presenting, place an "X" in the appropriate space in between the terms listed. For example, if you feel *extremely* honest, mark the space so designated; if you feel *extremely* dishonest, mark the other end of the scale accordingly.

Opinion of My Own Credibility

	extremely	quite	slightly	neutral	slightly	quite	extremely	
honest	___	___	___	___	___	___	___	dishonest
safe	___	___	___	___	___	___	___	unsafe
just	___	___	___	___	___	___	___	unjust
kind	___	___	___	___	___	___	___	cruel
friendly	___	___	___	___	___	___	___	unfriendly
trained	___	___	___	___	___	___	___	untrained
experienced	___	___	___	___	___	___	___	inexperienced
skilled	___	___	___	___	___	___	___	unskilled
qualified	___	___	___	___	___	___	___	unqualified
informed	___	___	___	___	___	___	___	uninformed
aggressive	___	___	___	___	___	___	___	meek
emphatic	___	___	___	___	___	___	___	hesitant
bold	___	___	___	___	___	___	___	timid
active	___	___	___	___	___	___	___	passive
energetic	___	___	___	___	___	___	___	tired

2. Rate yourself as you believe most other people would rate you.

How I Think Others See Me

	extremely	quite	slightly	neutral	slightly	quite	extremely	
honest	___	___	___	___	___	___	___	dishonest
safe	___	___	___	___	___	___	___	unsafe
just	___	___	___	___	___	___	___	unjust

kind	___ ___ ___ ___ ___ ___ ___	cruel
friendly	___ ___ ___ ___ ___ ___ ___	unfriendly
trained	___ ___ ___ ___ ___ ___ ___	untrained
experienced	___ ___ ___ ___ ___ ___ ___	inexperienced
skilled	___ ___ ___ ___ ___ ___ ___	unskilled
qualified	___ ___ ___ ___ ___ ___ ___	unqualified
informed	___ ___ ___ ___ ___ ___ ___	uninformed
aggressive	___ ___ ___ ___ ___ ___ ___	meek
emphatic	___ ___ ___ ___ ___ ___ ___	hesitant
bold	___ ___ ___ ___ ___ ___ ___	timid
active	___ ___ ___ ___ ___ ___ ___	passive
energetic	___ ___ ___ ___ ___ ___ ___	tired

3. Here, number all positions on each scale as follows:

___ ___ ___ ___ ___ ___ ___
  1   2   3   4   5   6   7

To determine your *trustworthiness rating*, add the results of the following scales together: honest/dishonest, safe/unsafe, just/unjust, kind/cruel, and friendly/unfriendly.

Total: ____

To determine your *competence rating*, add the results of these scales together: trained/untrained, experienced/inexperienced, skilled/unskilled, qualified/unqualified, and informed/uninformed.

Total: ____

To determine your dynamism rating, add the results of these scales together: aggressive/meek, emphatic/hesitant, bold/timid, active/passive, and energetic/tired.

Total: ____

Finally, in order to determine your overall credibility rating, total the results achieved for trustworthiness, competence and dynamism.

Total: _____

Follow this procedure for each credibility assessment.

Use the following point system as a guide to rate yourself:

0–15	You're Tops!
16–30	You're Super-Credible.
31–45	You have Potential.
46–60	You're in the Questionable Zone.
61–75	You're Having Some Trouble.
76–90	You're in the Woods. *(soon 11/1/94)*
91–105	Watch Out! You're Sinking.

Logical Appeals

When you use a logical appeal, you attempt to persuade your listeners by reasoning with them. Speakers who use logic analyze and understand their topics and, by so doing, help their audience reach what they believe to be appropriate conclusions. Two main types of logical reasoning have proven beneficial to speechmakers: 1) reasoning from induction, and 2) reasoning from deduction.

When you reason from specific cases to a general conclusion, you are using *induction*. Inductive reasoning is most useful to persuasive speakers when an audience holds a view opposite to their own. President Franklin D. Roosevelt used inductive reasoning when he addressed Congress and asked that a state of war be declared between the United States and Japan in 1941.

> Yesterday, the Japanese Government also launched an attack against Malaya.
> Last night, Japanese forces attacked Hong Kong.
> Last night, Japanese forces attacked Guam.
> Last night, Japanese forces attacked the Phillippine Islands.
> Last night, the Japanese attacked Wake Island.
> This morning, the Japanese attacked Midway Island.
> Japan has, therefore, undertaken a surprise offensive extending throughout the Pacific area.

In contrast to this, when you reason *deductively*, you begin with a general idea and then move to specifics. Thus, you would be reasoning deductively if you stated:

> The Conservative candidate does not merit our support.
> She wants to raise taxes.
> She wants to reduce unemployment benefits.
> She wants to eliminate day care programs.

Deductive reasoning has been found useful for speakers whose audiences are inclined to support their proposals.

When you reason inductively or deductively, you are using evidence to supply your listeners with logical reasons for believing your proposition. You need to realize, however, that human beings do not necessarily respond to reason alone.

Psychological Appeals

In addition to using personal and logical appeals, skilled persuaders also utilize psychological appeals. A psychological appeal works on the needs, desires, and feelings of an audience. Speechmakers who use a psychological appeal recognize that human behavior is always motivated; they realize that, if they are to motivate their audience to listen and respond to their ideas, they must design their speeches so that they appeal to the psychological needs and goals of their listeners.

A popular device used to analyze human motivation is Maslow's Need Hierarchy. In Maslow's model, our most basic needs are found at the base of the triangle and our most sophisticated needs at the apex.

According to Maslow, survival needs include a need for those things which help keep us alive. Under the heading of survival are shelter, food, water, and procreation. Safety needs include the need for security and the need to know that survival needs will be met. On the third level, love and belonging represent the need for love and the need for satisfying interpersonal relationships. Maslow believes that once the needs for love and belonging are met, esteem needs take over. Esteem needs include the need for acceptance and respect by others, as well as yourself. The efforts you make to reach goals and accomplish objectives

Figure 14–1. Maslow's Need Hierarchy Model.[3]

[3] Abraham Maslow, *Motivation and Personality* (New York: Harper & Row, Publishers, 1954), pp. 80–92.

are often attempts at satisfying your esteem needs. Finally, at the top of Maslow's Hierarchy is the need for self-actualization. When you meet this need, you realize your full potential; i.e., you become everything you are capable of becoming.

How does Maslow's Need Hierarchy relate to you as a speaker? Firstly, if used properly, it can help you decide the kinds of psychological appeals to include in your speech. It provides you with a series of categories under which you can organize your psychological proof. Secondly, it can help you design a speech with a particular audience in mind. For instance, if you are addressing an audience with a strong survival need; i.e., they lack the money to ensure adequate food and shelter for themselves and their loved ones, your appeal to the need for self-actualization would have little impact and would fall on deaf ears. Instead, you would be wise to appeal initially to the more basic needs of your audience. Thirdly, if what you advocate is going to conflict with one need level, you must be prepared to show your audience how what you you have in mind will satisfy the requirements of another need level. Try this.

SPEECH EXPERIENCE: Motivation Match

Step 1. Each of the following persuasive speech topics should be written on a separate card and placed in a container:
       a. Parenthood should be licensed.
       b. Nude bathing should be permitted on public beaches.
       c. Smoking should be forbidden in all public restaurants.
       d. The Jury System should be abolished.

Step 2. The items identified in Maslow's Need Hierarchy should also be written on separate cards and placed in a second container.

Step 3. One at a time, students should come to the front of the room, draw a card from each container, and formulate a statement that could serve as the basis for a motive appeal made to an audience listening to a speech on the selected topic.

Speakers can also persuade listeners by showing them how a problem or condition threatens their need satisfaction. The process of persuading by fear is ingrained in our culture. From childhood, we are bombarded by messages warning us that if we do not adopt certain beliefs or exhibit certain behaviors, our well-being and happiness could be threatened. For instance, a company which sponsors a popular brand of travelers checks on TV suggests that a failure to purchase their travelers checks could result in severe hardship and economic insecurity. Their commercials imply that, when traveling abroad, our survival and security needs are in jeopardy. Other advertisers appeal to our needs for acceptance, love, and esteem by urging us to conceal all bodily smells lest we offend friends, lovers, and employers.

On a more serious note, we are exposed to messages urging us to drive carefully, use seat belts, jog every day, refrain from smoking, have regular eye examinations, and eat a balanced diet. These warnings emphasize the consequences that we might suffer if we fail to take heed.

Fear appeals may be classified as high, low, or moderate. High fear appeals include vivid visualizations, references to pain, and emotionally charged words like *kill*, *maim*, and *torture*. Low fear appeals are based on logical analyses of a problem, utilize neutral wordings, and play down threats. Moderate fear appeals fall somewhere between these extremes. It should be noted that, just as low fear appeals may not arouse enough concern in an audience, high fear appeals may fail because they are too threatening. A study conducted by Irving L. Janis and Seymour Feshback demonstrated this. In their experiment, students, who were divided into high and mild fear appeal groups, were presented messages about brushing teeth. Pictures of dental abnormalities, rotting gums, and black tooth stumps were shown to the high fear appeal subjects. In contrast, those in the mild fear appeal group were exposed only to the mention of potential tooth decay problems. Curiously, the mild fear appeal was the most effective. The researchers noted that the high fear appeal message was tuned out by the audience because it was too frightening for them to consider. The mild fear appeal, however, aroused audience fears but did not scare receivers into not listening. It was also noted that all messages threatened the receivers themselves, but not their families. Strong fear appeals have been found to be more effective than low fear appeals, if the threat is to the receiver's loved ones. Witness the "What will they do when you are gone?" approach of certain insurance company messages.

Whatever you decide with regard to the use of fear appeals, suggest to your listeners that there are immediate actions they can take to remove the threats posed by inaction. The effectiveness of a fear appeal on your audience will depend on your ability to convince listeners that a threat is real but, at the same time, reassure them that by adopting your suggestions, they will avert or alleviate the possibility of any serious consequences.

In any consideration of persuasive appeals, public speakers need to know that the Maslow Hierarchy applies to the majority of people in most situations. As a speaker, it is important to know which appeal to use, under what circumstances it should be used, and how to support it with logical and personal proof. You will soon discover why logic, speaker credibility, and sound psychological appeal are such a winning combination. Read the following persuasive speeches. Make a special effort to identify the persuasive goal and specific persuasive strategies used in each.

Clarence S. Darrow

"I am pleading that we overcome cruelty with kindness and hatred with love."

CHICAGO, ILL., 1924—Clarence S. Darrow, at 65 years of age the most famous living advocate for the defense in criminal cases, who can boast that he has never seen a client executed, delivered here an appeal for mercy in concluding the most sensational murder trial of the century.

Mr. Darrow strove (and successfully) to

save from the gallows the youths Loeb and Leopold, both sons of relatively prominent Chicago families, who confessedly carried out the crime of mutilating and murdering a boy named Bobby Franks.

The trial lasted for months, not on the basis of guilt or innocence because it was preceded by a full confession in court, but on the sole question whether the youths should be hanged or imprisoned.

In his closing argument and plea to the court, Mr. Darrow seemed to push aside all the mountains of testimony that had been taken. He virtually admitted that he loathed both the case and his clients.

What made his plea notable even to those who in the press have been expressing open doubt as to his sincerity and speculating on the size of the fee paid to him—was its general mustering of arguments against the imposition of the death penalty for any crime.

The highlights of his argument follow:

There are causes for this terrible crime. There are causes, as I have said, for everything that happens in the world. War is a part of it; education is a part of it; birth is a part of it; money is a part of it—all these conspired to compass the destruction of these two poor boys.

Has the court any right to consider anything but these two boys? The State says that your Honor has a right to consider the welfare of the community, as you have. If the welfare of the community would be benefited by taking these lives, well and good. I think it would work evil that no one could measure. Has your Honor a right to consider the families of these two defendants? I have been sorry, and I am sorry for the bereavement of Mr. and Mrs. Frank, for those broken ties that cannot be healed. All I can hope and wish is that some good may come from it all. But as compared with the families of Leopold and Loeb, the Franks are to be envied—and every one knows it.

I do not know how much salvage there is in these two boys. I hate to say it in their presence, but what is there to look forward to? I do not know but what your Honor would be merciful if you tied a rope around their necks and let them die; merciful to them, but not merciful to civilization, and not merciful to those who would be left behind. To spend the balance of their days in prison is mighty little to look forward to, if anything. Is it anything? They may have the hope that as the years roll around they might be released. I do not know. I do not know. I will be honest with this court as I have tried to be from the beginning. I know that these boys are not fit to be at large. I believe they will not be until they pass through the next stage of life, at forty-five or fifty. Whether they will then, I cannot tell. I am sure of this; that I will not be here to help them. So far as I am concerned, it is over. . . .

But there are others to consider. Here are these two families, who have led honest lives, who will bear the name that they bear, and future generations must carry it on.

Here is Leopold's father—and this boy was the pride of his life. He watched him, he cared for him, he worked for him; the boy was brilliant and accomplished, he educated him, and he thought that fame and position awaited him, as it should have awaited. It is a hard thing for a father to see his life's hopes crumble into dust.

Should he be considered? Should his brothers be considered? Will it do society any good or make your life safer, or any human being's life safer, if it should be handed down from generation to generation, that this boy, their kin, died upon the scaffold?

And Loeb's the same. Here are the faithful uncle and brother, who have watched here day by day, while Dickie's father and his mother are too ill to stand this terrific strain, and shall be waiting for a message which means more to them than it can mean to you or me. Shall these be taken into account in this general bereavement?

Have they any rights? Is there any reason, your Honor, why their proud names and all the future generations that bear them shall have this bar sinister written across them? How many boys and girls, how many unborn children will feel it? It is bad enough as it is, God knows. It is bad enough, however it is. But it's not yet death on the scaffold. It's not that. And I ask your Honor, in addition to all that I have said, to save two honorable families from a disgrace that never ends, and which could be of no avail to help any human being that lives.

Now, I must say a word more and then I will leave this with you where I should have left it long ago. None of us are unmindful of the public; courts are not, and juries are not. We placed our fate in the hands of a trained court, thinking that he would be more mindful and considerate than a jury. I cannot say how people feel. I have stood here for three months as one might stand at the ocean trying to sweep back the tide. I hope the seas are subsiding and the wind is falling, and I believe they are, but I wish to make no false pretense to this court. The easy thing and the popular thing to do is to hang my clients. I know it. Men and women who do not think will applaud. The cruel and thoughtless will approve. It will be easy today; but in Chicago, and reaching out over the length and breadth of the land, more and more fathers and mothers, the humane, the kind and the hopeful, who are gaining an understanding and asking questions not only about these poor boys, but about their own—these will join in no acclaim at the death of my clients. These would ask that the shedding of blood be stopped, and that the normal feelings of man resume their sway. And as the days and the months and the years go on, they will ask it more and more. But, your Honor, what they shall ask may not count. I know the easy way. I know your Honor stands between the future and the past. I know the future is with me, and what I stand for here; not merely for the lives of these two unfortunate lads, but for all boys and all girls; for all of the young, and as far as possible, for all of the old. I am pleading for life, understanding, charity, kindness, and the infinite mercy that considers all. I am pleading that we overcome cruelty with kindness and hatred with love. I know the future is on my side. Your Honor stands between the past and the future. You may hang these boys; you may hang them by the neck until they are dead. But in doing it you will turn your face toward the past. In doing it you are making it harder for every other boy who in ignorance and darkness must grope his way through the mazes which only childhood knows. In doing it you will make it harder for unborn children. You may save them and make it easier for every child that sometime may stand where these boys stand. You will make it easier for every human being with an aspiration and a vision and a hope and a fate. I am pleading for the future; I am pleading for a time when hatred and cruelty will not control the hearts of men.

Red Jacket

"You have got our country . . . you want to force your religion upon us."

SENECA, N. Y., 1805—Red Jacket Chief, of the Seneca Tribe and dominant spokesman for the Six Nations, eloquently challenged the ablest spokesmen among the Christian missionaries in an address here, replying to appeals to the Indians to be baptized and thereby take one more step toward integration into the American community.

To the surprise of these spokesmen for the Christian church, the eloquent warrior and friend of the late General George Washington, told the junior race that in his view the Indians have a better religion and one with less division than the white man. For good measure, using quotations that might well have been taken from the Bible itself, he cited actions by the white man in encroachment upon Indian rights, in self-divisions over doctrine and in other matters, that constituted an indictment comparable with those spoken in earlier days by the great Reform leaders within the church itself.

For these reasons, as well as the simplicity of expression used by this warrior of warriors—whose name itself came from the wearing of a scarlet coat given to him long ago by British troops—his words are memorable. In his own language his given name is far more euphonious, being Otetiani, and his title as Chieftain even more picturesque—Sagoyewatha. But as Red Jacket he must be known to posterity.

Friend and Brother: It was the will of the Great Spirit that we should meet together this day. He orders all things and has given us a fine day for our council. He has taken His garment from before the sun and caused it to shine with brightness upon us. Our eyes are opened that we see clearly; our ears are unstopped that we have been able to hear distinctly the words you have spoken. For all these favors we thank the Great Spirit, and Him only.

Brother, this council fire was kindled by you. It was at your request that we came together at this time. We have listened with attention to what you have said. You requested us to speak our minds freely. This gives us great joy; for we now consider that we stand upright before you and can speak what we think. All have heard your voice and all speak to you now as one man. Our minds are agreed. . . .

Brother, listen to what we say. There was a time when our forefathers owned this great island. Their seats extended from the rising to the setting sun. The Great Spirit had made it for the use of Indians. He had created the buffalo, the deer, and other animals for food. He had made the bear and the beaver. Their skins served us for clothing. He had scattered them over the country and taught us how to take them. He had caused the earth to produce corn for bread. All this He had done for His red children because He loved them. If we had some disputes about our hunting-ground they were generally settled without the shedding of much blood.

But an evil day came upon us. Your forefathers crossed the great water and landed on this island. Their numbers were small. They found friends and not enemies. They told us they had fled from their own country for fear of wicked men and had come here to enjoy their religion. They asked for a small seat. We took pity on them, granted their request, and they sat down among us. We gave them corn and meat; they gave us poison in return.

Brother, our seats were once large and yours were small. You have now become a great people, and we have scarcely a place left to spread our blankets. You have got our country, but are not satisfied; you want to force your religion upon us.

Brother, continue to listen. You say that you are sent to instruct us how to worship the Great Spirit agreeably to His mind; and, if we do not take hold of the religion which you white people teach we shall be unhappy hereafter. You say that you are right and we are lost. How do we know this to be true? We understand that your religion is written in a Book. If it was intended for us, as well as you, why has not the Great Spirit given to us, and not only to us, but why did He not give to our forefathers the knowledge of that Book, with the means of understanding it rightly. We only know what you tell us about it. How shall we know when to believe, being so often deceived by the white people?

Brother, you say there is but one way to worship and serve the Great Spirit. If there is but one religion, why do you white people differ so much about it? Why do not all agree, as you can all read the Book?

Brother, we do not understand these things. We are told that your religion was given to your forefathers and has been handed down from father to son. We also have a religion which was given to our forefathers and has been handed down to us, their children. We worship in that way. It teaches us to be thankful for all the favors we receive, to love each other, and to be united. We never quarrel about religion. . . .

Brother, we do not wish to destroy your religion or take it from you. We only want to enjoy our own.

SPEECH EXPERIENCE: (Your Name)   , THE PERSUADER

Your goal is to plan, rehearse, and deliver a six to eight minute extemporaneous persuasive speech. On the day you present your address, hand in the following:
  a. a brief audience analysis in which you explain how you have adapted your talk to your listeners, and
  b. an outline and bibliography.

15

The Entertainer

Behavioral Objectives

After reading this chapter, you should have a better understanding of:

- the nature of a speech to entertain.
- why preparing a speech to entertain is serious business.
- how to select a topic for a speech to entertain.
- how to employ such humor-related techniques as exaggeration, understatement, word play, incongruity, and satire.
- how to analyze a speech to entertain.
- how to prepare, rehearse, and deliver a speech to entertain.

Introduction

While many of the talks you give as a speechmaker will probably be either informative or persuasive, you may be asked to speak at times in a situation where informative discourse or overt persuasion might be judged inappropriate. The type of speech you choose should be directly related to the nature of your audience, the occasion, and your subject.

SPEECH EXPERIENCE: THE INVITATION

1. The class should be divided into groups of four to five students each.
2. Imagine that you are a member of a committee that has been assigned the task of inviting an individual to speak at a class banquet. Since you have unlimited funds, money is no object. Whom would you select and why?

Questions About "THE INVITATION"

1. What criteria did you use to select your banquet speaker?

_____

_____

2. What positive qualities does your chosen speaker possess?

_____

_____

3. On what topic do you expect the speaker to talk?

_____

_____

4. How do you expect the audience to respond to the speaker?

_____

_____

Definitions And Goals

If you believe the banquet speaker you have chosen will be entertaining, you made a wise choice. The word "entertainment" comes from the Latin word, *tenir*, meaning "to hold." Thus, the deliverer of a speech to entertain should have the ability to hold an audience's attention without making heavy demands on the listeners' intellect. The speaker's prime aim should be to please and amuse listeners, rather than anger, disturb, or provoke them. If listeners sit back and enjoy themselves, the deliverer of the speech to entertain has succeeded.

Don't be misled. Preparing a speech to entertain is serious business. Like any other speech, the speech to entertain should have a central idea or thesis and be well-organized. By well-organized, we mean that it should be divided into three basic sections: 1) the introduction, 2) body, and 3) conclusion. The introduction should spark audience interest and set an appropriate mood; the body should develop the theme while sustaining an established mood, and the conclusion should restate the central idea and leave the audience amused. The speech to entertain is very much a speech. As such, it should be approached with the same careful planning and preparation ordinarily used in all public speeches. The materials to be included in a speech to entertain need to be relevant to the chosen topic.

While the topic for a speech to entertain should be appropriate to speaker, audience, and occasion, the list of potentially entertaining subjects is virtually limitless. You can probably transform an informative speech or persuasive speech into a speech to entertain by modifying either your perspective or your tone.

SPEECH EXPERIENCE: TOPIC TRANSFORMATIONS

1. Listed below are some general speech subjects. The instructor will write each subject on a card and place it in a box at the front of the room.

2. Each student will have a chance to come to the front of the room, draw a topic from the box, and, transform it into a speech to inform, to persuade, or to entertain.

Marriage	Children	Life in a Big City
Food	Animals	Dieting
Politics	Love	Exercise
The Armed Forces	Fashion	Flying
Travel	School	News Reporting
Work	The Telephone	Money
The West	Invetions	Babysitting
Television	Life on a Farm	Life in a Small Town

Questions About "TOPIC TRANSFORMATIONS"

1. What are the main differences between the specific topics you generated?

---

2. What types of speech topics did you generate to inform? to persuade? to entertain?

Hopefully, the preceding exercise has demonstrated that it is the way you treat a topic that matters. It should also be apparent that when you decide to treat a topic in an entertaining fashion, while you may still inform or convince your audience, your primary goal is to amuse and divert them. For this reason, speakers who seek to entertain usually rely heavily on humor. Here are a number of key humor techniques.

Techniques of Humor

Becoming familiar with basic techniques of humor can help prepare you to deliver an effective speech to entertain.

SPEECH EXPERIENCE: HEAR THE HUMOR

All students should complete Part I of this exercise. Then, choose either Parts II or III.

Part I

a. While watching television, tape record or videotape a short comedy segment of a variety special, a comedian's monologue, or a roast. Identify the humorous ingredients in your chosen selection, and note the type of audience response given to the speaker. Attempt to pinpoint elements in the speaker's material that caused this response. After you have completed your analysis, prepare to retell a segment of the speaker's material in a way that suits your own speaking style and personality. On an assigned day, you will deliver your presentation to the class.

b. Tell a favorite joke to the class. Then, adapt the joke so that it is appropriate for a different audience or occasion. You can do this by altering the basic situation, the character, the setting, or the punch line.

Part II

Identify a behavior or personality trait that you believe says something about what you are like or who you are. Develop a three to five minute speech to entertain in which you explain these perceptions of yourself.

Part III

Select a favorite fairy tale, nursery rhyme, or fable. Rewrite it so that it comments upon a social problem of the day. Deliver your thoughts in a three to five minute speech to entertain.

As you no doubt have realized, a workable sense of humor better enables you to deliver a successful speech to entertain.

Major techniques of humor include exaggeration and understatement, word play, incongruity and satire. Let us briefly examine each of these techniques.

Overstatement and Understatement

Overstatement and understatement achieve their effects by depicting a habit, custom, or trait in a way that is considered grossly inappropriate. In other words, when using either device, the way a typical person would act or speak is compared with what a particular person actually says or does. If the subject goes beyond or stops short of what we consider usual or adequate, we label that person as foolish or ridiculous. The following story illustrates how exaggeration may be used to achieve such an effect. It was developed by T. A. Wilson, Chairman of the Board of the Boeing Company, who incorporated it in a speech entitled "A Cloudy Future for Our Air Transportation Industry."

Speaking of personal affairs brings to mind a story during the early days of air travel when saving time wasn't always what the airlines provided. In the mid-1930's, the British decided to link the Empire with air transport. Their equipment consisted of large, but slow, airliners with limited range.

One of the first flights from London to Australia attracted a full passenger load. The plane took off and flew to northern France where it was delayed by an extended period of bad weather. It finally arrived in southern France where one of its engines failed and it was necessary to wait for another engine to be shipped by sea from England.

Other delays en route occurred in Rome, Cairo, the Middle East, and India. Finally, the flight reached Singapore where still more repairs were needed.

At this point, a lady passenger asked the manager in Singapore if he thought the airplane would arrive in Australia in the next few weeks because she was expecting a baby shortly.

"My dear lady," sniffed the manager, "You should never have commenced your trip in that condition."

She replied, "I didn't."

When exaggeration is used in reverse, we call it understatement. The following anecdote relies on understatement for its impact:

When a little girl asked why accused ax killer Lizzie Borden was shunned by her neighbors, her mother explained, "You see, that lady was very unkind to her mother and father."

Word Distortions

When you manipulate language to achieve humor, you distort the way words are commonly used. You can do this by altering familiar expressions, utilizing words that sound like other words, or relying on the double meaning of words. These examples achieve their effects through word distortions.

A cannibal mother held her young son by the hand and said, "I'm worried about him, doctor. He won't eat anybody."

A cannibal chieftain said to a newspaper editor whom he had just captured, "By sunset you will be editor in chief."

A research fellow at the University of Miami Marine Biology Lab was engaged in some rather esoteric research on ways to retard the aging process. His theory was based on the observation that some porpoises that had modified their diets to include low-flying seagulls seemed to live considerably longer. He had set up a research study in a corner of the Everglades, rather remote from the campus. In addition to the large tank for the porpoises, a number of huge, normally wild animals roamed the enclosure—which included a large, but often sleepy lion. One night, returning from an expedition to the shore to collect gulls for his voracious porpoises, he found the lion sleeping directly across the walk leading to the lab. As he stepped across the lion with a bag of seagulls on his shoulder, he was seized by waiting sheriff's deputies. The charge: Transporting gulls across a staid lion for immortal porpoises.

In *The Rivals* by Richard Sheridan, Mrs. Malaprop tells Lydia Languish, "the point we would request of you is, that you will promise to forget this fellow—to illiterate him, I say, quite from your memory."

Incongruity

If you expect one thing and, instead, you find something else, the contrast between what you expect and what actually occurs may be humorous. For instance, former Presidential candidate, Adlai Stevenson made use of incongruity in the following anecdote from a speech to entertain which he entitled, "A Funny Thing Happened to Me on the Way to the White House."

I, a Democrat, had just been elected governor by the largest majority ever received in Republican Illinois. And, here I am, four years later, just defeated by the largest majority ever received in Democratic America.

Incongruity is also present here:

A man was walking down the street with one foot on the curb and the other in the gutter. A police officer, noticing this, walked up to the man and said, "I'm arresting you for drunkenness." The man looked at the policeman and, with a sigh of relief, said, "Oh, thank God, I thought my leg shrunk."

Satire

Satire may be defined as exposing the folly or vice of individuals by making fun of human behavior, manners, or social customs. As a speechmaker, you can use either gentle or bitter satire; you can poke fun at human failings lightly, or you can be merciless. You can satirize or "poke fun at" yourself, soap operas, the world of advertising, the life of the jet set, high finance, or politics. In his speech "Is There Intelligent Life in Washington?", Lee Loevinger used satire to discuss the folly that was Watergate.

You may recall that a while back a fellow named Rexford or Robert or Richard Nixon, or something like that, used to stay at the White House when he was in Washington as he traveled between California and Florida. One day, when he was out of town, somebody started a rumor that he had taken the original copy of the U.S. Constitution. Nobody around Washington had used it for quite a while so they couldn't tell at first whether it was missing. However, a couple of Washington Post reporters printed a rumor that Nixon was going to trade the Constitution for the Magna Carta, which he liked better than the Constitution. This got Congress excited because it was trying to make its own deal with the British for the Magna Carta. As a result, Congress voted to terminate Nixon as caretaker at the White House and hired Jerry Ford.

After all this, it turned out that Nixon was trying to sell the Constitution to The New York Times for a million dollars. The Times was seriously considering the deal because it was running low on stolen government documents to publish. However, The Times finally turned the deal down because the editors decided that nobody was interested in reading the Constitution these days anyway.

As we see, speeches to entertain can serve useful and worthwhile purposes. They can help us maintain our sense of psychological balance by reminding us that we are human, fallable, and, sometimes, absurd. Comedy and humor are very much a part of our world; they are a part of us. The speaker who has a sense of humor can help strengthen us and our society by getting behind the fictions and facades we erect in order to show us who and what we are. Now that we have examined a number of characteristics of speeches to entertain, let us see how they can be applied. Read the following speeches of entertainment. Then make a special effort to identify those factors responsible for making them entertaining.

"Bosses, Baboons, Brains, and the Bicentennial: Anybody Can Be a Boss" [1]

It is a privilege—I think—to speak at Bosses Night, when the Minneapolis JayCees honor their bosses and present an award to Outstanding Boss of the Year, I did notice, though, that nobody assigned the speaker a topic. So, on my own, I chose "Bosses, Baboons, Brains, and the Bicentennial." That title shows you how things can break loose without the guidance of bosses.

Talking about bosses, like talking in public about one's income or religion, is not easy. It is especially not easy when bosses are present.

Someone, however, must have realized that I have very high qualifications to discourse on bosses. Anyone who has worked for both the United States Senate and the Chamber of Commerce of the United States cannot remain unacquainted with bosses. Also, I have been married to the same wife for more than 30 years.

Indeed, having experienced so many bosses, no self-respecting economist could resist the temptation to generalize about bosses. One must not, of course, indulge in mere prejudice or opinion as an economist, but one must search diligently for verifiable evidence, wherever it may be found.

---

[1] Carl H. Madden, "Bosses, Baboons . . . ," *Vital Speeches of the Day*, **42**: 445–8 (May 1, 1976).

One generalization, to illustrate, comes from survey interviews with bosses to determine their common interests. Elaborate computer analysis was required because of the varied sample. As you know, some bosses are thin, other not-so thin; some young, other not-so-young; some tall, some not-so-tall; some handsome, others not-so-handsome; some mild, some not-so-mild; and so on. (Of course, you know, there are no bosses who are fat, old, short, ugly, and ferocious except comic-strip characters like Mr. Dithers in "Blondie"). The computer revealed two highly significant common traits: most bosses are concerned with their health; and most bosses, facing a complex problem, turn to others for help.

Such research may be apochryphal if not downright spurious, but at any rate it hardly scratches the surface of the subject. No doubt, a big question for an inquiry into bosses concerns whether they are really necessary to peaceful existence. That is, do bosses in fact contribute positively to human welfare?

One place to start, especially to remind people of one's academic background, is with dictionary meanings. The word *boss* is entered just after the word *bosomy*, which as of 1611 meant "full of sheltered hollows." Is that juxtaposition mere coincidence?

As for the word *boss* itself, it comes from the Middle English *boce*, *bos* which was adopted without change of form (or pronunciation) from the Old French. After a few more abbreviations we can omit comes the puzzling news in brackets: "[In Middle English *boss* and *botch* are partly synonymous.]" Did the Middle English know something we did not realize about bosses?

Next, alas, we find that the first meaning of the word *boss* is: "1. a protuberance on the body of an animal or plant; a convex or knob-like process." Now, I have heard bosses called all sorts of things but never a *protuberance*.

Yet, this modest piece of research illustrates the pitfalls of the academic life. It is only after a good deal of further reading on page 206 of the *Oxford Universal Dictionary* that we learn the full scope of meaning of the word *boss*. True, a *boss* may be something like a Middle English *botch* (if not a modern *botch*), a kind of knob-like proturberance, convex, as it were. It may also, however, be "a water conduit, running out of a gor-bellied figure as in the Boss of Billingsgate." A gorbelly figure, by the way, for any of you who may have forgotten your basic gorbelly shape, is either (1790) "a protuberant belly" or earlier (1530) "a person with a protuberant belly." Also, we learn that a *boss* may be "a plasterer's tray, a hod," and you remember that's what a plasterer holds in one hand and then he flings plaster onto it in gooey piles, scrapes it around, and the like. And, too, as of 1695 a *boss* could mean, as a corruption of *bass*, "a seat of straws, a hassock."

Only after all that does my *Oxford Universal Dictionary* observe, without editorial comment, that about 1822 in the U.S. the word *boss* came to mean, as a slang expression, "A master; a business manager, anyone who had a right to give orders." This was shortly before the era of *laissez faire* began, around 1836, with the Free Banking Act in New York and state general incorporation laws, that led to a multiplication of *bosses*.

Bosses—And Baboons

Another approach to the question whether bosses are necessary is to seek the evidence of anthropology, to examine the social behavior of other animals. The behavior of monkeys and apes has always held great fascination for man. In recent years, this plain curiosity has combined with the anthropologist's desire to understand human behavior. The evolution of primate social behavior helps in understanding human behavior, since the development of man's social behavior has played an integral part in his biological evolution.

The answer given by research into primate social behavior is that bosses seem to be necessary. Some years ago Desmond Morris in his book *The Naked Ape* described baboon behavior, as observed by anthropologists who lived with baboons and observed them in their natural habitat. A classic account is that in 1961 of Washburn and Devore, "The Social Life of Baboons." They studied baboons to gain insights into the kind of social behavior that characterized the ancestors of man a million years ago. They studied 30 troops of baboons made up of 40 to 80 individuals each, in their natural setting in Africa. They found that "the social behavior of the baboon is one of the species' principal adaptations for survival."

And they found that the adults in a troop are arranged in a dominance hierarchy. The more dominant males, as it were, get feeding and resting positions of their choice. They will be more frequently groomed by others than will they groom them. When a dominant animal approaches, lesser animals move out of the way. If food is tossed between two baboons, the more dominant one will take it, whereas the other may not even look at it directly.

Status among male baboons in the dominance hierarchy depends on physical ability, fighting ability, and relationship with other males. A few dominant males in some troops stay together a lot and if one is threatened the others back him up. The few male dominants outrank any individual even though another male outside the group could defeat any member of it separately.

The cluster of dominant males decreases disruptions in the troop. Dominant animals will not allow others to fight back. They stop the bickering of others by threat-posturing. They thus protect weaker animals against harm from inside as well as outside. Conclude the authors, "So although dominance depends ultimately on force, it leads to peace, order, and popularity."

Today, anthropologists are studying the social behavior of animals more intensely. Studies range from the pioneering work of Jane Goodall, now going on for 15 years, in the hills of the Gombe Stream Chimpanzee Reserve in Tanzania on the shores of Lake Tanganyika, to the recent studies by Diane Fossey of gorillas in the mountain rain forests of Rwanda, to the studies by still others of orangutans in Borneo. Today, anthropologists realize that social behavior of the higher primates is more complex than a rigid dominance theory might suggest. Still, all the studies show the prevalence of dominance and leadership as a means of group order and survival.

Indeed, the prevalence of hierarchy is widespread in all animal life. It is not too much to say that in every animal species in which there is a social organization—ants, bees, the like—there is a hierarchy with dominance-submission relationships.

Bosses—And Brains

Of course, the mystery of profound relationships in human life only seems to deepen as knowledge grows. A brilliant *Time* magazine essay on leadership of July 1974 acknowledged that, much as we have studied the subject through the years, almost nothing is known for sure about what it takes to make a leader. Most often in baboon troops leaders are recognized by observing conduct, and we are not all that far ahead of the baboons in fact, despite elaborate processes in our own institutions for leadership training.

That is why the question of brains and leadership remains intriguing. *Harper's Magazine,* in its Wraparound feature for December 1975 tells about "The World of the Brain." The human brain is "a gelatinous three-pound lump of fat, connective tissue, spinal fluid, veins, and nerve cells—the last generating about 25 watts of total power." It guzzles a pint and a half of blood a minute. No matter what happens to the rest of the body, it takes its nourishment first. One minute without oxygen or glucose means unconsciousness; eight minutes means death.

The brain is divided into halves down the middle from front to back. The left side controls the right side of the body; the right side controls the body's left side. Each half can also be divided from back to front into three sections. Each of these sections is a legacy from a different epoch of man's evolution.

Closest to the spinal cord is the brainstem. It is known as the "old" brain or "reptilian" brain—because reptiles have brains like this that do similar things. Above and in front of that is the limbic brain or "smell" brain, or "old mammalian" brain. On top of that brain, completely enveloping it and dominating its appearance, is the heavily convoluted cerebral cortex, also called the cerebrum or "new mammalian" brain.

The brainstem—the "old, reptilian" brain—goes back in evolution some 200 million years. It seems to have the same function in all vertebrates. Listen to what it governs. It governs "gut" reactions, ritual behavior, courting and mating activity, the ability to find one's way home, rapport (or lack of it) with other animals, and the *sense of being a leader or a follower*. Says *Harpers* (for what it may be worth), "It has even been suggested that a politician's charisma is a function of his (or her) reptilian brain."

Is this perhaps why all the formula success books, including "The Power of Positive Thinking" and "How to Win Friends and Influence People" urge the practice of meditation, of "thinking positive thoughts," or what comes to prayer, self-hypnosis, and the like—so that the deepseated, 200-million-year-old "gut" impulses of the "reptilian" brain can be reached? Who knows. The new subject of mind research is trying to explore systematically the implications of new knowledge about the brain and its functions. However, for our purposes, we see forcefully that recent study of the human brain as well as of animal behavior attests to the ancient and powerful origins of hierarchical social relations and dominance-submission relations in humans.

Bosses—And Bamboozlement

But of course man does not live by his reptilian brain alone, even though all of us have known cases in which "gut" reactions, ritual behavior, courting and mating activity, rapport with others, and the sense of being a leader or follower come close to exhausting the recognizable activity of some people. Indeed, concerning these people we also sometimes wish they had sharpened a little more their ability to find their way home, taking their charisma along with them.

Because man does not live by the "old" brain alone, however, dominance-submission relations throughout history have often been overlaid with what can most briefly be called cerebral bamboozlement. No one can read such books as *Parkinson's Law* or *The Peter Principle*—in fact, few of us can withstand very much of the mumbo-jumbo of modern personnel doctrine—without looking about ourselves to see whether our wallets are still intact or whether our pockets may not have been picked. After that, some of us may even study these modern Machiavellis to learn more about how to climb the ladder up the hierarchy.

It's worth a moment or two to remind ourselves what these modern satirists say about how hierarchies grow. First, work expands so as to fill the time available for its completion. The number in a hierarchy thus may not be related to the quantity of work. Second, the law of triviality holds that the time spent on an agenda item will be in inverse proportion to the importance involved. Third, committees are organisms; they take root, grow, and multiply themselves. Fourth, superiors tend to multiply subordinates by dividing the work, thus introducing a bureaucratic disease referred to as "induced inferiority," also called *injelititis*. All of these laws and others are the discovery of C. Northcote Parkinson, then Raffles Professor of History at the University of Malaya in his 1957 book, *Parkinson's Law*.

Raymond J. Hill took this line of inquiry further, with the help of an elusive colleague, Dr. Laurence J. Peter—a man so terribly shy no one has ever seen him. Peter is a sort of academic Howard Hughes. The Peter Principle, as you all know, holds that in a bureaucracy, people are promoted to the highest level of their incompetence. This explains why so much goes wrong in modern life, and of course Dr. Peter marshals a great deal of evidence supporting the view that much does indeed go wrong in modern life. Dr. Peter explores not only the workings of the Peter Principle in raising incompetence to its highest level. He also explores the politics and psychology of hierarchiology and the pathology of hierarchical success. Indeed, he even propounds a doctrine—not so easy to grasp—of creative incompetence, a means by which each of us can avoid the ultimate promotion.

Finally, there is now a handbook for bureaucrats, prepared by James H. Boren, and though its title may seem frivolous, it contains much solid material. The title is, *When In Doubt, Mumble*. It is impossible to do justice to Boren in a brief space. He has, for example, formulated the handbook maxim "When in doubt, delegate." He explicates bureaucratic skills in communicating, such as how to issue the call to inaction, how to mumble with professional eloquence, how to master the art of pondering and how to write the all-purpose speech—the ghost-writer's dream speech.

His advice to Federal agency heads in testifying before Congress comes in cartoon form: "Smedley, the next time Proxmire asks about agency spending, don't start off by saying, 'Senator, would you believe . . .' "

If the modern U.S. and British analysts of the bureaucracy know more than they pretend in formulating their tongue-in-cheek laws, the entire aspect of behavior derived from dominance-submission relations and the threat posture has been fantastically elaborated by man. For baboons or gorillas, the threat posture is physically direct but for reasons of troop survival almost never comes to any harm. It consists of whomping on the chest, letting fly a few blood-curdling screams, flashing quite a few large and shiny teeth, and rushing at the victim, only to veer away at the last instant. Football linebackers such as Dick Butkus or Ray Nietschke illustrate the posture, but they hardly stop at posturing, as any former NFC fullbacks will tell you.

It is not that brute physical intimidation is gone from the life of man; far from it. It is surely a live form in our violent species, practiced seriously by terrorists, gangsters, cops, prison inmates, street criminals, and others in peacetime and by soldiers at war. Rather, it is that the entire aspect of behavior surrounding dominance and the threat posture throughout history has tended to be shrouded in a vast overlay of religious and ritualistic legitimacy given to various kinds of boss-men and boss-women—witch doctors, priests or priestesses, shamans, sun-gods or goddesses, kings or queens, nobles, and chieftains. Elaborate theologies of many settled cultures from ancient Chinese dynasties to the mysterious Mayan civilization have assured the magical or divine origin and legitimacy of specific forms of dominance-submission behavior. Viewed from the safe distance of the present, these past tapestries of power in part seem to be the essence of cerebral bamboozlement, as if among the ancient priesthood and nobility there were, so to speak, a lot of sly crocodiles ready to eat the unwary, the weak, the ignorant, the innocent.

Bosses—And The Bicentennial

But close up, in our own civilization, the dominance-submission issue has been deadly serious, a race between the cerebrum and the reptilian brain that remains far from won. Our bicentennial celebrates among other things the triumph of reason over ritualized religion in rejecting the divine right of kings and asserting the rights of man. Listen to the last written words of Thomas Jefferson, penned on June 24, 1826, to celebrate the Fourth of July on which he died:

"All eyes are opened, or opening, to the rights of man. The general spread of the light of science has already laid open to every view the palpable truth that the mass of mankind has not been born with saddles on their backs, nor a favored few booted and spurred, ready to ride them legitimately by the grace of God."

This is our Bicentennial Year—our celebration of a revolution. It is a revolution that, above all, asserts the value of giving ordinary men and women wider and wider personal opportunities. The chance for freedom, for an education, for freely taking part in public life, and for increasing our material well-being by working at jobs we choose— what a priceless heritage!

How ironic it is that, as the United States retreats from its peak as a world power, Freedom House in its annual survey just a week ago estimated that barely 20 percent of the world's population now live in free societies—only two dozen of the world's 150 nations can fairly be called democratic or capitalist.

This is our Bicentennial Year—our celebration of a revolution. Yet we are bereft of revolutionary ardor for the rights of man, well along the road *The Economist* of London saw us moving down some weeks ago, when it said:

"Two great empires have ruled the two centuries of industrial advance—the British from 1776 to 1876; the Americans from 1876 to 1976. But the Americans, on the eve of this Third Century, are showing the same symptoms of drift from dynamism as the British did at the end of their century. World leadership is therefore liable to pass into new hands quite early in the century 1976–2076. America's contribution in its Third Century will depend largely on how its three main institutions evolve in or out of pace with the changing times. These three main institutions are its business corporations, its government, and its mechanism for living together."?

How ironic that as America risks losing a sense of its own significance, it is the socialist states that, armed to the teeth, impose on their own citizens a rigid hierarchy of dominance that sneers at the rights of man. Years ago, Stephen Leacock, the Canadian essayist and economist, said about socialism:

"Socialism merely means everybody working along with everybody else for everybody's good, in cheerful cooperation and equality instead of each selfishly working for himself in a world of inequality and injustice."

It is surely queer of history that the idealistic and sophomoric dream of socialism has spawned tyranny of unprecedented scope, a Gulag Archipelago of 40 million to 80 million submissives to the iron will of a state supposed in the dream to wither away, themselves intimidated and then liquidated on the ritual altar of socialist conformity. It is surely queer of history that an ideology rejecting inequality in the economic system has spawned such unrelenting dominance-submission relations of the proletariat few to the supine masses.

This is our Bicentennial Year—our celebration of a revolution. To be here honoring the bosses of free men and women, who enjoy together and separately the protections of liberty and the blessings of a fruitful society, is indeed a privilege, when you think about it.

Contrary to the *London Economist*, I believe that the blessings of liberty have only just begun to flow in this land. To be sure, we are a minority in the world. To be sure we are a young nation in the family of nations. Ours, however, in the long evolution of mankind from the reptilian brain of 200 million years ago, to the dawning social behavior of ancestors a million years ago, to the palpable truth of Thomas Jefferson's rights of man, has been a move toward the light. The Declaration of Independence rings down the centuries on behalf of reason over ritual.

Our free government embodies the paradox of force and persuasion, for coercion—the opposite of freedom—is the essence of government. We do not deny that paradox. Instead, we seek a form of government that, so far as possible, protects freedom of thought and action by coercing those who would deny such freedom to others. We and our Constitution seek to secure conditions favorable to people in their individual pursuit of happiness.

We live in a society where (after 200 years under the same form of government) any person can aspire to be a boss or can seek to be his own boss or her own boss. And that, in a free society. I therefore salute BOSSES, BABOONS, BRAINS, and the U.S. BICENTENNIAL!

"After You Get Where You're Going, Where Will You Be?: Pucker Up And Let Her Go"[2]

Thank you, Mr. Chairman. This club wanted someone a little better known to speak to you today, so they first asked a prominent clergyman, but he couldn't make it. They then asked Mayor Olson, but he had other plans. They then asked Governor Ray, but he, too, had a conflict in his schedule. Would you believe that by the time they got to me, they were desperate for a speaker? Imagine . . . starting with a prominent clergyman and ending up with an unknown oil company executive . . . that's running the gamut from saint to sinner!

But your asking me to be here *is* a nice gesture, and I'm not used to receiving nice gestures because I *do* work for an oil company . . . and whenever I drive a company staff car with the company name on it, other motorists quite often give me *obscene* gestures. Since the energy crisis, I've seen enough upturned middle fingers to last me a lifetime.

As the father of four youngsters, I can applaud the Optimist Club's "Youth Appreciation Week" because we adults don't always take the time to really appreciate the youth of our community. So I want to talk about the most important person in the world—You! I salute you! *You* who are making worthwhile contributions in your school and in our community, or you wouldn't be here, but I must admit there are times when I wonder about my *own* kids.

Some people say I'm living proof that insanity is contagious and that I get it from my kids. Let me give you an example: I recently read that by the time the average person dies, he has spent two years of his life in the bathroom, three years in the car, and five years eating. That describes my teen-age son perfectly, and he isn't even 17 yet.

You should see his bedroom—it's a real disaster area. My son is an accident looking for a place to happen. He spends so much time in the family car that *his* rear end has to be checked every 5,000 miles. His friends are really something, too. His friends have tee-peed our yard so many times that we haven't had to buy toilet paper for over a year. It's saved us a lot of money.

Seriously, though, the Rockefeller Report on Education stated that what most people want—young or old—is not merely security, or comfort, or luxury. Most of all, they want *meaning* in their lives . . . objectives, convictions, substance, direction! This is a challenge of our time! A challenge for this affluent society.

So I would ask the question, "After you get where you're going, where will you be?" I know that when we're teenagers it isn't easy to know *what* we want to be or *where* we're going. We're a little indecisive and that's understandable. And sometimes we're like the teen-age boy who was madly in love with a girl and when they were walking home from their first date, the boy wanted desperately to give her a kiss, but being a religious youngster, he said out loud: "Father, father up above, should I kiss the girl I love." And a big, booming voice came from out of the sky and said: "Sinner, sinner down below; pucker up and let her go!"

Now the lesson to be learned from that is that if we *know* something is good and honorable and desirable, *don't procrastinate* . . . don't put things off . . . aim for the worthy goals and don't hesitate to pucker up and let her go. BE AN OPTIMIST!

Be like the young man who attended college but had to walk on crutches. He had

---

[2] Max D. Isaacson, "After You Get Where You're Going, Where Will You Be?", *Vital Speeches of the Day* 40: 204–5 (January 15, 1978).

a talent for friendliness and optimism. He won many scholastic honors and the respect of his classmates. One day, a classmate asked the cause of his deformity. "Polio," was a brief reply. "But tell me," said the friend, "with a misfortune like that, how can you face the world so confidently?" "Oh," he replied, "the disease never touched my heart." And Eleanor Roosevelt reminded us some years ago that "No one can make you feel inferior without your consent." Think about that for a moment.

And when Cathy Rigby, a champion gymnast, failed to win a gold medal at the Olympics, she never forgot what her mother told her afterward: "Cathy, doing your best is more important than being the best!"

One of my favorite parts of the Optimist Creed says we should be "too large for worry, too noble for anger, too strong for fear, and too happy to permit the presence of trouble." And it's amazing the capacity that some people have to accomplish this.

Not long ago, I was a member of a group listening to a talk by Elizabeth Kubler-Ross, internationally known psychiatrist who is an author of several books on death and dying and she related the poignant, true story of a black cleaning lady who worked in the doctor's hospital in Chicago, and it seems that whenever this black cleaning lady left the room of a dying patient, that patient—always, without exception—was happier and more at peace. Doctor Kubler-Ross was determined to find out why and called the cleaning lady in for a conference. There unfolded a story of great compassion.

This uneducated black cleaning woman confided that she had faced a great deal of fear and tragedy and poverty all her life, and told of the time she had her three-year-old son in a public health clinic, waiting for treatment for pneumonia. But while waiting for that treatment, the little boy . . . died . . . in her arms. And then she added: "You see, doctor, the dying patients are just like old acquaintances to me, and I'm not afraid to touch them, talk with them, or to offer them hope."

As a result of her tremendous rapport with these patients, the woman subsequently was promoted to a job of "special counselor to the dying" and works in that capacity to this day. She *was* too noble for anger, too strong for fear, and too happy to permit the presence of trouble.

Yes, the pessimist says his glass is half-empty, but the optimist says his glass is half-full . . . the pessimist says he's sorry that roses have thorns, but the optimist says he's glad that thorns have roses. And while they sound a good deal alike, there *is* a difference between being in a rut and in a groove.

If you want to be in a groove, if you want to be an optimist, I believe you'll be interested in the philosophy expressed in an article I recently obtained. This article is titled, "Invest It Wisely," and it says:

"If you had a bank that credited your account each morning with $86,400, that carried over no balance from day to day, and allowed you to keep no cash in your account, and every evening cancelled whatever part of the amount you had failed to use during the day, what would you do? Draw out every cent, of course!

"Well, you have such a bank, and its name is 'Time.' Every morning it credits you with 86,400 seconds. Every night it rules off, as lost, whatever of this you have failed to invest to good purpose. It carries over no balances. It allows no overdrafts.

"Each day it opens a new account with you. Each night it burns the records of the day. If you fail to use the day's deposits the loss is yours. There is no going back. There is no drawing against the 'tomorrow.' You must live in the present—on today's deposits. Invest it so as to get from it the utmost in health, happiness, and success?"

Finally, the Optimist Creed tells us to "press on to greater achievements of the future" and I want to leave you with a beautiful thought by some unknown author . . . perhaps a teen-ager . . . who wrote:

God said "Build a better world" and I said "How?" The world is such a cold dark place and so complicated now; And I so young and useless, there's nothing I can do. But God in all his wisdom said: "Just build a better you!"

SPEECH EXPERIENCE   (YOUR NAME)   , THE ENTERTAINER

Your goal is to prepare, rehearse, and deliver a three to four minute extemporaneous speech to entertain. On the day you speak, hand in the following:

a. an analysis of the techniques of humor you have incorporated in your address, and

b. an outline.

MEMORANDUM

TO: READERS

FROM: AUTHORS

MESSAGE:
IN THIS BOOK, WE HAVE SHARED WITH YOU OUR KNOWLEDGE AND EXPERIENCE ABOUT SPEECHMAKING. WE FIRMLY BELIEVE THAT YOU HAVE THE ABILITY TO BECOME AN EFFECTIVE PUBLIC SPEAKER. SPEECHMAKING IS AN ART AND, LIKE OTHER ARTS, IT REQUIRES A GREAT DEAL OF PRACTICE. NOW, WHAT YOU SHOULD DO IS CONTINUE USING THE COMMUNICATION GUIDELINES AND PRINCIPLES WE HAVE ADVANCED AND APPLY THEM TO YOUR DAILY NEEDS. SPEECHMAKING CAN MAKE A SIGNIFICANT DIFFERENCE, NOT ONLY IN YOUR LIFE, BUT ALSO IN THE LIVES OF THOSE IMPORTANT TO YOU.

RECOMMENDED READINGS

Barrett, Harold. *Practical Uses of Speech Communication*. 4th ed. (New York: Holt, Rinehart and Winston, 1977).

Bremback, Winston L., and William S. Howell. *Persuasion: A Means of Social Influence*, 2nd ed. (Englewood Cliffs, N.J.: Prentice-Hall, Inc. 1976).

Eisenberg, Abné M., and Ralph Smith. *Nonverbal Communication* (Indianapolis: The Bobbs-Merrill, Co., Inc., 1971).

————, and Joseph Ilardo. *Argument: A Guide to Formal and Informal Debate*, Second Edition. (Englewood Cliffs, N.J.: Prentice, Hall, Inc. 1980).

————. *Living Communication* (Englewood Cliffs, N.J.: Prentice-Hall, Inc., 1975).

————. *Understanding Communication in Business and the Professions* (New York: Macmillan Publishing Co., Inc., 1978).

Fletcher, Leon. *How to Design and Deliver a Speech* (New York: Harper & Row, Publishers, 1979).

Gibson, James. *Speech Organization: A Programmed Approach* (San Francisco: Rinehart Press, 1971).

————, and Michael Hanna. *Audience Analysis: A Programmed Approach to Receiver Behavior* (Englewood Cliffs, N.J.: Prentice-Hall, Inc., 1975).

Monroe, Alan, Douglas Ehninger, and Bruce Gronbeck. *Principles and Types of Speech Communication*, 8th ed. (Glenview, Ill.: Scott, Foresman and Company, 1978).

Nichols, Ralph A., and Leonard A. Stevens. *Are You Listening?* (New York: McGraw-Hill Book Company, 1957).

Ochs, Donovan J., and Anthony C. Winkler. *A Brief Introduction to Speech* (New York: Harcourt Brace Jovanovich, Inc., 1979).

Rodman, George. *Public Speaking: An Introduction to Message Preparation* (New York: Holt, Rinehart and Winston, 1978).

Wilson, John, and Carroll Arnold. *Dimensions of Public Communication* (Boston: Allyn & Bacon, Inc., 1976).

Zimmerman, Gordon I. *Public Speaking Today* (St. Paul, Minn.: West Pub. Co., 1979).

NAME INDEX

SUBJECT INDEX

SPEECH EXPERIENCE INDEX

WORK AREA

WORK AREA

WORK AREA

WORK AREA

WORK AREA

WORK AREA

WORK AREA